NOLS EXPEDITION
PLANNING

NOLS EXPEDITION PLANNING

**Dave Anderson
and Molly Absolon**

STACKPOLE
BOOKS

Published by
STACKPOLE BOOKS
5067 Ritter Road
Mechanicsburg, PA 17055
www.stackpolebooks.com

Printed in China

First edition

Cover photo by Ignacio Grez, NOLS instructor
Interior photos by Dave Anderson

10 9 8 7 6 5 4 3 2 1

NOLS books are printed by FSC® certified printers.
The Forest Stewardship Council™ encourages responsible management of the world's forests.

Library of Congress Cataloging-in-Publication Data

Anderson, Dave.
    NOLS expedition planning / Dave Anderson and Molly Absolon. — 1st ed.
        p. cm.
    Includes bibliographical references and index.
    ISBN-13: 978-0-8117-3551-3 (pbk.)
    ISBN-10: 0-8117-3551-6 (pbk.)
    1. Outdoor recreation—Planning. 2. Recreation leadership. 3. Adventure and adventurers. I. Absolon, Molly. II. Title. III. Title: National Outdoor Leadership School expedition planning.
    GV191.66.A64 2011
    790.06'9—dc22
                                        2010030637

About the Authors

Dave Anderson began instructing for the National Outdoor Leadership School (NOLS) in 1996. As a senior field instructor, Dave's specialties are rock climbing and mountaineering, developing related curriculum, and conducting staff trainings. He is also a professional photographer and writer and gives multimedia presentations about his personal expeditions around the globe. His expeditions have taken him to 15 different countries on four continents: from long traverses in the Wind River and Teton ranges in Wyoming, to Grade VI big walls in Pakistan, to mixed ascents in Patagonia, to crossing the Gobi Desert by camel. Find him at http://dea-media.com.

Molly Absolon, a NOLS instructor since 1986, lives and writes in Lander, Wyoming. She is an environmental educator, writer, and outdoor enthusiast who prefers to be on her bike or skis rather than at the computer. Her personal expeditions have taken her to Alaska, the Yukon, Nepal, India, Ecuador, and throughout the western United States. Now most of her adventures are closer to home with her daughter Avery and husband Allen O'Bannon. Molly dedicates this book to the memory of her late husband Peter Absolon, with whom she shared many years of adventure.

This book is dedicated to the memory of Peter Absolon—
husband, father, director of NOLS Rocky Mountain,
and longtime NOLS instructor—
who brought energy, enthusiasm, skill, and joy
to many expeditions for many people.

Contents

Acknowledgments   viii

Introduction   x

Chapter 1:   The Innate Desire for Exploration   1

Chapter 2:   Determining the Goal of Your Expedition   12

Chapter 3:   Choosing Your Expedition Team   19

Chapter 4:   Expedition Support   35

Chapter 5:   Researching Your Expedition   45

Chapter 6:   Red Tape   55

Chapter 7:   Budget and Funding   67

Chapter 8:   Equipment   79

Chapter 9:   Food and Fuel   105

Chapter 10:   Training   129

Chapter 11:   Health Considerations   143

Chapter 12:   Transportation and Lodging   157

Chapter 13:   International Logistics   175

Chapter 14:   Leadership   191

Chapter 15:   Expedition Behavior and Communication   209

Chapter 16:   Risk Management   221

Chapter 17:   Dealing with Adversity and Uncertainty   235

Chapter 18:   Leave No Trace   245

Chapter 19:   Recording Your Adventure   255

Chapter 20:   Personal Reflection and Heading Home   265

Bibliography   275

Index   279

Acknowledgements

NOLS has been planning and executing backcountry expeditions since 1965. Teaching technical skills and leadership in some of the world's most beautiful and remote wilderness is what we do, so it's not a surprise that this book has been a long time in the making. In addition to Dave and Molly, who have brought their experience together in this comprehensive handbook on how to plan and execute your own expeditions, there are a number of other parties whom I'd like to acknowledge here for their involvement with this book. Special thanks go to our risk management director, Drew Leemon, for his contributions to the leadership and risk management chapters; to Tod Schimelpfenig, the curriculum director at the Wilderness Medicine Institute of NOLS, for his keen input on the wilderness medicine and first-aid sections; to senior NOLS field instructor Nate Ostis for bringing a paddler's perspective to the overall narrative; and to John Gookin, NOLS' curriculum and research manager, for the incredible work he puts into the NOLS curriculum on a day-to-day basis. Thank you, too, to all the instructor reviewers who read and gave feedback on early drafts and interns who helped fine-tune some of the research details in chapter 5. Together, this group of professionals has created a valuable resource for outdoor enthusiasts who will take their adventures to the next level with a personal expedition.

Joanne Haines
NOLS Publications Manager
July 2010

We shall not cease from exploration
And the end of all our exploring
Will be to arrive where we started
And know the place for the first time.

—T. S. Eliot

Introduction

Who Is This Book For?

Have you ever read a travel book, attended a slide show, or thumbed through a stack of your friend's vacation photos from an incredible journey to a remote corner of the earth and wondered what it would be like to embark on such an adventure—to watch a herd of caribou cross an Alaskan river, to feel the strong wind of Patagonia on your face, or to share a pot of yak-butter tea with a Tibetan monk?

Some people contemplate such experiences for a few moments and then return to their everyday lives. For others, those exotic images float in their heads, refusing to let go while the thought of organizing and planning such an expedition becomes overwhelming.

The famous adventurer Bill Tilman said, "Any expedition worth doing can be planned on the back of an envelope." He and his main expedition partner, Eric Shipton, explored the remote, uncharted corners of Africa, Asia, and South America from the 1920s to the 1960s, sailing unknown seas, crossing barren deserts, and ascending high Himalayan peaks. They favored small expeditions that could move quickly and adapt to unknown terrain and logistical challenges.

Shipton and Tilman lived in a bygone era when the most important asset for an explorer was a strong will and the ability to commit months, if not years, to an expedition. While *NOLS Expedition Planning* embraces the core of Tilman's statement—that an expedition should be a streamlined and efficient endeavor—the modern day explorer is confronted by a host of hurdles to overcome when planning an extended expedition. Raising money, securing permits, assessing transportation options, selecting equipment, considering health and safety issues, and balancing limited vacation time are just some of the challenges of planning an expedition today.

NOLS Expedition Planning is a resource for anyone who has been inspired to step outside his or her comfort zone and explore the vast natural world. While first-time car campers and veterans of Himalayan expeditions alike will find much useful information in these pages, this book is primarily written for outdoor enthusiasts with basic wilderness living and travel skills who are seeking to take their adventures to the next level.

Why I Expedition: A Snapshot from Dave

The summit was the size of two pool tables pushed together and nearly as flat. I untied from the rope and let the unobstructed 360-degree view of the Karakoram Mountains sink in. Above me somber clouds began to weep a fine mist, reviving dormant clumps of lichen clinging to the rocks at my feet. Responding to the moisture, the lichen started painting the brown granite with vibrant strokes of neon yellow and pumpkin orange. Below in the valley, the straight borders of green potato fields, outside the tiny village of Khorkondas, were the only hint that humans inhabited the chaotic glaciated land. The rain intensified, softening the jagged skyline and obscuring other high mountain treasures behind a thin veil of moisture.

For the last six months, my expedition team and I had poured our energy into this expedition. Now we were standing together on the summit of Tahir Tower, a previously unclimbed 3,000-foot granite spire.

The impetus for this expedition came from a 2 x 3 inch photo in a Pakistan travel guide. The photo showed what appeared to be large granite cliffs somewhere in northeastern Pakistan. My team and I figured out where the photo was taken, applied for and received the necessary permits to access the area, raised the funds to make the trip happen, packed the right stuff, and all along kept our fingers crossed that the photo was not lying and there actually was something there to climb.

Why I Expedition: A Snapshot from Dave

Above: My expedition team—
Jimmy Chin, Steph Davis, and
Brady Robinson—in the midst of
planning for Pakistan.

Right: Jimmy shopping for spices
in a local Islamabad market.

Our small expedition team was composed of Jimmy Chin, Brady Robinson, Steph Davis, and me. Jimmy, Brady, and I work as field instructors for NOLS. Steph is a talented sponsored climber and writer. Though all the members of our small team had been on climbing trips out of the country, the complexity of this expedition was clearly going to be a big step for all of us.

As our planning began, we learned the photo was from the Kondus Valley in the Baltistan region of Pakistan. Unfortunately we also learned the Kondus was in a restricted military zone and had been closed to Westerners for the last 25 years. Despite this setback, the lure of unclimbed mountains persuaded us to try gaining access to the area, and we began filling out the necessary forms to enter the Kondus Valley. Six months later we were elated to learn that we had been granted a climbing permit by the Pakistani ministry of tourism. And though our enthusiasm was somewhat dulled by the reality that the Pakistani military, which ultimately controls the region, might not put much stock in our small piece of paper once we left the capital of Islamabad, we had a start.

Why I Expedition: A Snapshot from Dave

Steph posing next to a sign we saw more than once. If you're traveling internationally in remote countries, be prepared!

The next few months were a blur of applying for climbing grants, pursuing sponsorship, and collecting the right equipment. Before we left we had managed to pool together $15,000 and hoped it would be enough for our two-month expedition. With no real information about what types of terrain or weather conditions the approach and the climbing would include, we packed for every possibility—T-shirts to down jackets, rock shoes to ice axes, and everything in between. Our duffels multiplied like rabbits, and the only people who seemed happy with the huge amount of luggage were the airlines employees, who gladly charged us $1,500 in extra baggage fees. Nevertheless, a year's worth of planning was behind us at last, and we, along with our baggage, finally arrived in the much-anticipated city of Islamabad.

Once in Pakistan, we drove up to the small mountain town of Skardu, the jumping-off point for every expedition that seeks to explore the crown jewels of the Karakoram Range. In Skardu, we made arrangements to meet with General Tahir, the commander in charge of all the northern areas of Pakistan and on whose approval the success of our expedition hinged. The general greeted us in the well-maintained garden courtyard of the military compound in Kapalu. Standing over six feet tall and carrying his 250 pounds on a broad frame, he projected an aura of strength and respect. We were led to a large sitting room decorated with finely upholstered furniture.

Why I Expedition: A Snapshot from Dave

Above: Local residents helping us scope our objective, the Forbidden Towers.

Left: Steph packing one of our haul bags. It takes more than a little gear for a remote climbing expedition.

"So you are here to climb my mountains," he stated firmly, looking at each of us. Just as the pause began to turn into an awkward silence, the smile lines around his eyes crinkled into life, and he continued, "Good. I love the mountains, and there is much to explore in Pakistan."

As it turns out, as a young man the general had worked as a liaison officer for many foreign mountaineering expeditions. For the next hour he entertained us with nostalgic tales of the mountains and climbers he knew.

"But enough about the past," he said, pushing aside a plateful of hors d'oeuvres and unrolling a map across the large glass table. Balancing teacups on our knees, we stared down at the map. Not only was General Tahir enthusiastic about us climbing in the Kondus Valley, a place he had visited many times, but he went so far as to point out a spire at the mouth of the canyon that we might be interested in. Watching the general trace his finger across a map marked "Military Map—Top Secret" as he talked, my climbing partners and I were wide-eyed with the wonder

Why I Expedition: A Snapshot from Dave

Our successful expedition team on the summit of Tahir Tower. Previously unnamed, this peak now honors General Tahir, the Pakistani general who gave us our opportunity.

and excitement of becoming privy to information that we knew we did not have the clearance to see.

General Tahir continued, confirming that our permit from the ministry of tourism meant nothing there. In these remote mountains, the military, and ultimately Tahir, was in control. With a sweep of his hand over the map, he invited us to explore whatever we liked. The only stipulation was to send him some pictures of whatever we ended up climbing and to tell all our friends back in the States about the friendly people and great mountains of Pakistan.

Exuberant, but somewhat stunned by our good fortune, we piled our gear into hired jeeps, tied bandanas around our mouths and noses, and began the slow, dusty drive toward the unknown.

As we passed through one local police checkpoint after another on our journey to the "forbidden" valley, we found that the mention of General Tahir's blessing to enter the Kondus unlocked door after door and would-be roadblocks melted into the dust behind us. We continued on, higher and farther until we turned one tight corner and the mystery of the Forbidden Kondus evaporated. There before us, and only 300 feet from the road, was the giant tower the general had described. Closer inspection of the tower through our spotting scope revealed a continuous crack system that ran over 3,000 feet from the base all the way to the summit—this would be our route.

Why I Expedition: A Snapshot from Dave

The climb would take us several weeks to ascend, and we would have to haul up everything needed to live on the wall—camping gear, food, and a 300-pound barrel filled with drinking water. While we were organizing our supplies for the ascent, we had a constant stream of curious onlookers in our base camp.

Being the first Westerners that most of the locals had ever seen, we must have appeared to them as part circus freaks and part aliens. We used an unfamiliar tongue and wore strange clothes, the three men had long hair, and the woman was smiling and laughing all the time. But the main fascination was for all the equipment we had brought from the States—climbing gear, solar panels, satellite phones, and even a computer. Each day we would have 10 to 40 villagers in our base camp content to stare in silence at us and our gear.

Being a military zone, there was a squad of special forces troops stationed nearby, and they were frequent visitors to our base camp as well. The troops were well versed in basic climbing techniques to access their posts, some as high as 20,000 feet. They used carabiners and pitons, but modern climbing protection such as camming units were something they had never seen. One day we spent two hours teaching a squad of soldiers rope systems and modern climbing techniques. In exchange, despite our feeble protests, they proceeded to show us how to properly handle and fire AK-47s.

After shuttling all our gear to the base, we began climbing the shimmering wall of granite, following the giant dihedral that spread up the wall like an open book offering endless pages of spectacular climbing. Sweating with exertion and sometimes fear, our bounty at the end of each day was a new collection of sore muscles, worn skin, and a few more feet of elevation toward the summit. Sleeping on ledges and eating energy bars, we found a home in the vertical world.

The last thousand feet of the wall steepened and the rock quality deteriorated to the consistency of compacted sand dune. Jimmy led one particularly loose section, and while he was climbing, the rock disintegrated, sending him hurtling headfirst onto a ledge below. Miraculously, he received just a few minor lacerations and some bad bruises from the 30-foot fall. The near disaster made us think about how remote our expedition was from medical care, and we proceeded with a new sense of caution.

When we finally reached the summit, after days upon days of intense physical and mental effort, we were simultaneously ecstatic and exhausted. There were hugs and high-fives and a seemingly endless series of summit photos. Before I headed down, I watched a sliver of light cut through the clouds and ignite the

Why I Expedition: A Snapshot from Dave

shimmering glacier below as it ran through the endless rock walls and illuminated the high peaks, connecting me with the wildness of the Karakoram Range. In the end we named the granite spire Tahir Tower in honor of the man who, although he did not partake in any of the actual climbing, had given us the opportunity to try.

The storybook expedition came to an abrupt end on our return flight to the United States in the Chicago O'Hare Airport, where we were greeted by thunderstorms that grounded our connecting flight, causing an unexpected bivy at the airport. And once I was finally back in Salt Lake City, I stared at the empty baggage carousel for a good 30 minutes before I accepted that fact my luggage was still on an expedition of its own. Jet-lagged and suffering from a bout of traveler's diarrhea, I argued with the airlines about my lost bags. I had to start working a NOLS mountaineering course in two days and needed the gear that was now on its way to Jacksonville, Florida. Frustrated and tired, I got in my truck and started the five-hour drive to Lander, Wyoming.

Driving east along the highway, listening to a radio station in English and drinking water that didn't need to be purified, I was looking forward to sharing my adventures with friends and family waiting for me at home. Soon the monotony of the wide open landscape had me thinking back on the trip, remembering the wonderful people I had met and the unique cultures and amazing climbing I had experienced. The nuts-and-bolts reason for our success had to do with planning, permits, fund-raising, and technical climbing skill. But in reality it all started with one little photo in a tourist book, a lot of hard work, and of course luck.

Seven years have passed since the four of us stood arm-in-arm on the top of Tahir Tower. While the details of the expedition have faded somewhat over time, what remains unblinkingly clear to me is looking into the eyes of my three close friends on the summit and seeing the patience, courage, commitment, and friendship needed to make what was once just a dream a lifelong memory. ■

The National Outdoor Leadership School

In 1924, 16-year-old Paul Petzoldt found himself halfway up the Grand Teton in Wyoming. Dressed in cowboy boots and jeans, he and his friend Ralph Herron were caught by the fading light and an approaching storm. They spent the night crouched and shivering on a small rock ledge as the wind and snow pummeled them. During the sleepless night, they had plenty of time to think back on the boastful comments they had made to the locals about how they were going to make the second ascent of the Grand. Hopelessly unprepared for the alpine environment, their best option was to sit tight and hope the storm would break. Fortunately, by morning the quick-moving storm had passed, but the rocks were now encased in snow and ice. Using a borrowed pocketknife, Petzoldt chopped handholds and footholds out of the ice so that he and Herron could retreat back down the way they had ascended. Discouraged and physically drained, but with a new appreciation and knowledge of the mountain, they spent the day recuperating at their base camp whittling alpenstocks out of nearby pine boughs. The following morning they kicked steps up a snowfield and followed a weakness in the southwest face of the mountain, and by 3:00 p.m., they were slapping each other's backs in celebration on the summit.

Over the next three decades, Petzoldt became one the most experienced mountaineers in the United States. In 1938, he was invited to join the first American expedition to climb K2, the second highest peak in the world. While on the expedition, he set a record for the longest continuous time above 20,000 feet without supplemental oxygen. During World War II, Petzoldt served with the Army's 10th Mountain Division at Camp Hale, Colorado, teaching the ski troops safety and preparation techniques. He continued to be a driving force in wilderness education by helping establish the first American Outward Bound program in Colorado in the early 1960s.

While working at Outward Bound, Petzoldt recognized the need to teach the next generation of outdoor leaders. In 1965, he founded the National Outdoor Leadership School and set up operations in the small cow town of Lander, Wyoming. The first season, 100 students were issued wool trousers, heavy coats, and wooden frame packs, loaded into stock trucks, and set loose for a month in the wilderness of the Wind River Range. Today, NOLS educates over 13,000 students every year in a variety of outdoor and leadership skills in a wide range of environments worldwide using state-of-the-art equipment and a pool of talented NOLS instructors.

Though NOLS has evolved as it has grown, the philosophy inspired by Petzoldt is still firmly in place: "Take people into the wilderness for an extended period of time, teach them the right things, feed them well, and when they walk out of the mountains, they will be skilled leaders."

The core of his idea was the extended expedition, one of sufficient length to allow a person to practice the skills learned over and over again. That is the backbone of every NOLS course, and today the school is widely recognized as the world's leader in extended wilderness expeditions.

NOLS graduates take home much more than the specific techniques used to backpack, climb, paddle, or ski in the wilderness. More importantly, they also take with them lifelong skills that can be applied to a much broader range of challenges: how to communicate effectively with others, tolerate adversity, solve problems, and as Paul Petzoldt learned on the Grand Teton, how to make sound decisions.

Throughout this book we refer to and discuss many of the skills and philosophies of NOLS. However, *NOLS Expedition Planning* is not a substitute for attending a NOLS course or any other type of skilled outdoor instruction. In addition, there are several other NOLS publications that readers can reference to find more detailed information about certain outdoor topics than will be covered in this book.

The NOLS Reference Library

The National Outdoor Leadership School's Wilderness Guide by Mark Harvey
NOLS Backcountry Cooking by Claudia Pearson and Joanne Kuntz
NOLS Backcountry Nutrition by Mary Howley Ryan
NOLS Bear Essentials by John Gookin and Tom Reed
NOLS Cookery by Claudia Pearson
NOLS River Rescue by Nate Ostis
NOLS Soft Paths by Bruce Hampton and David Cole
NOLS Wilderness Ethics by Jennifer Lamb and Glenn Goodrich

NOLS Wilderness Medicine by Tod Schimelpfenig
NOLS Wilderness Mountaineering by Phil Powers
NOLS Wilderness Navigation by Darran Wells
NOLS Wilderness Wisdom by John Gookin
NOLS Winter Camping by John Gookin and Buck Tilton

How to Proceed

It is easy to get swept up by the image of an adventure, dreaming, for example, about a monthlong journey across the southern steppes of Patagonia on horseback with wind in your face and granite peaks spread across the horizon. But before you tighten down that saddle and head off on the expedition of a lifetime, there are many questions you'll need to answer:

> *Where is the best area for riding in Patagonia?*
> *How do I find a horse to lease?*
> *If I get hurt, will my insurance cover me?*
> *What is the weather like there?*
> *Are there any travel warnings for the area?*
> *What vaccinations do I need?*
> *How do I get a visa?*
> *Can I buy white gas for my camp stove in the country?*
> *How much food should I bring from home?*
> *How can I keep friends and family up-to-date on my expedition or how do I share my adventure with others once I'm home?*

This book is devoted to giving you the tools and resources you'll need to help answer questions like these. Every adventure has its own unique set of challenges and requires different preparation and execution, but the overall thought process is the same whether you're planning to climb Mount Kenya or backpack through the Grand Canyon.

THE INNATE DESIRE FOR EXPLORATION

Humans are born with a natural curiosity about the world around us. As soon as we learn to crawl, we begin exploring our surroundings from the ground up. The homes where we live seem at first like immense castles filled with endless nooks and crannies, containing a host of benign and dangerous items. Most of these unknowns are thankfully kept out of reach until we can learn to appreciate the power of electricity or the intrinsic value of a family heirloom. Once we learn to walk, the locked doors begin to open and our environment gets exponentially bigger and more complex. Whether chasing after frogs or shopping solo at the local grocery store, we are bombarded on a daily basis with new experiences and insights.

When do we stop exploring and learning? We hope never, but the demands of the modern world force us into daily routines where we often repeat a series of similar tasks and interact with the same segment of society. While curiosity about the world sometimes takes a backseat to responsibilities and societal obligations, it is still there in all of us, waiting for the next opportunity to set loose our five senses, to laugh, to cry, to learn, and to wonder.

A Brief History of Exploration

The world's very first explorers carried no maps and few, if any, supplies; they did not seek riches, fame, or enlightenment. Thousands of years ago modern humans simply wanted to see if it was any easier to survive in the next valley. Since these early adventurers left only bones and a few stone tools as evidence of their passage, scientists have had to piece together a time line of their migration using genetic analysis and archeological records. Although there is still much debate, most researchers believe that modern humans emigrated from Africa and colonized Asia,

Partial Time Line of the History of Exploration

356–323 BC

Alexander the Great explores (and conquers) Asia Minor, India, and parts of Africa.

AD 1265–1299

Marco Polo explores China and Asia.

1325–1354

Ibn Battuta explores Africa, Middle East, Asia.

1400–1800

Ocean-going voyages dominate exploration worldwide.

1804–1806

Lewis and Clark Expedition crosses North America.

1840–1870

Dr. David Livingstone explores eastern Africa.

1860

Robert Burke crosses Australia.

1838–1845

John Frémont explores western North America.

1911

Roald Amundsen reaches the South Pole.

1909

Robert Peary reaches the North Pole.

1953

Sir Edmund Hillary climbs Mount Everest.

Australia, Europe, and North and South America between 90,000 and 40,000 years ago.

The first written account of an expedition is from 2600 BC when an Egyptian expedition was sent to Byblos, in current-day Lebanon, to get cedar wood. Many of these early explorers were involved in trade or colonizing lands with advantageous resources. The Silk Road, the Northwest Passage, and shipping lanes to the New World are examples of important historical trade routes. Religion also played a major role in early exploration. The soldiers of the Crusades, pilgrims to Mecca, and missionaries spreading Christianity were some of the earliest adventurers. The 18th and 19th centuries, the Age of Enlightenment, saw a renewed emphasis on exploration for scientific purposes and to improve the body of knowledge and understanding about the earth.

By the 20th century, the period of colonization had passed and the world's ruling countries needed a new stadium to demonstrate their muscle and enhance national pride. Expeditions to the North and South Poles, the depths of the oceans, and the high summits were often fueled by patriotic fervor. In fact, British interest in the coronation of Queen Elizabeth II was almost overshadowed by the news that a British expedition had climbed Mount Everest in 1953. In the second half of the 20th century, the world's two superpowers, the United States and the Soviet Union, were not only engaged in a military arms race but also a nationalistic quest to be the first country to explore the moon and beyond. Today, advanced technologies developed for space exploration help make our lives here on earth safer and more productive.

The Personal Benefits of Expeditions

While survival, trade, wealth, religion, fame, and charting the unknown corners of the earth have all played a role in explorations of the past, this book deals with personal expeditions where the main goals are personal enlightenment and achievement.

When George Mallory set off to attempt Mount Everest in 1924, the media hounded him, trying to ascertain his motives for such a seemingly foolish endeavor. Frustrated at the press' lack of understanding and continual inane questioning of why he wanted to climb Everest, Mallory eventually blurted out the famous one liner, "Because it's there." But the extended version of his motives for climbing Everest, and his view of life, still rings true today:

> The first question which you will ask and which I must try to answer is this, What is the use of climbing Mount Everest? and my answer must at once be, It is no use. There is not the slightest prospect of any gain whatsoever. Oh, we may learn a little about the behaviour of the human body at high altitudes, and possibly medical men may turn our observation to some account for the purposes of aviation. But otherwise nothing will come of it. We shall not bring back a single bit of gold or silver, not a gem, nor any coal or iron. We shall not find a single foot of earth that can be planted with crops to raise food. It's no use. So, if you cannot understand that there is something in man which responds to the challenge of this mountain and goes out to meet it, that the struggle is the struggle of life itself upward and forever upward, then you won't see why we go. What we get from this adventure is just sheer joy. And joy is, after all, the end of life. We do not live to eat and make money. We eat and make money to be able to enjoy life. That is what life means and what life is for.
>
> —George Mallory

Most people can relate to Mallory's "sheer joy" benefit of going on adventures, but there is also growing scientific evidence that taking time off can have a positive effect on both your physical and mental health.

One study that surveyed 12,000 U.S. men who were participating in a heart disease prevention trial suggested that men who took vacations decreased their overall risk of death from heart disease by as much as 30 percent. The researchers found that some men in the survey had not taken any vacation time during the five-year study period. As a result, these overachievers had both the highest overall death rate and highest incidence of heart disease of any of the participants. The researchers concluded that vacations have a protective effect because they help you reduce your stress load, or at least allow you to take a break from the everyday stressors of the workplace.

A similar survey was conducted on women by the National Institute for Occupational Safety and Health (NIOSH) wherein researchers compared psychological stress, quality of marital life, and disruptive home life due to work among women who take vacations frequently and those who do not. Not surprisingly, women who took fewer vacations demonstrated higher levels of stress, depression, and home-life problems.

Recent Trends in Outdoor Recreation

Why are Americans so stressed out? One reason might be the relatively few vacation days we are allotted per year compared to the rest of the world. Unlike most modern industrial countries whose residents enjoy at least three weeks of paid time off, Americans average just 13 days of vacation per year.

Average Vacation Days by Country

Country	Vacation Days Per Year
Italy	42
France	37
Germany	35
Brazil	34
U.K.	28
Canada	26
Korea	25
Japan	25
U.S.	13

So what do most Americans do with their precious two weeks of vacation time away from the daily grind? We go shopping! The number one activity of domestic travelers is shopping, followed by

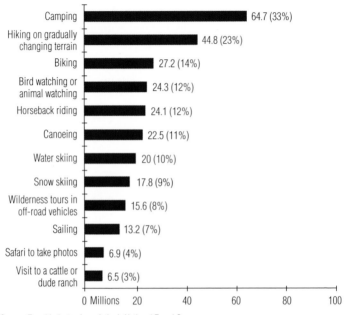

Soft Adventure Activities on Trips in the Last Five Years
(millions and % of 197.7 million adults)

Camping	64.7 (33%)
Hiking on gradually changing terrain	44.8 (23%)
Biking	27.2 (14%)
Bird watching or animal watching	24.3 (12%)
Horseback riding	24.1 (12%)
Canoeing	22.5 (11%)
Water skiing	20 (10%)
Snow skiing	17.8 (9%)
Wilderness tours in off-road vehicles	15.6 (8%)
Sailing	13.2 (7%)
Safari to take photos	6.9 (4%)
Visit to a cattle or dude ranch	6.5 (3%)

Source: Travel Industry Association's National Travel Survey

attending family and social events. But have faith—the third most popular vacation activity is camping.

One-third of U.S. adults say they have gone camping in the past five years. Camping vacationers tend to be married with children, and people who go camping also tend to enjoy hiking, biking, canoeing, and other outdoor activities. Fifty-nine percent of campers said they traveled with their spouses on their most recent outdoor vacation, and nearly half traveled with their children.

In addition, 98 million Americans have taken an adventure trip in the past five years. Researchers have defined adventure travel as a trip for the specific purpose of participating in an activity to explore a new experience. Often, these experiences involve the perceived and real risks associated with personal challenges in a natural environment or exotic outdoor setting. During the last five years, 67 million people participated in soft adventure activities like camping, canoeing, and easy hiking, while 6 million people partici-

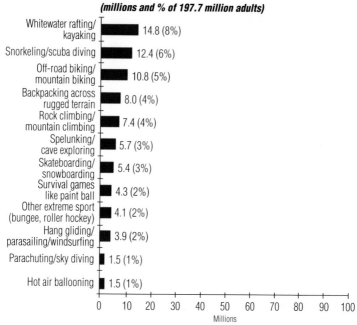

Hard Adventure Activities on Trips in the Last Five Years
(millions and % of 197.7 million adults)

Whitewater rafting/kayaking	14.8 (8%)
Snorkeling/scuba diving	12.4 (6%)
Off-road biking/mountain biking	10.8 (5%)
Backpacking across rugged terrain	8.0 (4%)
Rock climbing/mountain climbing	7.4 (4%)
Spelunking/cave exploring	5.7 (3%)
Skateboarding/snowboarding	5.4 (3%)
Survival games like paint ball	4.3 (2%)
Other extreme sport (bungee, roller hockey)	4.1 (2%)
Hang gliding/parasailing/windsurfing	3.9 (2%)
Parachuting/sky diving	1.5 (1%)
Hot air ballooning	1.5 (1%)

Source: Travel Industry Association's National Travel Survey

pated in hard adventure activities like whitewater rafting, scuba diving, and mountain climbing.

Living in the United Sates, we are also fortunate to have over 700 million acres of public land in which to recreate. These public lands are managed by four different federal agencies: the National Wildlife Refuge System, the U.S. Forest Service, the National Park Service, and the Bureau of Land Management. Recreational use, however, is not spread out evenly throughout our public lands. The National Park System, which has the least amount of acreage, has more visitor use than any of the other public lands. The National Parks also contain most of the well-known scenic natural attractions found in the United States. Unlike the other federal lands that have multiuse mission statements, which accommodate many activities such as logging and mining in addition to recreation, the National Park Service legacy is to protect our nation's natural treasures for the enjoyment of people now *and* for future generations. Accordingly,

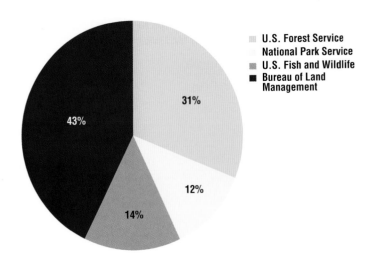

Division of Federal Land in the United States

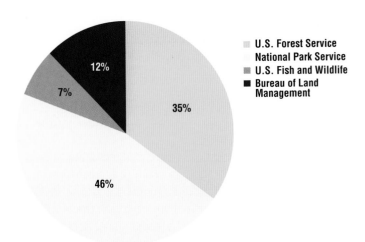

Distribution of Visitor Use

the Park Service is continually struggling to find a balance between providing for human enjoyment now, which can often mean building roads, hotels, restaurants, and trails, and protecting these wild places unscathed for the future, which is often best done by preventing the construction of these same things.

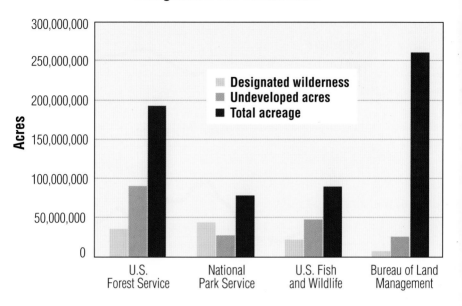

Furthermore, some of the most remote and untamed backcountry found on public lands in the United States has been set aside as wilderness areas. The Wilderness Act of 1964 defines wilderness as an area of generally undisturbed federal land without permanent improvements or human habitation that is protected and managed so as to preserve its natural conditions. Congress has designated over 106 million acres of federal land in units as part of the National Wilderness Preservation System. While current legislation prevents designated wilderness areas from being developed, there are tens of thousands more acres of federal land that meet the wilderness criteria but have not received the same protected status. These areas, such as the Arctic National Wildlife Refuge, are constantly under pressure from special interest groups looking for loopholes within the law to exploit our natural resources for profit.

Although the number of people who recreate on public lands has grown to a record high, the length of time these people spend on public land has shrunk. Partially due to an increasingly hectic lifestyle and fewer vacation days, the number of backcountry users in our national parks has steadily declined since the early 1990s. While this

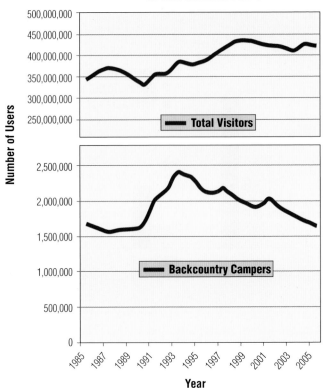

decrease might cause some federal land agencies to allocate more of their limited resources to the more popular park areas, it also means expeditions traveling to remote regions within public lands will encounter more of what they desire in the first place—solitude.

The United States was "settled" fairly recently in terms of human history, and in the process, many of its native peoples were removed from their traditional lands. Consequently, the federal lands where we recreate are for the most part uninhabited. In other areas of the world, however, designated parks and nature reserves often contain communities of people living within their borders. In Nepal, for example, Sagarmatha National Park not only has the mighty Mount Everest within its boundaries, but also 3,000 indigenous people. U.S. residents planning adventures outside the country should bear in mind that the term wilderness in other parts of the world may have a different meaning than they are accustomed to. Still, for many expeditions traveling abroad, this mix of cultural and natural splendor is part of the motivation for planning such a trip.

Summary

The word "expedition" carries an aura of importance. Tell a group of friends that you are going on vacation and you will receive some polite questions of feigned interest, but mention the word expedition and watch their expressions change to curiosity and be prepared for a barrage of questions. In today's regimented world, many people find themselves having less control of their daily lives: the "small-cog-in-a-giant-wheel" syndrome. Planning and successfully carrying out an expedition yields an incredible sense of accomplishment and purpose. But be careful, expeditions can become addictive. An adventure should be used to enhance your life, not escape from it. Writer and Nobel Prize winner Anatole France summed up the heart of any journey when he wrote, "To accomplish great things, we must not only act, but also dream; not only plan, but also believe."

DETERMINING THE GOAL
OF YOUR EXPEDITION

In today's information-rich society, inspiration for travel can come from a variety of sources—friends, TV, the Internet, books, and magazines. Goals for an expedition usually originate in two different ways: either you are looking for a place to pursue an activity like climbing, hiking, boating, or skiing—or you want to visit a place and choose an activity based on the options available there. Thinking about where your interest lies along this spectrum will help you define your expedition goal.

Once the concept for an expedition has been formulated, the next step is to write down your overall goal. Getting the objective down on paper or on a computer's hard drive will bring the idea out of the thinking phase and into the planning and doing phase.

Expeditions have a way of changing focus throughout the planning process, and written goals will serve as a reference point for all the expedition members.

Factors Affecting Expedition Goals

There are a multitude of overlapping and often antagonistic factors that can influence the goals and success of an expedition. These factors can be divided into three basic categories: known, variable, and uncontrollable.

KNOWN FACTORS
Known factors include the technical skills (e.g., experience with backpacking, first aid, climbing, foreign languages) and interpersonal skills (e.g., communication, leadership, and tolerance for

Objectives for an expedition can vary widely. Clockwise from top left: A family outing; a light and fast coastal hike; fly fishing in China; a new climbing route in the Rocky Mountains; summiting a peak in Alaska.

adversity) that you know you and your expedition mates possess. Determining how much the expedition will cost and how much money each team member can contribute is another known factor, as is the amount of time each participant can devote to the expedition. Known factors are somewhat controllable in the planning stage of an expedition—for example, expedition members can actively improve map-reading skills or get a part-time job to generate additional funds—but once the expedition begins, these factors become more static.

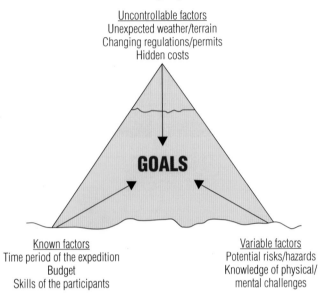

Factors Affecting Expedition Goals

Uncontrollable factors
Unexpected weather/terrain
Changing regulations/permits
Hidden costs

GOALS

Known factors
Time period of the expedition
Budget
Skills of the participants

Variable factors
Potential risks/hazards
Knowledge of physical/
mental challenges

VARIABLE FACTORS

Variable factors are those that can be researched or discussed before the trip begins and reassessed as needed during the expedition. Knowing as much as possible about the intended objective will improve the odds of an expedition accomplishing its goals. Expeditions traveling to previously unexplored regions or attempting new routes have much lower success rates. (Everest was attempted eight times over a 30-year period before Edmund Hillary and Tenzing Norgay finally reached the summit in 1953. Today, thousands of people have summitted Everest, and one in four people who attempt the peak reaches the summit.) Obtaining information about the climate and terrain, as well as reviewing other expeditions' experiences on similar objectives, will allow team members to get a feel for the challenges they will face. Discussing what level of risk individuals are comfortable with before the expedition begins will help eliminate surprises during the adventure and determine if the goal of the trip is realistic.

UNCONTROLLABLE FACTORS

While a realistic assessment of known and variable factors can help support an expedition's goals, uncontrollable factors can stop an expedition in its tracks. These factors include unpredictable environmental conditions, like the hundred-year flood that knocks out all the bridges to the base of the mountain you are trying to climb, or unpredictable political conditions, like a border crossing between two countries you planned on using that is closed indefinitely due to terrorist threats. While nothing can be done about uncontrollable factors, acknowledging their potential will mentally prepare the team members for the worst. Eric Shipton wrote, "Mountain exploration is like cooking eggs. Quite often you set out to make an omelet and end up with scrambled eggs."

Dave and the Birth and Culmination of an Expedition Goal

In the summer of 2003, I was looking for a new adventure—an exciting journey that could be undertaken with just a few close friends. I wanted something different than my normal climbing-based trips, and something I could sink my teeth into. Seeking inspiration, I spent an evening thumbing through my *National Geographic* collection, soaking up exotic images from far-flung corners of the seven continents. I found a plethora of potential trips, but nothing really grabbed me. As I returned the magazines to the bookshelf, a dusty, dog-eared paperback caught my eye: *The Long Walk* by Slavomir Rawicz.

The Long Walk is an incredible tale of human will and physical endurance set during WWII. In 1939 Rawicz, a Polish army officer, was captured by the Russian army. He was falsely accused of being a spy and sentenced to 20 years of hard labor in a Siberian gulag (prison camp). Knowing he would never live through his incarceration, Rawicz and six other inmates escaped and, over the next year, made their way on foot from Siberia to freedom in India, more than 4,000 miles to the south. They marched through the frozen taiga of Russia and across the scorching Gobi Desert of Mongolia before scaling the Himalayan Mountains in winter to finally arrive in the safe haven of India. Four of the prisoners perished from the elements,

Dave and the Birth and Culmination of an Expedition Goal

and Rawicz and two other survivors spent several weeks in the hospital recuperating from their ordeal.

Many scholars have questioned if Rawicz's story is true or just the ramblings of the author's overactive imagination. Could someone really survive a trek across Europe and Asia with just the clothes on his back? I didn't know, but as I looked at the paperback on my shelf, I knew I had found the objective of my next expedition—to retrace Slavomir Rawicz's *The Long Walk*.

I mentioned the idea to my main traveling partner and fellow NOLS instructor Ant Chapin. Ant and his partner, Keri Bean, had also read Rawicz's book and were excited about the potential adventure. Ant had lived and guided in Asia for half a dozen years, and his ability to make anyone laugh as well as his "get it done" attitude would be extremely helpful during our long walk. Keri had a sharp wit and had also traveled extensively around the world. The fourth member of our group would be Lauren Edwards; while she lacked the travel experience of the rest of us, she had studied Chinese in college (2,500 miles of our journey would be spent crossing China) and was one of the physically toughest people I knew.

So we had a capable team, but was the expedition feasible? Math has never been my strong suit, but Ant quickly pointed out that if we hiked 20 miles a day, it would take at least 200 days to complete the journey. None of us could devote that much time or money to the project. We adjusted our goals and determined we could allot three months for the trip, and we also decided to use whatever modes of travel that seemed appropriate to follow the path that Rawicz took more than six decades previously.

We spent a year planning the expedition, writing grants, selling T-shirts, applying for visas, scouring the Internet for information, working several jobs, pooling our resources, and procuring the necessary equipment. In September of 2004, Ant, Keri, Lauren, and I flew to Siberia, and as we disembarked the plane, our welcoming committee was a bone-chilling gale and an early season snowstorm. India seemed awfully far away.

Throughout our expedition, unpredictable weather, strange foods, unforeseen border crossing problems, and other logistical headaches challenged both our physical health and our sanity. We traveled by plane, train, bus, car, boat, horse, yak, and camel, and we wore the soles off our hiking boots. But three months later, I was riding in a rickshaw down Park Street in the sweltering heat and humidity of Calcutta, India. ■

Asking Yourself the Right Questions

Now that you have thought about the goal of your next adventure and the factors you need to consider, walk over to a mirror, look yourself square in the eyes, and ask yourself the following questions:

Is your expedition goal reasonable based on your skills and the skills of your teammates?

Can you really hike 20 miles a day on the Pacific Coast Trail to complete the expedition in the allotted time frame? Will the Spanish classes you took 10 years ago in high school allow you to buy supplies during your trek through the Ecuadoran rain forest? Your partner boulders hard in the climbing gym, but can he lead an ice climb rated WI4? Also consider your team's people skills. Will you be able to get along with your teammates when you're stuck in a tent with them stormbound for a week in Patagonia?

Can you devote the time necessary for planning and completing the expedition?

The amount of preparation needed for an expedition can be as short as an afternoon for a 10-day backpacking trip in a familiar area or as long as several years to procure the necessary permits and iron out the other logistics to attempt an unclimbed peak in China. It is easy to become hypnotized by the visions of a month-long expedition itself, but the adventure does not begin at the airport. The planning portion of an expedition can involve a serious time commitment. Free time is a scarce commodity in most people's fast-paced lifestyles; make sure you have enough extra time for the expedition or you will make yourself and everyone around you miserable.

Do you have or can you generate the funds necessary for the trip?

There is nothing more stressful than having to max out your credit cards before your trip even begins or having to back out on your partners at the last minute because you could not raise your share of the budget, leaving them in the hole in terms of a teammate and expedition funds.

Expedition Mirror

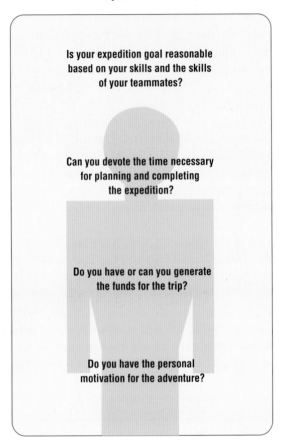

Is your expedition goal reasonable based on your skills and the skills of your teammates?

Can you devote the time necessary for planning and completing the expedition?

Do you have or can you generate the funds for the trip?

Do you have the personal motivation for the adventure?

Do you have the personal motivation for the adventure?

This is the most important question and the most difficult to answer. Take a long look in the mirror because only you can answer this question. Most people find that once they take the first step and commit to an expedition, the energy and motivation for the adventure become self-generating. While New Year's fitness resolutions often fall by the wayside at the first lapse in resolve, the thought of being dropped off with a 60-pound backpack in the Brooks Range of Alaska with 100 miles of rough terrain in front of you is a great motivator to get in shape.

CHOOSING YOUR EXPEDITION TEAM

After deciding on a goal, the next most important decision in planning is figuring out who is going on the expedition. The number of people who are needed to safely complete the expedition and what type of technical skills and people skills are required will vary depending on where the adventure will take place and the nature of the activity involved. The amount of risk the participants are willing to accept, as well as the manner or style in which the goal of the adventure will be attempted, can also affect the expedition's structure. Finally, the cost and how the funds will be generated will often have an influence on the size of the expedition.

NOLS advocates traveling with at least four people while on expeditions in remote regions. The rationale behind this number is that in the event of an emergency where one of the group members is injured or sick and no longer mobile, one person can attend to the ailing teammate and two people can go and get help; thus, no one is left on his or her own.

In some areas you are mandated by regulations to have a minimum number of participants. In Maine's Baxter State Park, for example, it is against regulations to venture into technical terrain without at least one other person. The Indian Mountaineering Federation requires that climbing teams who are attempting unclimbed peaks must comprise at least equal numbers of Indian nationals and foreign climbers. Research the area where you'll be going. Below is a list of some of the positive and negative attributes of different group sizes to consider.

Smaller Expedition Groups (4 or fewer people)	Larger Expedition Groups (5 or more people)
+ Ease logistics	− Complicate logistics
+ Are faster in technical terrain	− Are slower in technical terrain
+ Have less impact on the environment	− Have more impact on the environment
+ Are quicker to facilitate change	− Are slower to facilitate change
+ Are more efficient decision-makers	− Are slower to make decisions
+/− Have less structured leadership	+/− Have more structured leadership
+/− Have less potential for personality issues	+/− Have more potential for personality issues
− Have fewer resources to deal with hardship	+ Have more resources to deal with hardship

Considering a Solo Expedition

Traveling solo offers many benefits, such as low cost, efficiency, and a great sense of personal satisfaction. However, solo expeditions inherently involve more risk since there is no one else to help deal with difficult or dangerous events. Although traveling alone takes a certain mind-set and is not for everyone, some expeditions are often completed solo, such as through-hiking the Appalachian Trail (AT).

Each year between 400 and 500 people complete the more than 2,000-mile trail that usually takes around six months. One of the main reasons people attempt the AT solo is the difficulty in finding another person who has a similar hiking speed and can devote the time it takes to complete. Also, new lightweight back-packing gear makes it possible for a hiker to carry all his own gear instead of needing to divide heavier items, like a tent and stove, between several people. The trail is, for the most part, well marked and does not go through any technical terrain. While large sections of the route cut through remote wilderness regions, other portions have more access to facilities. As a result, through-hikers can mail resupplies to local post offices before the hike begins and pick them up along the way. Furthermore, although there have been a few incidents of violent crime against hikers on the trail, they are rare. In the event of an emergency, communication with the outside world has become easier in recent years due to increased cell phone coverage and reception throughout most of the trail. Although a relatively small number of people through-hike the entire AT, between 3 and 4 million people hike portions of the trail, so the potential of having someone to talk with or ask for help from is there if desired. For these reasons, hiking the AT alone is not an unreasonable endeavor.

Some expeditions are not viable solo adventures, though, such as a mountaineering trip to climb the Muldrow Glacier route on Denali in Alaska. The route involves 20 miles of hiking across tundra with several dangerous river crossings in grizzly bear habitat—just to reach the foot of the mountain. Once at the toe of the glacier, climbers still have to ascend over 14,000 feet of heavily crevassed snow and ice slopes on their way to the summit. The weather can be severe with temperatures often −20 to −50 degrees F, winds over 100 mph, and the potential for weeklong storms. Beside the obvious hazards, there are other handicaps to traveling solo on Denali. Without a climbing partner you would not need to carry a rope or other climbing safety gear, but you would still have to carry a mountaineering tent, stove, shovel, first-aid kit, repair kit, emergency communication devices, bear spray, maps/GPS—all of which would normally be split between at least two people. In addition to the dangers of ascending steep slopes and navigating around crevasses with no safety rope, a solo climber would also have to break trail the entire way up and down the mountain, essentially doing twice as much work as a party of two.

Safety and Style

After WWII, mountaineering expeditions attempting to summit the last unclimbed mountains of the world, including Everest, were often organized using military siege tactics. These expeditions were expensive operations that relied on large numbers of climbers and even larger numbers of support staff who slowly but steadily worked their way up the mountain. On Everest, the local guides or Sherpas would often fix ropes from the bottom to the top of the peak and set up and stock camps with supplies that would eventually enable a small team comprising the strongest climbers to attempt a summit bid. As a result of this style, many people's livelihoods in popular mountainous regions of the world, such as Nepal, have become directly tied to supporting larger groups of outdoor adventurers.

The trend has shifted a bit in recent years to smaller, more self-reliant expeditions. Equipment has become lighter and more reliable, and the fitness and overall technical skills of the participants have also increased, allowing expeditions to accomplish more with less gear and fewer people. In addition, smaller expeditions can move more quickly and, consequently, spend less time in hazardous terrain. Finally, the environmental impact is also reduced with smaller expeditions.

No matter the chosen activity or objective, whether climbing a mountain or running a river, the best way to succeed is to have adequate supplies, allowing you to wait out bad weather, and enough people power to share the work and absorb injuries or illnesses.

Costs

How the expedition is being funded and determining the major costs of the expedition will often have a direct effect on team size. If your expedition is fortunate enough to receive a grant or sponsorship money, you might try to keep the expedition team small. On the other hand, if all the members of the trip are splitting expenses, more participants can help defray big-ticket items like permit fees.

A single climbing permit for Mount Everest costs $25,000 for a single person, which does not include airfare, equipment, food, porters, or other in-country costs. However, for $70,000 you can purchase a permit that allows seven climbers to attempt the peak, which works out to $10,000 per climber; as mentioned previously, having more people could potentially increase the odds of reaching the top.

Local travel costs are often the biggest expenses of an expedition. Determining how many people and how much equipment will fit in a particular helicopter, small plane, boat, or land vehicle will also help determine the most economically feasible numbers for the expedition.

Leadership and Decision-Making

A small expedition of like-minded individuals functions like swimmers competing in the Olympic medley relay. Once the expedition begins, the team puts all of their effort into achieving the goal. Each person has his or her own strengths and takes on appropriate tasks and roles with little discussion. The whole process should happen seamlessly, but if one of the team members gets sick or injured, a small group might not be able to adapt to the misfortune.

A large expedition team can absorb unexpected challenges and continue forward; however, the pace of the larger group is much slower. A large group also requires a more structured leadership model to make sure all the group's resources are working together. In addition, people involved in large expeditions must communicate well or risk having their views get lost in the shuffle. Likewise, decision-making will have to be accomplished in a way that involves everyone or the expedition can grind to a halt.

Skills and Personality

Putting together a well-balanced, fun expedition team is a challenging task. The first step is to look at the expedition's goals and figure out what skills are needed to achieve those goals. Then you need to determine what skills you already have. While it is easy to focus on technical skills for a particular outdoor activity, there are

The Importance of Technical Skills vs. Personality Compatibility When Choosing Expedition Teammates

More Important		
Technical Skills	Multipitch rock climbing trip to Cochise Stronghold, Arizona	Mountaineering expedition to climb Mt. Logan, Canada
	Group guided natural history safari to Yellowstone National Park	Tandem canoe trip to Boundary Waters, Minnesota
Less Important		
	Less Important	More Important

Personality Compatibility

other attributes that are important to every expedition. These include judgment and decision-making, tolerance for adversity, and the ability to get along with people and be a supportive member of the group.

One tool that is helpful in organizing the attributes of the expedition team is an expedition questionnaire. See the following pages for an example that can be modified for any type of expedition.

In an ideal world, all members of an expedition would have excellent and equal technical skills and personal skills, and the blend of personalities would fit together like a jigsaw puzzle. Unfortunately, this is not the norm, and deciding who should be included in an expedition often boils down to finding a balance of skills based on the objective of the expedition. The chart above categorizes several types of activities based on the importance of technical skills versus personal skills. The lower left quadrant, for example, contains a guided natural history trip to Yellowstone National Park. This trip would require few technical skills, and guides as well as a preestablished itinerary would provide structure. A group trip will allow participants to gravitate toward or away from other people on the expedition.

Expedition Questionnaire Template

What is the main reason you want to go on the expedition?

_____

_____

_____

List five adventures similar to this expedition that you have attempted in the last 10 years.

	Date	Activity	Location
1.			
2.			
3.			
4.			
5.			

Please list outdoor activities you participate in.

Frequency: once a month, once a week, several times a week

Proficiency: beginner, intermediate, expert

	Activity Type	Frequency	Proficiency
1.			
2.			
3.			
4.			
5.			

Courses and other instruction/training (NOLS, Outward Bound, private guiding): _____

First-aid training and other certifications: _____

Highest formal education received:_____

Have you been treated for any physical or psychological illness or injury in the last six months? If yes, please describe. _____

Expedition Questionnaire Template

Do you have any other preexisting medical or mental history that could affect you during the expedition? _____

_____

Do you have any allergies (food, animal, plant, medication)? _____

_____

Food preferences: _____

Do you smoke? _____

Do you drink alcohol? _____

Do you snore? _____

Do you speak any foreign languages? Please list languages and level of fluency.

_____

Do you have any other skills that could be utilized during this expedition?

_____

Do you have the funds and time available to commit to this expedition?

_____

What has given you the greatest sense of accomplishment in the last five years?

_____

What do you do for work?_____

Favorite books:_____

Favorite music:_____

Religious denomination: _____

References: Please list three people who have been on trips with you and their contact information.

1._____

_____

2._____

_____

3._____

_____

Find the right blend of personal compatibility and technical skill in your teammates based on your expedition objective.

A tandem canoe trip to the Boundary Waters would require more technical skills. The trip takes place in a remote area and, with just two people on the expedition, personality compatibility would be an important consideration.

An example of an activity that would require a high level of skill from all the participants would be a multipitch climbing trip to Cochise Stronghold, where all the participants need to be able to climb the intended routes. While certain types of routes, such as big wall climbs, can take multiple days to complete and demand increased compatibility, single-day endeavors allow more personal space and switching of climbing partners.

Lastly, attempting the highest peak in Canada, Mount Logan, via the King Trench Route does not require highly advanced movement skills on snow and ice, but the remote location and danger of crevasses necessitate the need for the climbers to be roped together whenever they are traveling. In addition, the extreme weather can cause expeditions to be tent-bound for extended periods of time; thus, being able to get along with your partners is extremely important.

A Monumental Achievement of Two Strangers

On January 22, 2006, Børge Ousland and Mike Horn listened to the departing helicopter's blades slice through the frigid Arctic air. They had just been dropped off on Cape Arkticheskiy, Russia, the most northern vestige of land on earth. Ousland and Horn were relative strangers before the expedition, and now it was just the two of them with 620 miles of treacherous shifting ice between them and their goal of being the first people to reach the North Pole in winter. Not only would they face one of the most inhospitable places on earth during its coldest, most physically demanding times of year, but they would also have the mind-bending challenge of doing the two-month expedition in the complete darkness.

Ousland is the world's greatest living polar explorer. He usually travels alone, carrying, pulling, and sometimes swimming with all of his food, fuel, and equipment. He was the first person to reach the North Pole solo in 1994, the first to cross Antarctica solo in 1996, and the first to complete a solo crossing of the Arctic Ocean in 2001. However, going to the North Pole in the dark of winter was a much more dangerous endeavor. He would be shackled to an enormous sled of gear, like a chain gang inmate voluntarily serving a sentence of solitary confinement in a dark wall-less prison, where the only contact with the living world would come in the form of marauding 1,300-pound polar bears. Ousland soon realized that to increase his chances of success and getting back alive to his wife and son, he needed someone to share not only the physical ordeal but the psychological burden as well. However, the Arctic is an unforgiving training ground for would-be explorers; one simple mistake, like removing a glove at the wrong time, can result in a frozen hand, the end of the expedition, and possible death. What Ousland needed was a competent partner, an equal.

Enter Mike Horn, a native South African living in Switzerland who had amassed an impressive expedition résumé. He had swum the length of the Amazon River and had circled the earth following the equator using nonmotorized travel. But what ushered Horn into the elite world of extreme Arctic explorers was his 12,400-mile 808-day continuous circumnavigation of the Arctic Ocean. And just to make this colossal feat a little more challenging, he completed the human- and sail-powered quest against the prevailing winds and currents. While on his epic journey, Mike had learned how to navigate through the disorienting pack ice in the dark by reading the signs of windblown snow, something that Ousland had

A Monumental Achievement of Two Strangers

little experience with. He had also gone 57 days without seeing another living creature and had held on to his sanity.

Besides having parallel skills and experiences in the polar regions, Ousland and Horn had other similarities as well. Both were family men whose first priority was not reaching the pole, but making sure they returned home after the trip with all their fingers and toes and, most of all, their lives. In fact, both men had abandoned at least one previous expedition when the risks had become too great. On the surface, these two lovers of the frozen world seemed like a perfect match, but inside the two men were very different. Ousland was a master in expedition preparation and custom-designed much of his own equipment, but his almost manic attention to detail had given him a "my way or the highway" reputation. Horn, on the other hand, had been a competitive multisport athlete and had seen combat as a commando fighting guerrillas in Angola. While he was also an exceptional planner, Horn was inclined to mix it up and let his strength and wits carry him through difficult conditions. Recently, Ousland had switched from attempting expeditions solo to traveling with partners. Horn, however, had completed all of his adventures solo. The big question was could a lone wolf like Horn learn to run with the bossy Ousland, another alpha male?

In the dark cold of midwinter, Ousland and Horn left Cape Arkticheskiy and cautiously ventured out to test the thin pack ice and their new expedition partnership. Horn's snow navigating skills and Ousland's high-tech gear worked well together, and they made steady progress toward their goal, but interpersonal friction soon developed between them. With no light, their faces bundled in layers of fleece, and the wind stealing their words as soon as they left their lips, the subtleties of communication were nearly impossible. In the beginning, the two rugged men just kept to themselves. But after a broken tent pole sparked a heated argument, Horn and Ousland retreated to their tent to vent their concerns. With the silence broken, they acknowledged the small behaviors driving them apart and agreed to communicate more effectively. Sixty-one days after leaving Russia, they walked arm in arm to the northern apex of the globe. They were hungry, bruised, and slightly frostbitten, but Ousland and Horn had achieved together what would have been impossible alone. ■

Finding People

Most people planning adventures look to friends and family when putting together their expedition team. If that does not pan out, the next step is usually getting recommendations for potential partners from people you know. Other resources for finding suitable team- mates include clubs and organizations such as the American Canyoneering Association, Appalachian Mountain Club, or Ameri- can Alpine Club. These organizations often have trainings and get- togethers where you can meet people of similar skills and interests. Many colleges and universities have outing clubs that are often open to both students and members of the community. Online maga- zines, like *Expedition News*, and print magazines, like *Rock and Ice* and *Climbing Magazine*, have classified sections that often include advertisements for expeditions looking for additional members. Ernest Shackleton placed one of the most famous advertisements for expedition members in the *Times* of London in 1901. He and Robert Scott were sailing to Antarctica on an attempt to be the first people to reach the South Pole: "*Men wanted for hazardous journey. Small wages. Bitter cold. Long months of complete darkness. Constant danger. Safe return doubtful. Honour and recognition in case of success.*"

Also, in the last 10 years, the Internet has given birth to literally hundreds of online forums devoted to every type of outdoor activity. Most of these forums have sections devoted to looking for partners. By asking appropriate questions, you can get a good idea of people's experience, interests, and some of their personality traits.

Expedition Tryouts

Regardless of how you come into contact with your new teammates, it is a good idea to double-check their skill levels. Certain outdoor pursuits, such as climbing or paddling whitewater, have very defined ratings concerning terrain, but winter camping or ultralight back- packing does not, so it is important to meet with people face-to-face to determine what their actual level of skill is. Before hiking the Pacific Crest Trail with a new partner, for example, a long weekend backpacking trip would be a good arena to analyze her skills, fitness, and personality as well as for her to see yours. You can also use this tryout to determine if an expedition partner underestimates or over-estimates her abilities, which will be important information in determining how she will function during the expedition.

Contact Person

While most expedition members put considerable thought into whom they will be traveling with during the expedition, they often forget about one of the most important members of the team—the home contact person. The contact person does not partake in the physical portion of the expedition but is involved in the planning process and is a vital link between the expedition and the rest of the world during the adventure. The main role of the contact person is to help in the event of an emergency and keep a written copy of the itinerary of the expedition—who, where, when, and how—in addition to a list of emergency contact information.

Information to Leave with a Home Contact Person

EXPEDITION INFORMATION
Overall itinerary
Satellite/cell phone number
Expedition e-mail or Web site
Copies of permits
Lodging reservations
Local outfitter/guide contacts
Local transportation reservations
Travel insurance
Rescue plan/insurance
Emergency funds

PERSONAL INFORMATION
Driver's licenses
Passport copies
Visa copies
Travel reservations
Health insurance
E-mail addresses
Family contacts

LOCAL EMERGENCY CONTACT
U.S. consulates
Local government and police
Medical facilities
Rescue services
Local weather
Local news

Today, many guided expeditions have dedicated information technology employees who download and post text, images, and movies sent via computer and satellite phone to expedition Web sites. This might seem like overkill for a small expedition, but if providing regular updates about your progress is important to family, friends, sponsors, and other interested people, having a contact person to transcribe phone calls or organize and post updates to an expedition Web site can reduce the amount of time you spend in low-speed cyber cafes and increase the time you spend in the field.

Essential Skills or Excess Baggage?

After filling out the expedition questionnaire, answering questions about cost commitments, and having a tryout, you'll want to weigh each potential partner's strengths and liabilities. You might write out the pros and cons as in the example weighing Sue's suitability for a 10-day backpacking trip along a section of the Colorado Trail (page 34).

The trip is tentatively planned for August and will cover a 50-mile stretch of the trail with several climbs up to 12,000 feet with an average elevation of over 9,000 feet, much of it above tree line. Looking at our hypothetical partner, Sue, we can see that her positive attributes are that she is a strong hiker and can deal well with the rigors of the trail; she is also great at interpreting topographic maps, which will be helpful as the section of the trail above tree line is poorly marked. In addition, she can afford the trip financially, has enough free time to help plan and carry out the expedition, and has a great sense of humor. Putting all the positives together, she seems like an ideal partner.

Sue's list of potential liabilities, however, includes a few serious concerns and one red flag. Since you will be sharing a tent and food with Sue, snoring could be a problem as well as having to change your normal rations to eliminate the pasta and cheese that she is allergic to. The fact that she has not gone on a trip longer than a weekend is not a big deal, but you should expect to hear about the desire for a hot shower more than once. She is not a morning per-

The fun factor. Having expedition mates with whom you can laugh and play is a good standard to start with when picking your team.

son, which could be an issue when you are trying to get an early start to hike up and down one of the high passes before the inevitable afternoon thunderstorms develop. But the most important factor that you should question is the fact that she has never been above 5,000 feet. Most people can adapt to higher elevations given an appropriate amount of time to acclimatize, but some people's bodies never adapt and they suffer constant acute mountain sickness if they try to go above 10,000 feet. Unfortunately, there is no test to predict how people will react to altitude. If you're a gambling person, you could take a chance that Sue will probably be able to deal with the high elevations, but you could hedge your bet and tell her she needs to do a short trip to altitude before she can go on the Colorado Trail trip.

While developing logical criteria for determining the expedition team is helpful, leave room for your heart. Before you make your final decision try to imagine a variety of situations that you might encounter during the expedition, both the good and the bad, and think about whom you would want by your side.

Potential Partner's Pros and Cons for a
10-Day Backpacking Trip on the Colorado Trail

Sue's strengths	Sue's liabilities
Strong hiker	Not a morning person
Lots of disposable cash	Never done a trip longer than a weekend
Flexible schedule	Snores
Good map-reading skills	Allergic to wheat and dairy
Great sense of humor	Never been above 5,000 feet

4 | EXPEDITION SUPPORT

Once you have an idea about where you want to go, what you want to do, and who can come on your expedition, next is determining how to best execute your objective:

Guided: Hire a guide service or tour operator to do all the logistical work; all you have to do is train, pay, and show up.

Supported: Plan your own trip, but rent gear or logistical help from a local source.

Self-sufficient: Plan and execute the entire expedition yourself, which is really what this book is all about.

There are a number of criteria that can provide a framework for determining what level of support is best for your expedition—type of activity, logistics, environmental factors, emergency scenarios, time, and money:

Skills: Do you and your group possess the technical skills to complete the goal of the trip within a fair margin of safety?

Logistics: Does anyone in your group have the capability or expertise to secure the necessary permits, arrange for transportation and lodging, and perform other logistical duties inherent in an expedition?

Location: How much experience does the team have in the environment or countries you will be traveling through? Are you ready and able to interact with the people and cultures where the expedition will take place?

Emergency procedures: In the event of an emergency, will you be able to organize or recruit the necessary resources needed to help while on the expedition?

Time: Do you have time to organize logistics *and* learn or practice the skills necessary for your expedition? Will you be sacrificing the quality of one while preparing for the other?

Money: What are your financial constraints? Are there ways to save money with a guide or an outfitter?

As an example, let's use a weeklong bird-watching expedition to Ecuador with four friends. The main reason for going on the trip is to try and see the rare pale-headed brush finch that was thought to be extinct, but in 1999 a small population was rediscovered in the Yunguilla Nature Reserve in southern Ecuador. All of the people in your group are experienced birders, and two have even gone on birding trips to Ecuador in the past. One in your group speaks fluent Spanish, and everyone else knows enough to get by. Having gone on several trips as a group before this expedition, you know everyone possesses decent general outdoor skills, and two in the group have current wilderness first-aid certificates. What the group does not have is a lot of time: only one week for the whole trip. Two or three days will be eaten up by the international flights alone, leaving less than five days to travel to the reserve, look for the finch, and return to the airport. After weighing the options, each of the members in your group decides to book his own flights and hotels and to purchase his own food during the expedition, but you will use a local tour operator to provide an expert birder as well as a vehicle and driver for the time you are in Ecuador. Using a local guide will increase your chances of seeing the finch, aid in identifying other species, and be a valuable resource in the event of an emergency.

Guided or Supported Expeditions

Tour operators and guide services are companies that are already equipped and in business to offer a specific type of trip in a specific area. If you decide to hire such a company to assist you, you may need to decide between a prepackaged tour or developing a personalized itinerary.

Packaged tours offer several distinct advantages over personalized itineraries. The main advantage is the amount of time and effort you will save in terms of planning and expediting the adventure. Having all of the logistics taken care of allows you to focus on the experience itself without having to worry about all the small details. This, of course, comes with a price; prepackaged tours are usually much more expensive than doing all the legwork yourself, but they are often cheaper than designing a tour to follow your specific itinerary. The cost of these established trips are fixed, and as a client you are usually not responsible for covering unexpected expenses such as an increase in permit fees or porters demanding a higher daily wage.

Since tour operators and guide services want to make as much money as possible and do what they need to put a trip together that people will enjoy and recommend to future clients, established tours develop an itinerary that delivers high client satisfaction. Package tours are also open to the general public, and unless you can fill up all the slots with your expedition teammates, the tour will include other clients with possibly different expectations and personalities. Having control over your own itinerary does give you the freedom to change your logistics during the expedition instead of having to follow the company's time frame.

Packaged Tour	Personalized Itinerary
Costs usually fixed	Costs widely variable
Less research and planning required	More research and planning required
Overall outcome more known	Overall outcome less known
Less individual logistical freedom	More individual logistical freedom
Less control over group dynamics	More control over group dynamics

If you decide to hire a guide for a personalized itinerary, instead of signing on to a prepackaged trip, find the best service that you can afford. The more risks involved in an expedition, the more research you should do before hiring a guide. While choosing a poor natural-history guide for the Ecuadoran birding expedition example might decrease your chances of seeing the bird, choosing an unqualified mountaineering guide service to climb Mount Everest could get you killed. Fortunately, most types of guided activities do have a certification process, but it varies widely depending on the nature of the activity and the country in which it takes place. (See Choosing the Right Company.)

Finally, if you want the freedom of your own itinerary and don't feel you need a guide, but you would like help with gear and supplies once you arrive at a location, many tour operators and guiding companies can also service your expedition as outfitters. Food, equipment, and knowledge of an area are services they can provide for expeditions as short as a few days or as long as several months.

Choosing the Right Company

After deciding what level of support your expedition needs, do your research. Talk with a friend who has used the same service, read travel magazines and books that give recommendations, surf the Web looking for comments from other people who have used a particular company. Read all you can find about the organization that you want to hire, and then contact them directly and ask questions to round out your knowledge about them. Below is a list of sample questions:

Company history: How long has the company been in business? How long has it been operating in the area you want to visit? How long has it been running a particular tour or providing the advertised service?

The longer the company has been in business or running a particular service or trip, the more detailed the logistics and the better the outcome. The longer the company has been in business, the more experience it has had to deal with all the problems that can arise on a tour or expedition. In some areas of the world, permits, local governments, and cultural norms can change quickly. If a tour operator or guide service has not run your chosen trip in the last 10 years, things could be very different today.

Credentials: What type of permits/certifications/insurance does the company have to operate in the location where you'd like to go?

In the United States, most guiding, particularly mountaineering, takes place on either state or federal lands, and public land bureaus issue a variety of permits or concessions to businesses wanting to operate within these lands. U.S. governmental agencies do not have systems in place to evaluate the competency of guiding organizations, so concessions are given on a first-come basis to companies that have the required paperwork, insurance, and permit fees. The number of permits issued is often fixed, and once a company obtains a permit it is usually theirs indefinitely as long as they pay their fees and do not violate the terms of the permit. As a result, individual guides have little incentive to seek out certification unless they work for a company that has a concession. However, some land managers now require the organizations to have various levels of certification, and guiding companies that already have permits are requiring their guides to be certified before they can work.

Guide history: What experience and training does the guide have? How long has the guide worked for the company? How many times has the guide led the specific trip you're interested in? What level of first-aid training does the guide have? What trainings and certifications related to the specific activities you will be participating in does the guide have?

In Europe, guides have been employed to help their clients ascend the Alps ever since the Italian Jacques Balmat guided Dr. Michel-Gabriel Paccard to the summit of Mont Blanc in 1786. It is not surprising that the foremost mountaineering certification organization, the International Federation of Mountain Guides Associations (IFMGA), originated in Europe. Since 1966, the IFMGA has established guiding standards in mountainous regions and has expanded its certification process to include hiking, trekking, and ski guides as well. These professionals are certified to guide almost anywhere in Europe and other participating countries.

Other activities, such as canyoneering, have followed suit and developed various certification organizations. In the United States, Mexico, and Central and South America, the American Canyoneering Association certifies guides. Its counterpart in Europe is the Commission Européenne de Canyon (CEC). The new Commission Internationale de Canyon, also called the International Association of Professional Canyoneering Guides, has also been established to unify canyoneering techniques worldwide.

In Africa, the Field Guides Association of Southern Africa has a rigorous education and testing procedure to ensure that individuals working as safari guides are properly qualified to safely lead and inform clients about the environments they visit. The Kenya Professional Safari Guides Association also has a testing procedure to raise the level of guiding within Kenya.

Each of these organizations offer certifications for different types of outdoor activities; some certifications are required by land managers or governmental agencies and some are not. If this sounds confusing, it can be, and to make matters worse, it's hard to tell what the certifications really mean. For example, let's say that you are looking into hiring a guide service to take you heli-skiing in Alaska. The guide sends you his resume with a list of certificates like PSIA Alpine Level II and USSA Coaching Alpine Level 200, which are great, but they pertain to teaching and coaching skiing in lift-operated areas. A much more important certification would be a Level III Guides Avalanche Certification, which covers decision making in avalanche terrain and managing avalanche hazards in the backcountry. So remember to research the certifications your guide is claiming, and make sure they are relevant to the activities he or she will assist with on your expedition.

It is common in the U.S. guiding industry for guides and outdoor educators to have at least a Wilderness First Responder certificate. While a guide with good skills can quickly adapt to a new situation, knowing the specific area is also very important.

Price: What is included in the price, and what other types of expenses should you expect? Are meals, lodging, local travel costs, and group equipment like tents, stoves, and technical gear included? What is the tipping protocol? Do you give one tip to the head guide or tip everyone individually, and what is the standard rate?

Make sure you know exactly what the total cost will be so you can compare several quotes.

Accidents and Emergency Procedures: Has the company or guide had any accidents in the past that required medical attention? Has anyone ever died during a trip? These are tough questions to ask, but a reputable company will be prepared to answer them.

What if someone becomes ill or is injured during a trip? What type of communications systems will the guide or operator have? What types of evacuation services are possible in the area the expedition will take place? Where is the nearest medical facility and what standard of care can you expect?

In the United States, we may have access to highly trained rescue personnel, but in some parts of the world you are on your own if you need help, and it is a good idea to know what you are getting yourself into. Access to and quality of medical care can vary depending on the location. See chapter 11 for some suggestions for emergency procedures and health insurance options in international locations.

Cancellation policies: What type of cancellation and refund policy does the company or guide have? Does the company require a deposit? When will you be notified if a trip is cancelled?

If a tour is cancelled just days before it is scheduled to begin, it will be extremely difficult for you to make other arrangements. Purchasing trip insurance from a third party is a wise investment if the tour operator's refund policy does not seem adequate.

References: Does the company or guide have references you can contact? These references will be from people who had positive experiences with the outfitter, but it is still worth communicating with them to get an overall feel for the company.

Packaged Tours: What is the maximum and minimum number of participants the trip will have? What is the guide-to-client ratio? What level of fitness is expected of the participants? What is the typical profile of a client?

Many packaged tours will have certain operating parameters. Asking these types of questions will help you determine if a packaged tour is a good fit for your expedition objective. Likewise, the more information you can find out about the company's typical client will help determine if you fit the profile the company is targeting, again, leading to a higher likelihood that the match will be a good fit.

Ecotourism: Does the company minimize their impact in the areas they operate? Do they build environmental and cultural awareness and respect? Do they provide direct financial benefits for conservation as well as empowerment for local people? Are they sensitive to a host country's political, environmental, and social climate, and do they support international human rights and labor agreements?

Ecotourism is one of the most popular catchwords in the travel industry today. Almost every outdoor travel–related company touts its operation as being eco-friendly, but the definition of ecotourism has been debated ever since the word was introduced 20 years ago. In a broad sense, it means responsible travel to natural areas that conserves the environment and improves the well-being of local people.

Finally, after you consider all of the tangible factors in selecting a service, ask yourself if you really like the guide or company. Whether you are hiring a person for a monthlong climb up Aconcagua or a two-week river trip down the Grand Canyon, you will learn more and have a better experience if the guide is someone you want to hang out with.

Dave Finds the Devil in the Tour Operator

"Damn it, you try it, Mark," I said, dropping the padlock against the canoe. Frustrated, I stood sucking in the thick August air while swatting at a cloud of voracious mosquitoes, lamenting the fact that our weeklong adventure in the Pine Barrens of southern New Jersey had just ground to a standstill. Over the past three days we had hiked close to 30 miles of the Batona Trail that runs down the spine of the 1.1 million acres that make up the Pine Barrens. For the final leg of the journey, we had planned to canoe down the narrow, twisting Batsto River. A local outfitter named Wallace Stark had chained the canoe to a tree at the Hampton Furnace put-in so it would be there when we arrived. The only problem was the key Wallace had given us did not fit the lock.

Wallace was a friend of a friend who ran a small guiding operation in Burlington County, New Jersey. We based our whole trip on his advice, gleaned through just one phone call with him—a decision we would later regret. "I'm a Piney through and through, lived here all my life," Wallace said as he shuttled us to the Batona trailhead, his monologue filling the cramped cab of the pickup with various facts about the Pine Lands. "You know, over 400 species of birds have been seen here. There are all kinds of carnivorous plants like the Venus flytrap. You shouldn't have too much trouble with mosquitoes this late in the summer, but watch out for the Jersey Devil."

"The Jersey Devil?" Mark questioned.

"No, not the professional ice hockey team," Wallace replied, "But the original New Jersey Devil, a fierce creature that is part horse, bat, and rat and roams the Barrens terrorizing people. There haven't been any sightings lately, but folks claim it's still out there."

Back at the locked canoe we cursed our Jersey Devil, Wallace Stark. The year was 1983, long before the age of cell phones, leaving Mark and me to free the canoe on our own. The pitch pine Wallace locked the canoe to was over a foot in diameter, but looking up, we noticed it was a branchless dead snag only 20 feet tall. By first leaning the canoe against the tree and then standing on Mark's shoulders, I hoisted the canoe up on end and, after much effort, flipped the loop of chain over the top of the tree, freeing the canoe. For the next two days we peacefully navigated the clean, dark water of the Batsto River. At the takeout, we waited two hours

Dave Finds the Devil in the Tour Operator

past our predetermined pickup time and then lifted the canoe to our shoulders and started the two-mile forced march to Wallace's house. The temperature was close to 90 degrees F, and our feet were blistering from the scorching blacktop. A steady stream of cars passed us, honking horns at the two wayward sailors with a great aluminum albatross balanced on their necks.

"Do you smell food?" Mark asked, his voice echoing from under the gunnels of the canoe. We followed the seductive aroma of a summer barbecue for the last half-mile straight to a dilapidated two-story house. And there before us stood Wallace, wearing a dirty "Interstate Barbecue" apron and sipping a Budweiser tall boy with half a dozen crushed soldiers lying at his feet.

"Howdy, boys, you're just in time," Wallace greeted us, waving his spatula at the slabs of hamburger on the grill like he had somehow planned this whole scenario.

Dripping with sweat we unceremoniously dumped the old canoe on the driveway with a loud thud. "Careful boys, that is my livelihood you've got there," Wallace said, gazing at the beat-up boat like it was a prized piece of art.

Incredulous, I spun around, intent on giving Wallace the full fury of my pent-up anger for all his misinformation, botched logistics, and general lack of anything resembling a professional operation. Instead I turned and found Wallace holding two ice-cold beers at arm's length, smiling and saying, "Isn't that river one of the most beautiful places on earth? Grab some buns, the burgers are ready."

Wallace might have been a totally incompetent businessman, but he did know how to please people. With my resolve for retribution waning, I slumped to the ground in the shade of a sweet bay magnolia tree and set about expanding my shrunken stomach with several burgers.

Sensing his moment, Wallace confessed, "I guess today was the day I was suppose to pick you guys up at Batsto. I'm real sorry, boys, I know I should write things down; my memory hasn't been too good these last few years. But I do know one thing," he said slapping me on the back, "I know you are smart boys and I'm sure glad you figured things out." ∎

RESEARCHING YOUR EXPEDITION

You are likely to feel overwhelmed when starting your research on an expedition, like the artist standing in front of a breathtaking landscape with a blank canvas, wondering how to capture the scene with a brushstroke. But the more you learn about your craft, the less daunting and more fun it becomes.

NOLS instructors Andy Tyson, Molly Tyson, and Sarah Hueniken meet over maps of China for a personal trip. None of them are new to expedition planning, yet they all still take the necessary steps.

Resources

People you know who have gone on similar expeditions are the most important resource in researching a potential adventure. While tour operators will often emphasize the positive aspects of a trip and downplay the negatives in order to get your business, your friends and family probably won't hesitate to regale you with stories about how it rained everyday and the nasty bout of food poisoning they had during their stay. You can ask them the questions that you might not want to post on an online travel forum or ask a travel agent, like how hard was it to get used to dealing with the squat toilets found in most of Asia and the Middle East.

NOLS publishes a number of great resources that can aid your planning. Books on subjects like risk management, wilderness ethics, and various technical skills can be found at www.nols.edu/store.

You know your friends' strengths and weaknesses when it comes to travel, and they know yours as well. When you ask them how challenging it is to buy train tickets in Moscow if you don't speak or read Russian, they can take into account your tolerance for adversity when answering the question.

If you don't have any friends who have been where you want to go, any large bookstore has rows devoted to travel guides for just about any destination that you might want to visit. While some of the information might become dated—especially prices—it is usually representative of what people experience when traveling to a particular area.

The Internet is another good resource in travel and adventure tourism research. While many people use the Internet to book components of their expedition, the real power of the Internet lies in the wealth of resources and previous experiences that you can find on Wikipedia, travel Web sites, travel forums, travel blogs, photo-sharing Web sites, and Google Earth.

Lastly, outdoor clubs and societies as well as other adventure travel organizations are great resources for dialing in the details of your desired expedition. Below is a list to get you started:

American Alpine Club
www.americanalpineclub.org

Located in Golden, Colorado, the Henry S. Hall Jr. American Alpine Club Library and Colorado Mountain Club Collection is an internationally known resource on alpinism, climbing, and mountain regions and cultures. You can conduct an online search yourself or get help from the research librarian. The American Alpine Club also publishes a book of notable climbs and expeditions completed or attempted each year.

The Banff Centre
www.banffcentre.ca/mountainculture
107 Tunnel Mountain Drive or Box 1020, Banff, Alberta, Canada

Mountain culture programs at the Banff Centre promote the understanding and appreciation of mountain places by creating opportunities for people to share and find inspiration in mountain experiences, ideas, and visions.

The Royal Geographical Society

www.rgs.org

1 Kensington Gore, London, England

Established in 1830 to promote "the advancement of geographical science," the Royal Geographical Society is a British organization for geography and geographers. Today their headquarters is a dynamic world center supporting geographical learning, research, education, expeditions, and fieldwork, as well as promoting public engagement and informed enjoyment of our world.

The Alpine Club of Britain

www.alpine-club.org.uk

55/56 Charlotte Road, London, England

The Alpine Club, the world's first mountaineering club, is Britain's only national club for alpinists. Since it was founded in 1857, its members have been at the leading edge of worldwide mountaineering development and exploration. The club provides a forum for sharing experiences and information.

The Explorers Club

www.explorers.org

46 East 70th Street, New York

The Explorers Club is an international multidisciplinary professional society dedicated to the advancement of field research and the preservation of the human instinct to explore. Since its inception in 1904, the club has served as a meeting point and unifying force for explorers and scientists worldwide.

What to Research

The table on pages 50–54 gives a general idea of the best times to travel to different areas of the world for climbing, hiking, canyoneering, river running, and natural history observation. The best time period is considered to be the time when the specific region has weather most conducive for the given activity. This table can be used one of two ways once you have an expedition goal in mind: First, if you know you'd like to climb in Northern Africa, you can narrow your trip dates to the ideal months. Or if you know you'll have four months off starting in July and would like to plan a long trek, the table breaks down the best places to do so worldwide.

Once you decide where and when to go on your expedition, next you should research the rules and regulations specific to the country you are traveling to (chapter 6) and transportation and lodging en route to your destination as well as during your expedition (chapter 12). The initial preparation stages should include research into planning your funding (chapter 7), equipment (chapter 8), and food and fuel (chapter 9). Keep in mind that some of your research into these topics will hinge on whether your expedition will be entirely self-sufficient or guided or outfitted to some degree.

All the tools you have at your disposal for solid research and planning.

	DEC	JAN	FEB	MAR	APR	MAY	JUN	JUL	AUG	SEPT	OCT	NOV
Antarctica	Sea Kayaking	Sea Kayaking										
	Trekking Climbing	Trekking Climbing										Trekking Climbing
Africa												
Northern Africa		Trekking	Trekking		Trekking Climbing	Trekking Climbing				Sea Kayaking	Sea Kayaking	Trekking
Tanzania/Kenya		Climb Mt. Kenya Climb Kilimanjaro	Climb Mt. Kenya Climb Kilimanjaro	Whitewater Kayaking and Rafting	Whitewater Kayaking and Rafting	Whitewater Kayaking and Rafting	Whitewater Kayaking and Rafting		Climb Mt. Kenya Climb Kilimanjaro	Climb Mt. Kenya Climb Kilimanjaro		
Rwanda/Uganda		Birding							Wildlife Safaris			
	Mountain Gorilla Viewing	Mountain Gorilla Viewing	Climbing					Mountain Gorilla Viewing	Mountain Gorilla Viewing			
	Whitewater Kayaking and Rafting	Whitewater Kayaking and Rafting						Whitewater Kayaking and Rafting	Whitewater Kayaking and Rafting			
	Trekking	Trekking						Trekking / Climbing	Trekking / Climbing			
Southern Africa						Sea Kayaking	Sea Kayaking					
					Trekking	Trekking				Trekking	Trekking	
			Whitewater Kayaking and Rafting	Whitewater Kayaking and Rafting						Whitewater Kayaking and Rafting	Whitewater Kayaking and Rafting	
								Wildlife Safaris	Wildlife Safaris			Birding
Oceania												
New Zealand			Trekking Climbing	Trekking Climbing				Sea Kayaking	Sea Kayaking	Whitewater Kayaking and Rafting	Whitewater Kayaking and Rafting	
Papua New Guinea			Whitewater Kayaking and Rafting	Whitewater Kayaking and Rafting			Trekking	Sea Kayaking				
Tasmania	Sea Kayaking											
	Trekking / Climbing	Trekking / Climbing										

	DEC	JAN	FEB	MAR	APR	MAY	JUN	JUL	AUG	SEPT	OCT	NOV
Australia: Queensland, Northern Territory, Western Territory										Sea Kayaking		
								Trekking / Climbing				
					Whitewater Kayaking and Rafting							
Australia: New South Wales/Victoria										Sea Kayaking		
					Trekking Climbing							
						Whitewater Kayaking and Rafting						
North America												
Mexico				Sea Kayaking							Sea Kayaking	
	Mountaineering Trekking in Baja											Mtneering Trekking in Baja
		Rock Climbing								Copper Canyon Trekking		
		Whitewater Kayaking and Rafting									Whitewater Kayaking and Rafting	
Arctic and Subarctic U.S. and Canada							Sea Kayaking					
								Trekking Wildlife Viewing			Polar Bear Ecotourism Churchill, Manitoba	
Rocky Mountains Western/Northwestern U.S. and Canada							Mountaineering					
								Sea Kayaking				
								Trekking Climbing				
Southwestern U.S. (including California)						Whitewater Kayaking and Rafting						
					Canyoneering Trekking Rock Climbing						Canyoneering Trekking Rock Climbing	
						Sea Kayaking (California)						
Midwest/Eastern U.S.							Whitewater Kayaking and Rafting					
								Sea Kayaking				
							Whitewater Kayaking and Rafting					
Southern U.S.			Sea Kayaking					Trekking / Climbing			Trekking Rock Climbing	
		Trekking Rock Climbing						Whitewater Kayaking and Rafting				

	DEC	JAN	FEB	MAR	APR	MAY	JUN	JUL	AUG	SEPT	OCT	NOV
South America												
Central America			Sea Kayaking			Whitewater Kayaking and Rafting						Sea Kayaking
		Trekking Wildlife Tours										Trekking Wildlife Tours
Ecuador	Trekking					Sea Kayaking / Whitewater Kayaking and Rafting					Trekking	
	Climbing Sierra Region						Climbing Sierra Region					Climbing Sierra Region
Bolivia and Peru						Whitewater Kayaking and Rafting						
							Sea Kayaking					
							Trekking / Climbing					
Argentina			Whitewater Kayaking and Rafting									
			Sea Kayaking									
		Climbing Aconcagua										
		Lake District Trekking and Climbing										Lake Dist. Trekking Climbing
Patagonia			Sea Kayaking								Sea Kayaking	
		Whitewater Kayaking and Rafting										
		Trekking Climbing										Trekking Climbing
Tierra del Fuego			Sea Kayaking / Whitewater Kayaking and Rafting						Whitewater Kayaking and Rafting			
		Trekking Climbing										
Columbia and Venezuela	WW K&R	Trekking / Climbing				Sea Kayaking						
Brazil		Whitewater Kayaking and Rafting			Trekking			Amazon Trekking and River Travel			Trekking	

	DEC	JAN	FEB	MAR	APR	MAY	JUN	JUL	AUG	SEPT	OCT	NOV
Asia												
Tibet-China	Trekking Lower Elevations					Climbing / Trekking	Sea Kayaking / Whitewater Kayaking and Rafting					Climbing / Trekking
Japan					Trekking	Sea Kayaking	Whitewater Kayaking and Rafting	Mt. Fuji Trekking, Northern Islands				
Nepal	Trekking Lower Elevations				Trekking / Climbing				Whitewater Kayaking and Rafting		Trekking / Climbing	
India	Trekking Southern Areas	Whitewater Kayaking and Rafting				Sea Kayaking				Whitewater Kayaking and Rafting	Trekking in Southern Areas	
India						Trekking and Climbing in Most Northern Regions					Trekking and Climbing in Most Northern Areas	
Pakistan						Whitewater Kayaking and Rafting	Climbing / Trekking					
Bhutan		Whitewater Kayaking and Rafting			Trekking / Climbing		Sea Kayaking	Climbing / Trekking	Whitewater Kayaking and Rafting		Trekking / Climbing	
Kazakhstan, Kyrgyzstan, Tajikistan, Turkey							Sea Kayaking		Whitewater Kayaking and Rafting			
Mongolia					Gobi Desert			Whitewater Kayaking and Rafting / Trekking		Gobi Desert		

	DEC	JAN	FEB	MAR	APR	MAY	JUN	JUL	AUG	SEPT	OCT	NOV
Thailand, Malaysia, Vietnam, Laos, Southern China	Sea Kayaking / Whitewater Kayaking and Rafting											Trekking Northern and West Coast
		Trekking and Rock Climbing Northern and West Coast Regions										
						Trekking Southern and East Coast Regions						
Indonesia	Sea Kayaking											
		Whitewater Kayaking and Rafting										
						Sea Kayaking						
								Trekking				
										Whitewater Kayaking and Rafting		
Philippines				Sea Kayaking								
						Whitewater Kayaking and Rafting						
			Trekking									
Europe												
Scandinavia, Russia				Whitewater Kayaking and Rafting								
							Sea Kayaking					
Central/Eastern Europe								Trekking / Climbing				
									Whitewater Kayaking and Rafting			
							Trekking / Climbing					
Southern Europe							Sea Kayaking					
									Whitewater Kayaking and Rafting			
							Trekking / Climbing					

RED TAPE

Rules, Regulations, and Common Sense

Rules and regulations to some, red tape to others: Regardless of how you look at it, most expeditions are going to have to jump through a certain number of hoops in order to achieve their objectives. It may be as simple as stopping in at the backcountry rangers' office to secure an overnight camping permit, or it may mean applying months or even years in advance for permission to travel through a restricted area. Do your research and know what is required for your expedition so you don't end up being turned back from a border crossing or checkpoint or getting fined because you don't have the proper paperwork completed.

Access

Public access to the world's wild places is governed by a wide range of factors: Local government, land ownership, land management policies, environmental considerations, national politics, civil unrest, global tensions, and popularity are just some of the things that might affect the ease with which you gain permission to access an area.

DOMESTIC EXPEDITIONS

Obtaining access for expeditions in the United States is relatively straightforward. Most of the large uninhabited regions in the United States are public land. National parks, national forests, state lands, Bureau of Land Management (BLM) acres, and wildlife refuges all preserve wildlands for conservation, recreation, and resource use. Public lands have different guidelines for balancing multiple uses depending on their managing agency and its mandate, but most allow some form of visitor access. Access to private property is much less certain.

Public Land

Look up the area you plan to visit on a land ownership map to determine which agency manages it, and then call that agency or check its Web site to find out about the policies for backcountry travelers. Many national forests and BLM lands have very few restrictions on travel. Some simply ask you to sign in and out at the trailhead; others require backcountry permits; a few have special camping regulations for more popular destinations; while still others have no special requirements at all.

Most national parks, on the other hand, require visitors to camp in designated areas and may have regulations on activities such as climbing that could affect your plans. For example, Devils Tower National Monument in Wyoming has a voluntary ban on climbing in June to promote understanding and encourage respect for the American Indian tribes who consider the tower a sacred site, as well as closures of certain climbs other parts of the year due to wildlife considerations like prairie falcon nesting. Arches National Park in Utah does not allow climbing on any arch or natural bridge

U.S. Government Land Management Agencies	
Department of the Interior	**www.doi.gov**
National Park Service	www.nps.gov
Bureau of Land Management	www.blm.gov
Bureau of Reclamation	www.doi.gov/bureaus
U.S. Fish and Wildlife Service	www.fws.gov
Bureau of Indian Affairs	www.bia.gov
Department of Agriculture	**www.usda.gov**
U.S. Forest Service	www.fs.fed.us

that is named on the U.S. Geological Survey 7.5-minute topo-graphical map for the area. Popular backcountry trips—the White Rim mountain bike trail in Canyonlands National Park and private river trips through Grand Canyon National Park, for example—have limitations on the number of people allowed each year. For these areas, you often need to apply for a lottery well in advance of your travel dates, and you still may not be guaranteed a permit. See the list of land management areas and their Web sites on page 56. For state lands, check the state's Web site.

Private Land

Private lands in America are sacrosanct. No landowner is required to grant you permission to cross his or her property. That said, many will if you ask.

Individual landowners—farmers, ranchers, or corporations—are usually best approached with a phone call or letter requesting permission to access their land. Outline your plans clearly and indi-cate your understanding of courteous behavior while crossing or recreating on private land: This includes packing out trash, avoiding livestock, leaving gates as you find them, using fires with permis-sion only, and other practical methods for minimizing the impact of your presence. If you plan to engage in activities that may be per-ceived as hazardous, landowners may require you sign some kind of waiver. People do not want to be held responsible for your actions on their land, and if they feel they could be sued in the event of an accident, they are likely to deny you access. Polite, hum-ble attitudes will get you further, but remember, access to private land is a privilege that can be given and taken away with no cause or explanation, so treat it carefully.

Tribal lands are considered independent sovereign nations. Although technically under the jurisdiction of the Bureau of Indian Affairs, which is part of the U.S. Department of the Interior, Indian reservations have their own rules and regulations regarding public access. Often people are allowed to camp, hike, hunt, or fish within reservation boundaries if they hire a guide or buy a permit. You can call the tribal office to find out what is and isn't allowed on the lands and what permits cost. On the Wind River Reservation in Wyoming, for example, you may backpack on reservation lands with an annual trespass permit that costs $80 per year for Wyoming residents, $120 for nonresidents. The fees are a deterrent to many would-be visitors, and as a result, this section of the Wind River Mountains contains some of the wildest, most pristine alpine scenery in the entire range—an unexpected benefit of having to pay.

INTERNATIONAL EXPEDITIONS

Every country has its own rules and regulations regarding access to its mountains, rivers, lakes, and forests, so we can't stress enough that your first step in ensuring that you secure the necessary permits and permissions for your desired destination is to do your research. Again, one of the easiest ways to gather this information is to talk to people who have traveled in the area before. You can connect with past visitors through mountaineering organizations, trekking groups, hiking or climbing clubs, and adventure travel agencies. Like the United States, many countries have a mountaineering association or federation that serves as an information clearinghouse for trekkers or climbers. You can find information about climbing in Pakistan from the Alpine Club of Pakistan, while the Indian Mountaineering Federation serves a similar function in India. Still, there may be places where little information exists. In the early days of

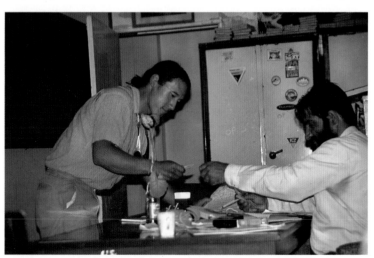

Jimmy Chin arranging for a climbing permit at the Ministry of Tourism in Pakistan.

NOLS' Patagonia operation, for example, an instructor went to pick up a course at a roadhead only to discover a large military base right where he was scheduled to meet the students. The base had not appeared on any maps. Chilean soldiers escorted the students across the property and everything worked out, but the instructor said it was a bit of shock to drive up and find soldiers, barbed wire, and a checkpoint where he expected no more than a wide spot in the road. Again, do as much research as you possibly can.

Visas and Travel Advisories

The U.S. Department of State (www.state.gov) provides information about travel in various countries around the world, including specifics about visas, travel safety, health, custom regulations, and so forth. While the site does not include specific information about permits for climbing or travel in a given nation's mountains or forests, it will outline the steps you must take to enter and leave the country without hassle.

The State Department recommends overseas travelers register with the U.S. embassy or consulate in the country they are visiting to make their presence and whereabouts known in case of an emergency, such as an evacuation of U.S. citizens in the event of a natural disaster or civil unrest. You can register online, and it is recommended for the following cases in particular:

- Travelers who intend to remain in a country longer than one month
- Travel in a country that has an unstable political climate or is undergoing a natural disaster
- Travel in a country where there are no U.S. officials, in which case you should register with the embassy or consulate of an adjacent country, leave an itinerary with the Consular Section, and ask about a third country that may represent U.S. interests in the country you plan to visit.

Timing

Make sure you plan ahead to allow yourself plenty of time to secure visas and permits, particularly permits for more popular peaks or rivers. You may want to consider teaming up with others for a permit or attaching yourself to a group to use its permit for a particular mountain or route. Look at climbing or boating forums online or in advertisements in the back of magazines for people looking to pool together in a group for permitting purposes. There are some obvious potential pitfalls to going this route, but it has worked in the past for individuals unable to raise the necessary funds to pay the high fees for popular summits.

Dave's Red Tape Obstacle Course

Seven years ago I opened a climbing magazine and was captivated by a steep, glaciated peak erupting out of dense jungle with its summit shrouded in a swirl of mist. The caption identified the peak as "Takpa Shiri," an unclimbed 7,000-meter peak in the Arunachal Pradesh region of India. Dangling off the northeast corner of the country, the unclimbed peaks of Arunachal Pradesh or "Dawn-Lit Mountains" looked ripe for the picking.

Greg Child, an Australian mountaineer who took the photo and is one of a handful of Westerners who have attempted to climb in this region, said, "It was one of few mountain ranges in the world that climbers can point to and say, 'All these peaks are unclimbed.'" As I researched the area more, I learned there are good reasons why these peaks remained unclimbed. Just the approach to the mountains is an expedition in itself. The average rainfall is more than 10 feet per year, which has produced an impenetrable malaria- and leech-infested jungle, hundreds of miles of roadless forest that you have to hack your way through with a machete before you even glimpse a view of the mountains. The thick vegetation has allowed the indigenous people to develop unique cultures in neighboring valleys separated by as little as 20 miles of forest. Some of the cultures had developed fierce warring and head-hunting traditions, where the women tattooed their faces and put large pugs of stone through their pierced nostrils to make themselves unattractive and less likely to be taken hostage by rival tribes.

The mountainous region of Arunachal Pradesh has rich history. The British first carved a trail through the dense jungle on their way to Tibet. In 1939, the globetrotting explorer Bill Tilman came to the area in hopes of climbing virgin peaks. He never even saw any of the mountains he came to climb and barely escaped with his life after catching malaria.

Dave's Red Tape Obstacle Course

In 1959 the Dalai Lama used the old British trail through the remote area to make his escape from the Chinese. The Chinese later invaded, causing great hostilities between the two countries. In fact, the boundary line between India and China is still disputed to this day. Not more than a handful of expeditions have braved the horrendous approaches and piles of governmental red tape and fewer still have stood on the summit of any peaks. In 1999 famed mountaineer Doug Scott, accompanied by Greg Child, made the first and only attempt on Takpa Shiri. Due to an extremely wet year, even for Arunachal Pradesh, they barely saw the peak and left the mountains hobbling from illness, injury, and the ridiculous regulations they endured on the approach to base camp.

While most normal people would steer clear of such an inhospitable place, the challenges of trying to climb in the Dawn-Lit Mountains had a hypnotic effect on me, drawing me in like a moth to a candle. The big question was how badly would I get burned. In the spring of 2005, I applied for and received the prestigious Shipton-Tilman Award from Gore and Associates for an expedition to try to climb Takpa Shiri. On the application, one of the questions was, "Do you have the necessary permits to access and climb your objective?" Like the answer to many things in life, I responded that I was in the process of receiving said permits. In reality, before I had the money in hand I had done very little groundwork in gaining access to Takpa Shiri. I did have a good knowledge of how the Indian Mountaineering Foundation worked. A vestige from India's colonial rule, the IMF had a long list of requirements that had to be fulfilled and typically a lot of money had to be paid in peak fees, liaison officer support staff salaries, local tariffs and fees, not to mention the cost of hiring a local tour operator to provide the logistical support to get us to the base of the peak.

I knew the planning of the expedition would take a considerable amount of time and effort, but I was a bit naive and overconfident due to previous successes climbing in remote regions in other parts of the world. The first indication that things might not go as planned was when I contacted Harish Kapadia, the local expert on all things involving mountains in India.

Dear David,

Thank you for your email. I am excited that you are planning a trip to the Arunachal Pradesh. However, the peak Takpa Shiri is actually located in China not India, and you will have no success if you try and apply for permits with the IMF. The peak Doug Scott and Greg Child

Dave's Red Tape Obstacle Course

attempted is actually not named and consequently not known by the IMF. As an unclimbed peak there will be additional fees for the climbing permit, and the climbing team must be made up of at least 50 percent Indian nationals. You should allow at least six months once you have all the necessary forms filled out for the IMF to process your paperwork. Unfortunately even if you do get a permit from the IMF, since the peak you want to climb lies on the border of China and India, the military could forbid you to travel there, and then there is also the local police who control the access roads.

Sincerely,
Harish Kapadia

Okay, so I did not even know the name of the peak, small setback. It also made sense that Indians should climb the unclimbed peaks of India, but doubling the number of people on the expedition would also double the costs. After months and months of trying to find a tour operator willing to try to help me get the permits, I was finally making headway, until I learned how much they would charge to get us to base camp—close to $40,000. This fee would be in addition to airfare, peak fees, our liaison's and his cook's salary, climbing and camping equipment, food, and other costs.

"There are no roads in this region, the vine bridges that cross the glacially fed rivers are constantly being washed away, and we will have to built new ones perhaps on both the way in and out of the mountains. . . . Porters are unreliable in this region and sometimes disappear into the jungle, never to be seen again. . . . We will need extra money for bribing the local politicians . . . but if the helicopter has been fixed since the last accident we will be able to fly over the most difficult section of the approach."

It soon became clear that the cost of the expedition, while not as expensive as climbing Everest, was going to be more than half of my yearly income. I would like to say that I was able to persevere against the odds and climb the mountain formerly known as Takpa Shiri, but in the end we changed objectives and climbed a magnificent peak in the Genyen Massif of China several hundred miles to the north. So the dream of climbing in the Arunachal Pradesh disappeared more because of the mountains of paperwork, unjustified expenses, and ridiculous permit requirements than the leech-infested jungles guarding the Dawn-Lit Mountains. ■

Private Land Ownership Overseas

Attitudes toward land ownership and access vary in different parts of the world. In New Zealand, for example, people commonly pull off the side of the road and camp regardless of where they are and who may own the surrounding property. It's worth investigating the norms for public trespass in the places you travel before you park your car and pull out a tent. As in the United States, you must respect the rights of landowners and treat their property with courtesy and care wherever you are to ensure both your continued access and the access of those who follow.

Special Considerations Affecting Access

CIVIL UNREST, CRIME, AND TRAVELER SAFETY

Often the features that draw us as explorers are also the boundaries between nations: huge mountain ranges, deep river valleys, expansive deserts, features that provide natural obstacles and barriers to travel and communication, or walls for a nation's self-defense. For these reasons, dream destinations can also be the site of political turmoil and access may be difficult or dangerous.

In 1998, internationally known alpinist Ned Gillette was murdered in his tent while he camped in the Haramosh Valley of Pakistan in what appears to have been a botched robbery attempt. Climbers Beth Rodden, Tommy Caldwell, and two other companions were taken hostage by rebels at gunpoint and held for several days during a climbing trip in Kyrgyzstan in 2000. More recently, the American war in Afghanistan has spilled over into Pakistan, while to the south Pakistani tension with India over ownership of Kashmir continues to make the area unstable and risky for travelers. But conditions change quickly. Just four years after the end of a long and bloody civil war between the Nepalese monarchy and Maoist rebels made travel to that country dangerous, tourists are returning to Nepal in record numbers to explore its spectacular wilderness.

International travelers venturing into political hot spots should use caution. Read up on any travel warnings, follow the political situation in the country where you hope to travel, and talk to people

Even though Jimmy got the permit from the Ministry of Tourism (page 58), permission wasn't granted until our team checked in with the military. (The full story is on pages xi–xvii.)

who have visited the area. It's important to understand what is going on politically and socially in the places you travel to prevent accidentally stumbling into a bad situation. Americans are not always viewed favorably overseas, so your national identity alone may be enough reason not to visit a particular place at a particular time. Or you may need to hire security guards during your expedition. Regardless of your decision whether to go, travel with sensitivity and cultural awareness. Remember you are a guest, and be sure that you treat the place you visit with respect and care.

ENVIRONMENTAL PROTECTION

Domestically and internationally, recreational use of wild lands may be curtailed to protect sensitive environments from further degradation. Trails may be closed or rerouted to prevent erosion, and travel may be restricted in some areas to avoid trampling delicate plants. In New England, off-trail travel above tree line is prohibited at all times because the alpine environment is too fragile to sustain the impact of the huge numbers of hikers who visit the area. Some places have seasonal closures to protect species during vulnerable times of the year: Breeding and nesting make animals particularly sensitive to disturbance so often these areas will be closed to visitors while such activities occur.

Closures are usually designed to ensure one of the following: the fulfillment of land management mandates, protection of special values or threatened and endangered species, managing environmental threats, or preserving cultural resources. You may be asked to avoid an area because of extreme fire danger or to avoid ground-nesting shorebirds. Climbing crags are often closed seasonally if peregrine falcons are nesting in the area, while cliff dwellings, granaries, and other historical structures may be fenced off to intruders to preserve their integrity. Please respect these closures. Avoid disappointment by checking into potential closures before you go. Once you are there, recognize that the regulations are intended to protect the natural and cultural heritage of the area, not to prevent you from bagging your peak or completing your hike.

Disregarding closures may mean little more than a ding to your karma, or you may find yourself facing stiff penalties. In the United States, laws such as the Endangered Species Act and the Antiquities Act of 1906 make certain actions not only disrespectful but also illegal. Damaging or removing artifacts—arrowheads, pottery shards, and remains of historical buildings and structures—can result in large fines and jail time. Killing or injuring an endangered species can also mean facing legal retributions.

Make sure you understand the laws regulating natural resource protection for the area you plan to visit and follow the regulations. It's not worth landing in jail over an arrowhead on your mantel. In the absence of laws, take a moment to consider the moral implications of your actions. Ayers Rock, or Uluru as the Aboriginal people know the iconic Australian monolith, is open to climbing under a 99-year lease between the Australian government and the area's traditional Aboriginal landowners. However, these people, known as the Anangu, do not climb the rock because of its great spiritual significance and would prefer visitors also demur from the activity out of respect. Unfortunately, most people do not abide by their request.

Throughout the world, you will encounter similar taboos surrounding certain sacred places. The decision to act against local customs—to visit a closed holy site, climb a sacred mountain, deface rock art, or alter a prehistoric ruin—is at the very least bad juju and disrespectful of the local wishes. Obviously in the absence of laws, the choice is yours, but make your decision with an understanding of the local history and customs. Think about how you would feel if visitors treated an area of spiritual significance to you without honor before deciding to ignore local requests. Remember, there are other mountains to climb, other valleys to visit.

BUDGET AND FUNDING

Creating a Budget

A realistic budget is critical for any expedition for two reasons. First, it helps team members understand their financial commitment to the expedition, and second, it can be used to secure funding if you decide to seek outside support. A basic budget can be broken down into four categories for organizational purposes: travel/accommodations, equipment, food, and fees or other miscellaneous expenses.

TRAVEL AND ACCOMMODATIONS

For many expeditions, this is the big-ticket category. If you are leaving the United States to travel, getting to and from your destination

For all the things pictured here, a good budget makes the plan a reality.

will cost money, maybe a lot of money. Travel within the States can be quite economical, but even here associated expenditures will need to be included in your budget to ensure the cost of your adventure is shared equitably among the team.

Here are some examples of the type of line items you may include on your budget spreadsheet for travel and accommodations:

- Airline tickets
- Baggage fees
- Transportation to and from airport if needed (shuttle, taxi, include parking fees)
- Transportation at destination if needed (shuttles, trains, car rentals, buses)
- Gas and mileage if driving (IRS standard mileage rate for reimbursement as of January 2010: 50 cents per mile)
- Hotels, campgrounds, overnight accommodations to and from trailhead
- Cost for transportation support (such as shuttling cars between roadheads, hiring porters or pack animals, paying outfitters and bush pilots)

You can get some pretty hard numbers for these categories, so you should be able to budget the cost of travel and accommodations with a high level of accuracy. If you talk to outfitters, suppliers, or other service providers on the phone, ask them to send you written confirmation of your agreed-upon price. You don't want to turn up at a remote airstrip expecting to pay $1,000 for a flight into the mountains only to find out the pilot had not included the cost of your baggage in his calculation.

EQUIPMENT

Once you've come up with your gear list, place values beside all group equipment to calculate the total cost for your expedition. You may decide to include personal gear in this exercise if people have to purchase expensive specialized items for the trip (such as a winter sleeping bag or a new paddle). If individual group members are supplying gear for the whole team to use, such as a tent, include the value of that item in the total. Expeditions are hard on gear: Inevitably things get lost, broken, or just worn out by use; to pre-

Be sure to budget a little extra for those pieces of gear you may not have thought about before leaving home, like a machete to bushwhack through the thick forests of Patagonia!

clude having anyone feel they've given more to the team than others, figure out a way to reimburse people for the team's use of their personal gear. You could "rent" a piece of equipment from a team member for the trip, subtracting the value of the item from his or her overall financial contribution to the expedition; people could receive some other piece of equipment specially purchased for the trip at the end of the expedition in trade; or you may decide it's a wash because everyone is contributing and no one cares about specifics. The key thing to remember is that everyone needs to understand and agree to the system to value personal equipment before you implement it. Your budget should account for:

- Group camping equipment
- Expedition-specific equipment (technical gear)
- Communication equipment (cameras, computers, phones)
- Maps and GPS

FOOD

Use your expedition menu to determine how much you expect to spend on food during your trip. Make sure you include the cost of meals on the road to your destination in your total. Often these restaurant meals can be quite pricey. It can be tricky to come up with accurate numbers if you intend to shop overseas for most of your supplies. Use the Internet or guidebooks, or talk to someone who has traveled in the area about food prices. In general, food in Europe or New Zealand and Australia is expensive. You can expect to pay as much or more than you'll pay in the United States in the grocery store, particularly if the dollar is weak. Asia, South America, and Africa are cheaper, so your food costs should be significantly lower.

Be sure you include:

- Per diem for all expedition members for travel to and from your destination
- Estimated cost for food and fuel on the expedition
- Salary for cooks (if applicable)

NOLS instructors Jared Spaulding and Josh Beckner in Argentina, preparing for an expedition into Piritas Valley with Dave by tapping into their food budget.

FEES

This category should include any expenses you expect to incur including the cost of permits, entrance fees to national parks or preserves, entrance or exit fees for your destination country, immunizations, doctor's visits, extra health or rescue insurance, membership dues, hut fees, tips, bribes, and so forth. Do a little research before you go to make sure you know what types of fees you can expect on your route.

GENERATING A SPREADSHEET

Once you have researched the type of costs you are likely to encounter and have estimated realistic numbers for your expenses, create a spreadsheet. You have plenty of options for software to use, or a handwritten spreadsheet can work as well. The key is to have an organized visual document that everyone on your team can read and understand.

Using Your Budget

All of us have probably had one of these kinds of conversations: You are sitting around with a bunch of friends over dinner and you start talking about how much you want to climb Denali or fly into a hut in the Selkirks to ski. Everyone nods, talks about the following year, and sounds really excited about the idea. But when you follow up a month later, you find out that for most of the group the talk was just that: talk. They have no intention of going to Alaska or Canada with you, and they never did.

Sealing the deal and actually getting your friends to commit to an expedition can be surprisingly difficult. The distance between dreaming and making that dream a reality is further than you'd imagine. Former NOLS chief mountaineer and current executive director of the American Alpine Club Phil Powers used to tell people that you needed money—cold hard cash—up front from everyone, even your closest friends, to ensure their commitment to the expedition. Without putting down some kind of security deposit well in advance of your departure, it's all too easy for an individual to bail at the last minute without feeling any pain just because he or she has suddenly fallen in love or gotten cold feet.

How big a deposit do you need? The amount varies, depending on the type of trip and the up-front expenses you expect to incur, but a good rule of thumb is to have everyone contribute from 25 to 30 percent of his or her total cost for the trip. This gives you money to use for purchasing permits, gear, food, and other items before you leave and should be enough to secure people's commitment. In general, it is recommended that the down payment is nonrefundable. If people drop off the team, they lose their money unless they can find someone to fill their spot who is acceptable to the entire team. There may be special circumstances where you decide to refund the money, such as a death in the family or an injury. But for the most part, stick to your guns and keep the deposit; otherwise you may find yourself with a hefty bill and no one to share the cost.

Some people advocate having team members sign a formal contract once they commit to the expedition. Such a contract should include:

- Expedition mission
- Itinerary
- Budget with cost per team member
- Amount of down payment and conditions for refunds
- Guidelines for removing team members for non-performance or for team members who want to leave of their own accord

A contract may be more formal than you want for your group. While they are essential for a team made up of strangers, contracts can feel cold and impersonal with your friends. That said, talking about money and interpersonal relationships can be harder with friends than strangers, so it may help to have your expectations lined out clearly and concisely on paper even if you are traveling with your best buddy.

APPOINT A TREASURER

Again, the idea of having a treasurer for your expedition sounds awfully formal, but even a straightforward trip to Alaska can cost a couple of thousand dollars before it's over. You can easily end up with strained relationships if people don't feel as if the cost of the trip is being shared equitably. An expedition treasurer is in charge of the budget. He or she keeps track of expenses and makes sure your expenditures are keeping pace with what you budgeted. If you are spending too much, the treasurer should inform the team so you can decide how to remedy the situation. You may need to change your plans, cut the trip short, or agree to contribute more money to complete the expedition.

One technique many teams use is to establish a kitty or a pool of money to be used for incidentals such as taxi fares, entrance fees, tips, meals, gasoline, and so forth. Each team member contributes an equal amount to the kitty. The amount will vary depending on the type of expenses you anticipate. The treasurer can keep track of the kitty, and when it starts to run low, get more funds from team members. Alternately, people can pay their own way as they go, or you can keep track of who is paying for what and balance things out at the end.

Finding Additional Funding

The simplest type of expedition involves coming up with a budget, dividing the total cost among team members, and having everyone cough up his or her share. This works for most of us on most of our trips, but occasionally your dream will be bigger than your pocketbook. In that case, there are options. Grants, fund-raising, even selling spots on your team can help you generate enough money to make your dream a reality.

GRANTS
Once you start looking, you'll discover there are numerous grants available to support wilderness adventure expeditions. Corporations, clubs, and foundations are just some of the organizations with money set aside for this purpose. Many of them target specific people: women or young explorers (18 to 25 years old) for example. Others seek to promote expeditions that push the boundaries of human accomplishment, add information to our world's knowledge, or explore remote regions. You may find there is a perfect niche for your expedition. Don't try to force your goals and skills to

match a grant, however. You could end up strapped to a commitment that doesn't fit your dream if you plan your expedition with funding criteria coming ahead of your team's passion.

Go online and start researching what's out there. Start early. Many grants only consider applications once a year and if you miss the date, you miss your shot at the money. If you find a good fit for your expedition, be professional, thorough, and honest in completing the application. The competition is stiff for funds, so if you want to compete, you need to stand out.

Some of the options available for expeditions include the following:

National Geographic's Expeditions Council: Funds a wide range of exploration and adventure around the world. Grants range from $5,000 to $35,000 and can be used for direct field expenses such as transportation, supplies, permits, fees, and so on.

Alpine Ski Club: Based in Great Britain, the Alpine Ski Club for ski mountaineers awards monies for expeditions with an element of exploration or research and especially focuses on young skiers.

American Alpine Club: Manages a number of different grants, most honoring climbers, mountaineers, and skiers who have lost their lives. These grants are typically designed to carry on the legacy of the individual being honored. There are grants named for Mugs Stumps, Karen McNeill and Sue Nott, Scott Fischer, Hans Saari, and Galen Rowell, to name a few. AAC gives out $50,000 annually. Most of their grants target expeditions that "push the envelope of human accomplishment in mountain and polar environments."

Explorers Club: Offers grants to students conducting individual scientific or exploration research projects through their respective schools. Grants range from $500 to $1,500.

Gore's Shipton-Tilman Grant: Provides $30,000 per year divided between three to six expeditions whose missions pay tribute to the spirit of adventure embodied by Eric Shipton and H. W. Tilman. Specifically, successful applicants, according to the grant's Web site, are small and unencumbered teams of friends with "daring and imaginative goals."

Polartec Challenge Grant: An international outdoor adventure award program that provides grants to "low impact teams who respect local culture and environment and serve as role models to outdoor enthusiasts worldwide." Grants can be awarded to support any activity in any part of the world.

ADOPT A CHARITY

You may be able to raise funds to offset the cost of your expedition and at the same time support a good cause. People have climbed in support of finding a cure for cancer and to raise awareness of world hunger. There are climbs against poverty or for peace. There are countless causes out there that merit attention and funding. The trick is whether you can raise enough money to pay for your trip and actually have a significant amount left over to give back to the cause. No one wants to find out that rather than giving money to MS, they've supported your personal hiking trip along the Na Pali Coast of Kauai, except maybe your parents or grandparents. Expeditions for a cause need to be legitimate, and that takes a lot of planning. The best bet if you want to investigate this route is to contact the group or people who work for the cause you seek to support and find out if you can partner with them to make your effort a success. You may be able to tap into the organization's fundraising machine, or perhaps they are willing to help you spread the word to their membership.

The downside to trying to use your expedition to support a cause is that you need to raise more money than you would need to if you were simply paying for your trip, and you need to dedicate time and energy to a public relations campaign. The process involves soliciting donations, seeking publicity, and creating marketing materials (Web site, brochures, logos). And you are not done when the trip is over. You will need to follow through with donors to demonstrate your achievement and the wise use of their funds. That said, you may really want to promote a cause for personal reasons, and if that is the case, go for it. Dedicating your expedition to a worthy cause is admirable and can be successful if you work hard.

Apply for sponsorships that are in line with your expedition objective and with companies for which you have a passion.

On the other hand, if you are just looking for funding, think twice before you decide this method is your golden goose.

SPONSORSHIP

Some outdoor equipment and clothing companies sponsor athletes or expeditions with gear, clothing, or money. Again, most corporate Web sites will give you information on the type of athletes and expeditions they sponsor. In general, you should be prepared to:

- Demonstrate your competency and experience with a detailed list of past accomplishments
- Explain how your expeditions will be valuable for product testing or visuals (promotional photographs, videos)
- Demonstrate that you and your team are pushing the extremes of your sport, are unique in some way, or are going to a new area; that is, show what makes your expedition unique

Hints for Grant and Sponsorship Success

- Make sure to read application guidelines thoroughly, talk to people at the company or past recipients to ensure your application is professional and targeted.
- Proofread your work. Nothing undermines a good application like typos or obvious cut-and-paste errors.
- Be realistic in your goals and representation of yourself. Let your accomplishments speak for themselves.

THE DOWNSIDE OF SPONSORSHIPS OR GRANTS

Besides taking a considerable amount of time just to apply for support, sponsorship comes with responsibility and sometimes-unexpected burdens. Former NOLS instructor Chris North and a climbing partner were able to convince a magazine to sponsor their expedition to attempt an unclimbed face in southern New Zealand a few years ago. The route was long, hard, and remote. At first Chris was thrilled to receive the funding, but then he was informed that both his and his partner's photography skills were inadequate, so the magazine was sending a photographer along to record their adventure. The photographer's presence completely changed the experience. Not only was he less competent and fit, he also required supervision in the technical terrain they encountered. They traveled slower than they had planned and ended up spending an extra night on the wall. Plus he was a stranger. The climb was successful but stressful. Chris says now he'd think twice before agreeing to such a stipulation.

Sponsorship, grants, and outside funding put pressure on you to perform in a certain way and under specific time constraints. Suddenly you are responsible for an expedition that is newsworthy, exciting, photogenic, and maybe a bit epic. Daily blog updates have become the norm on many big expeditions and may be expected of you as well, which means all the ups and downs of your trip are played out in a public arena: something you may be perfectly fine with or something that may affect the interpersonal dynamic of your trip negatively. None of these factors are necessarily a show-stopper, but they are things that everyone on the team needs to understand and agree to before you accept funds from outside sources.

8 | EQUIPMENT

Coming up with an equipment list can be daunting. There's so much to consider, buy, and know how to use. You always need a few camping basics, regardless of the number of days you'll be out. Add on any technical gear that may be required by your objective, and things start getting complicated. The good news is that planning your first expedition is usually the hardest. Once you've come up with a basic list, you'll never have to start from ground zero again.

Personal Gear

This is the best place to start. Your personal gear includes your clothing, your sleeping system, and any individual technical gear you may require, such as a harness, ice ax, life vest, or paddle, depending on the nature of your expedition. For ease of planning, start by answering some simple questions:

- Where are you going (e.g., mountains, desert, ocean)?
- What range of temperatures do you expect?
- What kind of weather conditions are likely (e.g., snow, rain)?
- What kind of footgear is required (e.g., hiking boots, climbing shoes, ski boots, waterproof shoes)?
- How long will you be gone?
- Do you require any specialized technical equipment for your objective (e.g., climbing gear, snow travel equipment, paddling gear)?

With this basic information in mind, it's time to start fine-tuning what to bring, categorized by body parts: head, feet, hands, upper body, and lower body. Then you will add sleeping systems,

A reasonable amount of personal gear for a 30-day hiking expedition.

toiletries, personal items (e.g., books, headlamps), and finally your individual technical gear.

Even with a list like the one on pages 81–83, you have to make a lot of decisions. Do you want to wear a soft-shell jacket or Gore-Tex? Will approach shoes suffice, or do you need heavy hiking boots? Many of these decisions ultimately come down to personal preference, so it helps to test out your gear before launching on a big trip. You never want to try out some newfangled gadget or piece of clothing for the first time high up in the Andes, especially if it is critical to the success of your endeavor.

Once you've narrowed down your options, line them out on the floor and try out different combinations. Ultimately you want to take the minimal amount necessary, so figuring out clothing and equipment that is multifunctional is beneficial. For example, a bandana can be worn French Foreign Legion–style under a ball cap to keep the sun off your neck; it can be used as a washcloth or sweatband; and you can clean your sunglasses with it. A white lightweight synthetic hoodie shirt can be a base layer worn under warmer clothes, or it can be a great sun shirt with the hood pulled up to shade your head and neck.

Personal Gear Checklist

	Basic Trekking or Camping in Mild Weather	Kayaking or Rafting	Winter Camping or Mountaineering
Upper Body	1 synthetic base layer (mid- or lightweight)	1 synthetic base layer (mid- or lightweight)	2–3 synthetic or wool base layers (minimum one mid-weight and one expedition weight)
	1 lightweight pile, wool, or down sweater	1 lightweight pile, wool, or down sweater	1 insulating layer (down or synthetic-filled, or heavy-weight pile jacket)
	1 windshirt or windjacket with wicking liner inside	Wet suit and dry-top combo okay; full dry suit recommended for river expeditions	1 windshirt or windjacket with wicking liner inside
	1 rain jacket		1 waterproof storm jacket (Gore-Tex or equivalent)
	1–2 T-shirts (synthetic best)	PFD	Women: 1 synthetic sports bra or tank top
	Women: 1 synthetic sports bra or tank top		
Lower Body	1 pair synthetic bottoms or lightweight polyester hiking pants	1 pair synthetic bottoms or fleece pants	1 pair synthetic bottoms (mid- or lightweight)
	1 pair windpants or waterproof/breathable pants (rain pants optional)	Wet suit and dry-pants combo okay; full dry suit recommended for river expeditions	1 pair stormproof pants (e.g. Gore-Tex, water-resistant, soft-shell, etc.)
	1 pair nylon shorts (can be zip-off hiking pants)		1 pair insulated pants or shelled polypropylene
Underwear	2–3 pairs, synthetic materials best for quick washing; shorts with liners best for men	2–3 pairs, synthetic materials critical to keep you warm when wet	2–3 pairs, synthetic materials critical to keep you warm when wet
Head	1 sun hat	River helmet	1 visor or sun hat (optional)
	1 lightweight wool or pile hat	Neoprene skullcap or balaclava	1 wool hat or pile hat
	1 bandana (optional)		1 neck gaiter, scarf, or balaclava
			1 insulated hood (optional)
			1 bandana (optional)
Hands	1 lightweight pair of gloves, wool or synthetic (optional)	Waterproof neoprene gloves or poagies	1–2 lightweight pairs of gloves (wool or synthetic)
		Paddle	1 pair of insulated gloves or mittens
			1 pair of mitten shells

Personal Gear Checklist continued

	Basic Trekking or Camping in Mild Weather	Kayaking or Rafting	Winter Camping or Mountaineering
Feet	2–3 pairs wool or synthetic socks	Closed-toe river shoes with sticky rubber and laces or Fastex buckle system	3–4 pairs wool or synthetic socks
	Hiking shoes or boots	Gore-Tex booties (attached to dry suit)	Hiking boots (plastic or leather, weather and activity dependent)
	1 pair gaiters (optional)	2–3 pairs Neoprene or wool socks	1 pair gaiters (supergaiters helpful for winter camping and glacier travel or high-altitude mountaineering)
	1 pair camp shoes or sandals (optional)		1 pair insulated booties or camp shoes (depends on whether camping on snow)
	1 pair neoprene socks (optional, helpful in rainy or wet places or if you anticipate many river crossings)		1 pair neoprene socks (optional, helpful in rainy or wet places) and/or vapor barrier socks
Sleeping system	1 sleeping pad	1 sleeping pad	1½ or 2 sleeping pads (depends on whether camping on snow)
	1 sleeping bag (weight is temperature dependent)	1 sleeping bag (weight temperature dependent)	1 sleeping bag (weight temperature dependent)
	Compression sacks for pad and sleeping bag (optional)	Compression sacks for pad and sleeping bag (optional)	Compression sacks for pad and sleeping bag (optional)
Personal technical gear	Expedition dependent: could include things like a backpack, hiking poles, harness, climbing shoes, binoculars for a birding trip, etc.	Rescue equipment for each paddler: 3 rescue pulleys 3 locking carabiners 2 prusiks 1 high quality throw bag with ⅜" spectra line. 1 15' piece of 1" tubular webbing 1 knife 1 whistle 1 collapsible folding saw	Expedition dependent: could include things like harness, ice ax, boots, skis, sled, snowshoes, avalanche beacon, shovel, probe, etc.

Personal Gear Checklist continued

	Basic Trekking or Camping in Mild Weather	Kayaking or Rafting	Winter Camping or Mountaineering
Toiletries	Toothbrush Toothpaste Comb Dental floss with needle for emergency sewing repairs Personal hygiene products Contact lens solution Sunscreen Lip balm, etc.		
Extras (expedition dependent)	Camera Money, credit card, passport, driver's license Book, notebook, pencil or pen Headlamp Lighter or matches Sunglasses Trekking poles Umbrella Binoculars Spare batteries for all electronic devices, consider portable solar-panel recharger Fishing rod, tackle, flies or lures 1–2 water bottles or bladders Bowl, spoon (cup optional)		

On long, overseas expeditions, you'll need to consider travel clothes as well. Travel clothing should be comfortable, wrinkle-proof, and presentable. You want to look neat and professional, especially if you are part of a big expedition that has to deal with the bureaucracy of permits, government officials, and the like before you head into the mountains. Loose clothes made from lightweight cotton blends or synthetic materials with lots of pockets work well on international flights, and they are easy to rinse out in a motel room and stand up to the wear and tear of long days of use. Give them a test run and make sure they are comfortable before you go.

MATERIALS

At NOLS, down was considered a bad word for many years, but times have changed. With the new lightweight water-resistant fabrics available for both jackets and bags, many instructors and

Strengths and Weakness of Fabrics Used for Outdoor Clothing

Fabric	Strength	Weakness	Best Use
Down	• Lightweight and compressible • Good warmth-to-size ratio	• Loses all insulating properties when wet • Difficult to dry	• Ideal for cold temperatures or dry climates
Wool	• Maintains insulating properties when wet • Less smelly than some synthetic materials	• Can be itchy • Sometimes bulky or heavy (newer wool items are better) • Can be expensive • Dries slowly	• Ideal for base layers, pants, or sweaters if drying time and weight are not your primary concern
Synthetic: polypropylene, Capilene, and others	• Maintains insulating properties when wet • Dries quickly • Relatively inexpensive	• Can be smelly	• Ideal for base layers • Good for wet conditions
Synthetic filling	• Lightweight • Maintains insulating properties when wet	• Bulky, hard to compress • Degrades over time, losing its insulation values	• Great for wet conditions or cold temperatures where space is not a concern
Gore-Tex	• Waterproof • Somewhat breathable	• Can be heavy and bulky • Expensive	• Ideal for winter and wet conditions
Coated-nylon	• Waterproof • Inexpensive	• Nonbreathable	• Good rain layer in warm temperatures or for non-rigorous activities like nature observation
Soft-shell	• Water-resistant • Breathable • Flexible • Nonbulky	• Expensive • Not entirely waterproof • Can be hot	• Ideal for skiing or climbing when you don't expect too much rain
Cotton	• Cool • Keeps the sun off	• Cold when wet • Slow to dry • Little insulating value	• Ideal as a sun shirt or for hiking in hot climates and for travel clothes

students go into the mountains with down these days. Cotton was also often frowned upon, but on a hot desert trip, you will probably live in a long-sleeve cotton sun shirt. There are no hard-and-fast rules for which materials are best. You just need to recognize the strengths and weakness of the options available for your clothing and make decisions accordingly.

LUXURIES

In addition to your essentials, you may want to pack a few extras to pamper yourself with on a long trip. For expeditions where you plan to establish a base camp, you may want to consider a deck of cards or a travel-sized board game like cribbage or backgammon. A book can help you pass the hours, and an MP3 music player can provide some diversion. Remember, anything you bring will endure a lot of wear and tear, and weight is always a factor, so keep the word luxury in mind when picking out extras for your trip. You don't need them, and they should be the first to go if weight and space become an issue.

Passing the time tent-bound with a good book can help keep you and your expedition mates sane.

JEWELRY

Take a moment to think about the implications of wearing jewelry before you travel. Many people wear some jewelry—rings, earrings, a necklace, or other piercings—without even thinking about it. Jewelry can make you a target of theft, and bracelets and rings can be dangerous when you are climbing. In freezing temperatures, earrings can increase your risk of incurring frostbite, and in some places certain forms of jewelry may not be culturally acceptable, such as earrings on men or nose rings on anyone. So while jewelry may be important because it makes you feel connected to people and events back home, and it may be an integral part of your personal identity, make sure you've considered the implications of wearing it before you encounter an unfortunate situation.

Group Gear

Group gear can be broken down into camping gear and technical gear—everything that your team will share during the course of the expedition. Here's the rub: Group gear is going to get beat up, so it is important to determine beforehand how you plan to share the financial burden of providing or replacing equipment that will be used by everyone.

You may decide to use an individual's gear—say your personal tent—for the trip. If you do, your team should discuss whether you will be compensated for the use of the tent, or whether there is enough sharing among the group to ensure everyone is contributing equally. Sometimes you may need to purchase equipment specifically for your expedition. If this is the case, again you need to determine how you are going to pay for the equipment and who will get to keep it after the trip is over.

If you plan to use personal gear as shared equipment, make sure to label items with a permanent marker or color-coded tape so you come home with the same equipment you brought. Carabiners and other types of climbing gear are notoriously difficult to differentiate without labeling.

Take time to coordinate items such as rechargers, solar panels, and spare batteries. People don't like to leave home without the tools they need to keep their precious iPod or camera working for the duration of the trip, but you don't want to end up in the field with multiple chargers that are all the same. That's just a waste of weight and space.

CAMPING GEAR

The type of camping gear you take is determined by your destination and objective. A two-week trip in Utah's canyon country may require a minimum of gear: Depending on the time of year it may be warm and dry there, bugs aren't often a concern, and you can sleep under rock overhangs in many places, so you may opt not to even bring a shelter. On the other hand, an expedition in the Alaska Range requires a four-season shelter that can withstand high winds,

Threading a Speedy Stitcher for some serious gear repair. Don't forget to plan for contingencies by packing a group repair kit.

The size of your backcountry kitchen and amount of food fluctuates not only with team size, but also with activity. The two people on the left are going light and moving camp every night on a hiking trip. The cook in the center could be cooking for either a group at a climbing base camp or for hungry paddlers on a rafting trip. The third example shows a one-pot meal, such as one you'd eat while weather-bound high on a mountain, like our friend to the right.

big dumps of snow, and maybe even hordes of mosquitoes on the approach. Once you've lined out the conditions you expect to encounter, you can use the following checklist to plan out your group gear needs.

When selecting your group gear, light is good but not necessarily best for everything. Don't sacrifice durability and reliability to save a little bit of weight. Make sure the equipment you select is high quality and will not fail you midtrip. Cooking on a fire while glacier camping is simply not an option; if your stove fails you above tree line, your trip is over.

Seam Sealing

Most tents are not seam-sealed against moisture when you purchase them, so before you leave, set up your tent outside and coat all external seams with seam seal or silicon seal. Follow the manufacturer's recommendation for the type of sealant appropriate for your shelter. Make sure you do this well before you leave. If you pack your tent with the sealant still wet, the seams will stick together and smell. Regardless of their dryness or wetness, you'll be much happier in a storm if the seams are keeping out the rain.

Make sure to choose an appropriately sized shelter for the number of members on your expedition.

Group Expedition Gear

	Summer conditions	Winter conditions	Water-based
Sleeping system	• Fly or lightweight tent with mosquito netting, smallest size to accommodate group	• Four-season tent or fly, smallest size to accommodate group • Shovel for digging snow shelters (one for every four people unless there is avalanche concern, then one per person)	• Gore-Tex bivy sacks or ultralightweight tent or fly
Kitchen	• Stove with windscreen, fuel bottles, and lighter • 1–2 four-quart pot with lid for every four people • 1 frying pan for every four people (optional) • Water bladder for carrying water • Mixing spoon, ladle, spatula, knife • Spice kit • Hand soap or sanitizer	• Stove with windscreen, fuel bottles, and lighter • Stove pad if cooking on snow • 2 four-quart pots with lid for every four people (volume is critical for making water from melting snow) • 1 frying pan for every four people (optional) • Water bladder for carrying water (unnecessary if melting snow for water) • Mixing spoon, ladle, spatula, knife • Spice kit • Hand soap or sanitizer • Lantern	• Stove with windscreen, fuel bottles, and lighter • 1–2 four-quart pot with lid for every four people • 1 frying pan for every four people (optional) • Water bladder for carrying water • Mixing spoon, ladle, spatula, knife • Spice kit • Hand soap or sanitizer
Latrine kit	• Spade for digging catholes • Toilet paper and garbage bag • Individual, commercially available sanitary bags for carrying out human waste (e.g., Wag Bag) • You may want to establish a group latrine in some base camps. Check into recommended practices at your destination.		
Bear camping	• Electric bear fence, rope for hanging food, or bearproof canister for food storage • Bear spray • Carrying firearms in Arctic regions may be recommended in some places. Check with local authorities.		
Communications	• Cell phone or satellite phone (see pages 100–101) • Global positioning system device (GPS) • Computer (optional) • Spare batteries or portable electronic power source • SPOT (Satellite Personal Outdoor Tracker)		
Maps and paperwork	• One set of maps (1:24,000 topographic preferred) or charts per two people, stored in waterproof bag • Copy of any necessary permits • Guidebook or route information (2 copies)		
En route to destination	• Oversized duffels for transporting gear • Transportation Security Administration (TSA)-approved locks		
Optional group library and entertainment	• Reference materials (bird or flower books, history book, etc.) • Games, cards, leisure reading, etc.		

Group Expedition Gear continued

	Summer conditions	Winter conditions	Water-based
First-aid kit	• Face shield or pocket mask • Wound closure strips • Cravats • Tegaderm or OpSite or other flexible, breathable bandage • Eye pads • Band-Aids • 3"x4" gauze pads • 3"x3" gauze pads • Gauze rolls • Tweezers/safety pin • Ibuprofen or other over-the-counter pain medication • Betadine (topical antiseptic for wound cleaning) • Tincture of benzoin (skin protectant when bandaging or taping) • Antibiotic ointment • Cortisone cream • Thermometer • Latex gloves • Ziploc bags and biohazard stickers • Ace bandage • Athletic tape • Soap sponge • Moleskin, molefoam, or blister pads • 2nd Skin • Mirror • Scissors		
Repair Kit	• Barge cement or epoxy • Duct tape • Seam grip • Cord locks (6 each) • Fasttex buckle to fit various sizes • Galvanized wire, 8" • Ladder lock buckle, 1" • P-cord, 30' • Ripstop tape, 8"–12" • Sewing kit • Zipper slider of various sizes • Speedy Stitcher • Tent pole splint with duct tape • Zipper pulls, 5 and 7 (3 each) • Zipper stops (6 each) • Stove replacement parts (pump, valve, cleaning tool, oil, etc.) • Pliers, vice grip, or multitool • Spare ski binding or crampon screws and parts (expedition dependent)		
Drug Kit	*Note: Many items on this list require a prescription, so consult your doctor and get detailed protocols for use of all drugs.* • Pepto-Bismol (to sooth digestion) • Antacid tablets (to combat acid reflux or indigestion common at altitude) • Antidiarrheals, e.g., Imodium • Monistat (for yeast infections in women) • Antihistamine, e.g., Benedryl (for allergic reactions) • Throat lozenges • Benzocaine, e.g., Orabase-B (topical anesthetic for dental problems) • Altitude sickness drugs (e.g., Diamox, Decadron) • Painkillers (e.g., Vicodin, Percocet) • Antibiotics (e.g, Zithromax for respiratory infections, Keflex for soft-tissue infections, Cipro for bacterial diarrhea, etc.) • Antimalarial drugs • Sleep aids or sedatives		

Molly's Cooking Gear Woes

Years ago, I was offered a job as the cook on a three-week educational expedition to the coastal rain forests of Ecuador. I eagerly accepted the offer, ignoring the fact I did not speak Spanish, had never planned menus or cooked for more than a few friends, and had no real knowledge of South America. I was sure it would be fine. I figured the food did not have to be extravagant, and I would be traveling with Spanish speakers, so things should work out.

The expedition began in Quito with a shopping trip. A local man who was helping us with logistics took me around town to find my cooking equipment and supplies. Unfortunately, his English was limited and my Spanish did not go much beyond a few key phrases: "Where is the bathroom?" "My name is Molly," and "How are you?" So we communicated with lots of pointing and some made-up sign language.

In the shops that lined the streets of Quito, we found kerosene-burning stoves and large aluminum pots, plastic wash basins, utensils, and jugs for water and fuel. Back at the hotel, we laid out the equipment and packed it as carefully as we could in large duffel bags, padding things with spare clothes and sleeping bags. The stove and pots looked flimsy, and I wasn't even sure they would survive the journey to our destination: a bus ride, boat trip, and two days of mule packing. My anxiety increased when I watched one of the mule handlers beat his mule to force it between two trees, where it was wedged by the load on its back. Something had to give, and I worried what it might be.

Once we reached the village where we were to spend our time, I tentatively unpacked. A few of the food bags had exploded, leaving one load coated in pink sugary lemonade and hardened white flour. The aluminum pots were dented and misshapen, but usable. One stove had snapped in half, and the other was perilously close to breaking, but looked salvageable. I prepared my first meal that night without too much trouble, but it was downhill from there. I had never used kerosene to cook with, and the one functioning stove quickly gummed up from the poorly burning fuel. I tried to figure out how to dismantle the stove to clean it, but could not figure out how to take it apart. Plus I feared that, once apart, I'd never be able to reassemble the thing. Eventually, the stove began an ominous cycle where it would flicker down to a single flame, roar back to life, and then flicker again. I

Molly's Cooking Gear Woes

shook the stove and swore at it, and for a few minutes it would flare up, roaring enthusiastically before fading again. Finally the shaking stopped working, and the stove died once and for all.

My coworkers (two guides hired for their Spanish and knowledge of the area) had no more expertise with stove repair than I, so I switched to cooking on fires. I set up my kitchen in the dirt beneath the house where we were staying, which was raised off the ground on stilts to keep out insects, snakes, and water. I would get up early and go searching for wood; gingerly exploring the jungle near the village, sure I was going to run into a deadly bushmaster somewhere in my rambles. Once I returned to my kitchen bearing a load of wood, I checked for other creepy crawlies and set up to cook, trying to blockade myself from the attentions of roaming pigs and goats. The wood was consistently green and smoldered more than blazed, making the cooking process take much longer than it would have on a camp stove. Breakfast routinely meant rising in the dark at 5:00 a.m. for breakfast at 8:00, and I had to start cooking dinner at 4:00 p.m. for a 7:00 meal. Then there was the cleanup, but at least that was relatively easy. There's not much you can do to destroy a plastic wash basin.

The trip was still exciting, but I could have explored more had my gear been up to par. As it was, I learned to make do, which is a good skill, but not the reason I had traveled to Ecuador. ■

NAVIGATIONAL TOOLS

First and foremost, you'll need topographic maps for your expedition. The level of detail and accuracy of such maps varies around the world. For the most part, you'll be looking for maps with a 1:50,000 metric scale where two centimeters on the map represent one kilometer on the earth. Ironically, the United States is the only developed nation without a standardized civilian topographic map series in the 1:50,000 metric scale. The United State's equivalent to such maps in terms of usability is the U.S. Geological Survey's (USGS) 1:24,000-scale, 7.5-minute maps. These maps are detailed—one inch on the map equals 2,000 feet on the ground—and contain lots of useful information for hikers; however, unless you plan to stick to traveling in the United States, the fact that they are nonmetric makes it hard to use them in correlation with the rest of the world's mapping systems.

Go online to locate maps for your area of interest. For the United States, start with the USGS Web site (www.usgs.gov), where you can download an index to help you determine which maps you'll need for the area you plan to travel. You can then purchase maps either through the USGS online store or locally at an outdoors store. The entire contiguous United States is available in a 7.5-minute map—57,000 of them are required to depict the continental United States, Hawaii, and its territories. Alaska has 7.5-minute maps for Anchorage, Fairbanks, and Prudhoe Bay. For the rest of the state, you'll have to use 15-minute maps, which cover a wider area but offer less detail because of the smaller scale.

Commercial topographic maps—such as the Trails Illustrated series—are made for national parks and popular recreation areas like the Wind River Mountains. These maps are useful because the details included are determined by the area's recreational value rather than its latitude and longitude. This means you won't end up spending your entire trip in the corner of four different maps, which is often the case with 7.5-minute maps. You can also purchase software programs that allow you to print your own topographic maps. These programs are pricey and require large printers, so unless you plan to print a lot of maps, it's probably not worth the expense. Some outdoor retail shops have in-house printers that you can use to print maps.

For international maps, start your search on the Internet. There are a number of different online retailers offering all types of maps for sale. Ideally, you want to find 1:50,000 topographic maps for the area you intend to visit. If you have trouble determining your best option from the Internet, it's worth talking to people who have traveled in the area before. They may have suggestions for a map brand or series that provides the most accurate, detailed, and up-to-date information, particularly for countries without a national mapping program to produce standardized maps.

Start your map search with omnimap.com or maps2anywhere .com. Both Internet sites have a comprehensive list of destinations

*Guidebooks, maps, and navigation equipment are considered group gear.
Divide them up accordingly.*

and the types of maps available for the region. Their indexes include maps that cover large areas, which can be helpful for your big picture planning. You can buy maps through these sites as well.

Beware that in some parts of the world—such as India and Pakistan where borders are contested—detailed topographic maps may be considered classified information available only to the military. Check with people who have traveled in the area before to find out how strictly these kinds of rules are enforced. Often you can just hide such maps in your backpack at checkpoints or park boundaries and pass through without issue.

Compasses

Although not necessary if you have good topographic maps, a compass can be useful for orienting your map or pinpointing your location. You don't need anything fancy, just a standard orienteering compass with a movable dial marked with a compass rose (the cardinal directions and degrees), a base plate bearing a direction-of-travel arrow, and a magnified north-seeking needle. With this simple tool, you can perform most basic orienteering techniques.

One navigational trick to help minimize your need for the compass is to familiarize yourself with the general lay of the land at the start of your trip. Do the mountains trend north-south? Where does the sun rise and set? Are the rivers generally flowing in one direction? These kinds of big-picture landmarks can help you get your bearings and develop your sense of direction so you have an idea where you are heading without having to resort to your compass. For example, in the Wind River Mountains in Wyoming, the range generally trends north-south. If you are standing on a high peak staring out across the plains, you know you are looking either east or west. Add in the placement of the sun, and you can get a good sense of your orientation. But when clouds close in, blocking out the sun and hampering your views, it's a good idea to have your compass for backup. Compasses are particularly useful in feature-less areas: Big glaciers, high alpine plateaus, and open mesas can all be hard to navigate without a compass to keep you on track.

Practice using your compass before you go, especially if it's been a while since you put one to use. Map reading and compass use are skills that require practice to maintain accuracy. If you are rusty, it's worth polishing up on the techniques you'll need before you have an emergency where accuracy is critical.

Essential Compass Skills

- Orienting a map with a compass
- Shooting a bearing from the land and from a map
- Following a bearing
- Triangulation for pinpointing location

Global Positioning Systems

Global Positioning Systems (GPS) use satellite signals to triangulate your location. The degree of accuracy is remarkable. You can hone in on a specific location within inches with the right equipment. Hunters use GPSs to pinpoint their location when hunting in dense trees and brush; pilots use them to find drop zones or remote landing strips. You may find yourself using a GPS for resupplies, evacuations, rendezvous, or rescues.

GPSs are notorious for being misused. Search–and-rescue professionals joke about having to look for lost hikers armed with a fancy GPS but who are unable to transfer the information on their receiver to the map. They know where they are if you ask them to tell you their lat/long, but don't know what that means. To use a GPS effectively, you have to know how to plot waypoints—which means you must know how to find either latitude/longitude or Universal Transverse Mercator (UTM) coordinates on your map.

In general, you probably do not need a GPS unless you anticipate the need to communicate with someone in the air, you have to find a specific location (say a cache), or the landscape through which you are traveling is featureless, making map reading difficult (you are deep in the forest with limited views or the terrain is flat and you have no topography to use for pinpointing your location). In these situations, a GPS can be vital.

Technical Group Gear

The nature and objective of your trip will dictate your choice of technical gear. You may need multiple racks of climbing protection, swift-water rescue gear, or nothing more than shared camping gear.

To ensure you have the right equipment, do your research. If you are climbing, talk to people who have been to the area you are visiting, who have climbed the route or a route nearby, and who know what kind of rock to expect and what gear you might need. In the absence of first-hand knowledge, guidebooks or trip reports may help.

Guidebooks for alpine rock routes or trekking trips are often left intentionally vague to leave you with a sense of adventure. You

This is where it gets fun—sorting your technical gear! Molly Tyson takes inventory in China (above). Steph Davis and Jimmy Chin sort out who needs what in Pakistan (left).

should be able to discern the general nature of most routes from the descriptions, however. In the absence of any route information, at least find out what kind of rock you'll encounter at your destination: Granite demands very different gear from limestone. That information alone may dictate what protection you bring along.

If you are trekking, you'll want to do the same kind of sleuthing to determine what technical gear you may need. For example, some routes require ropes for navigating fourth-class terrain or to set up a tyrolean for a river crossing.

If you are paddling, again start with guidebooks to find out the type of water you'll encounter and what crafts are recommended. Some people paddle the Nahanni River in Canada's Northwest Territories in sea kayaks, which allows them to carry lots of gear. Sea kayaks perform adequately in flat or moving water—up to class II—but are not designed for whitewater, so they would probably not be the craft of choice for the Middle Fork of the Salmon River in Idaho. Guidebooks will also give you an idea of how long the trip will take, where you can camp, and what kind of equipment you'll need to carry to be self-sufficient.

COMMUNICATIONS

Today you can follow climbers up Everest and read an explorer's blog from Antarctica. Modern communication devices have shrunk the world and left us expecting—even demanding—instant communication with our loved ones (and fans) back home. But the reality is you can't always guarantee you'll be able to achieve contact unless you are willing to spend a fair bit of money, and even then, technology or connections may not work 100 percent of the time.

Radios

Radios that are small enough and light enough to carry on a remote expedition are limited by their transmitting power and the need to have line of sight to the receiving radio; mountains, hills, and ridges block the signal. A repeater installed on a ridge can repeat the signal over the terrain obstacle. Marine and aircraft VHF radios generally work well because terrain features do not block the signal, so you have a clear view of the sky and a plane flying overhead.

In most parts of the world, satellite phones, which are both lighter and more compact, have replaced radios for outside communications in all but a few situations. In some instances it is still important to carry a ground-to-air radio if you know your support will be from aircraft.

If you have a big team that will be spread out over your route during the expedition, handheld walkie-talkies can be a convenient, easy way to maintain contact with each other. Today's walkie-talkies come with a variety of functions. Most have a two- to five-mile line-of-sight range, but there are models that are more powerful. Some walkie-talkies come with a GPS system built in, and others have a weather alert function. You can choose which options make the most sense for your needs; often all you really want is to be able to check up on each other during the course of the day, and for that you just need a basic model.

Cell Phones

This day and age, most everyone—from your rickshaw driver in Asia to the maid in your motel room in Yosemite—carries a cell phone, and coverage is pretty much universal in populated areas. However, you shouldn't rely on cell phone coverage in remote or unpopulated locations where service is often spotty and unreliable.

If you discover that cell phones work where you plan to travel, beware: Most American cell phones and phone plans will not work overseas. To function internationally, you can contact your service provider to see what international plans they have available; rent or purchase a phone and a subscriber identity module (SIM) card; or if you have an unlocked cell phone, buy a SIM card to make your personal phone work wherever you travel.

The bottom line is, you need to check into the communications network available at your destination. Find out how widespread coverage is and whether you can unlock your phone without compromising its usability. Much of this information is available on the Internet.

Satellite Phones

Satellite phones, or satphones, are a type of mobile phone that transmits voice and data signals to orbiting satellites that then relay the signals to ground stations and existing land lines, cell services, or the Internet. The satellites are basically orbiting repeaters. Satellite phone systems may utilize constellations of orbiting satellites and provide coverage around much of the earth; examples of this type of system are Iridium and Globalstar. Other systems utilize satellites in geosynchronous orbit that appear, from earth, to stay "parked" over the same part of the earth. These systems may provide communication only in certain areas or, if there are multiple satellites, may provide coverage over a larger area. The Thuraya system, which provides coverage over Asia and much of Europe, is one such system. TerreStar is developing a similar system for North America.

Satphone technology is continually improving, and handsets are becoming smaller, lighter, and more powerful and use a smaller antenna. The TerraStar handset is advertised to be the size and weight of a current smart phone and is both a cell phone and satphone. Satphones are the most popular form of external communications for expeditions into remote areas where cellular service is unavailable or unreliable. Satphones may allow travelers to access e-mail and can provide live-feed blogs so friends, family, and fans can follow an expedition.

There are some limitations to satphones, however. They are basically line-of-sight transmitters so they need a clear view of the sky in order to transmit and receive from the orbiting satellites. So, for example, in canyon country where your view of the sky is limited by cliff walls, a satphone may not work well because it loses the line-of-sight to the satellite as it moves through the sky. With systems that use a constellation of satellites, you may have calls dropped due to the technological complexity of transmitting the signal from the phone to a satellite (and often relayed to more than one satellite) to the ground station and out to the receiver. Any of the links along the way can fail, resulting in a dropped call. Frequent users of satphones learn to just call back.

While satphone service providers may claim worldwide coverage, be aware that in some countries, such as Burma and India, possession of a satellite phone is illegal, and in other circumstances a country may not have granted permission to the satphone service provider to use their airspace to transmit. So in parts of the Himalaya—such as the Karakorum in Pakistan and the Nanda Devi area of India—if you ask about satphone use you'll likely be told no.

Satphones are also expensive, both for the handsets and for the airtime. Prices will likely slowly come down as technology develops and competition heats up, but in the meantime, renting a satphone for the duration of your expedition is often your best bet. NOLS Rocky Mountain in Wyoming, for example, both owns and rents satphones to outfit its courses. During the peak season, in order to have enough phones to go around, the school rents extra satphones for $5 a day.

Personal Locator Beacons

A cheaper alternative to the satphone is a personal locator beacon (PLB). PLBs are data transmitters only and do not allow for two-way voice communication. They are specifically designed and intended for land-based situations as opposed to aircraft (ELTs) or marine vessels (EPIRBs). They are designed to send a distress signal and the latitude and longitude coordinates of your location via satellite; when received, the information initiates a search-and-rescue operation. There are different types of PLBs, such as the SPOT, the McMurdo Fastfind, and the ACR SARLink. The SPOT is relatively inexpensive ($169 in 2010) but requires an annual subscription fee ($100–$150 in 2010). The Fast Find at $300 and SARLink from $400–$500 are more expensive but do not require subscriptions.

The SPOT uses a privately owned satellite constellation system operated and maintained by Globalstar. A private company (GEOS International Emergency Response Center) receives the distress signal and coordinates a search and rescue using local SAR authorities and resources in the country the signal came from. The Fastfind and SARLink systems use the Cospas-Sarsat satellite system of geosynchronous satellites that are operated and maintained by government agencies including the United States, Canada, and others. A government agency receives the distress signals (NOAA in the United States) and contacts local authorities based on your location coordinates to initiate a SAR mission.

PLBs do not have worldwide coverage because some countries, such as India, do not allow their use and in NOLS' testing of SPOTs we found they were unreliable in Chile and New Zealand. The manufacturer of Fastfinds notes that they need to be purchased in the country in which they will be used. This technology is evolving and we expect that limitations will become fewer as the systems gain acceptance.

All of these devices need to be registered in your name so when a distress signal is received the authorities can verify that the unit is on an expedition (as opposed to an accidental activation). The SPOT device, because it is a private system, has some other potentially useful functions. On your registration page you can enter a predetermined message for the Help and OK functions and program whom you want these messages to go to—usually not SAR authorities, but rather family or friends. These functions can be used to request non-emergency help or simply to let people know that things are going OK. SPOT includes a link to Google Earth with your location coordinates. For an additional fee there is a tracking service—you leave the unit on and it transmits your location to your contact people with the Google Earth URL at regular intervals. The Delorme company, maker of GPS devices, has developed a way to transmit text messages from one model of its GPS units via the SPOT satellite system, which became available in July 2010. These are text messages you can create and send from wherever you are. It is still only one-way communication, but you could inform someone of the specific situation you're in.

Dave finds a local equipment store for a few extras on a personal expedition in Nepal.

The Fastfind only transmits the distress signal. The ACR units have an OK function, similar to SPOT's. The OK signal is really a unit self-test function that is routed to up to five contacts that you set up ahead of time. This service requires an annual subscription ($40 in 2010).

PLB technology will likely advance rapidly in the future as the cost of these units decreases and the features they have improve due to competition.

Summary

Once you have an idea of your objective and the equipment you'll need to achieve it, spread all your gear out on the floor. Make a list of what you need and check it off, noting the actual piece you plan to bring to make sure everything is in place. Inspect your equipment for its condition, replace worn items, and consider contingency plans. Should you bring an extra set of stoppers in case you need to back off your route and want to leave inexpensive gear in the anchors? Will you need to place bolts? Again, consider multifunctional gear to prevent redundancy and cut down on weight: Varying lengths of tied webbing slings are more versatile in the mountains than sewn quick-draws for example.

You may also be able to purchase some gear at your destination. Clothes, shoes, even used climbing gear, are available all over the world, often for much less money than they cost in the United States. This is definitely a good option when you are traveling in places where a certain style of dress is both more culturally appropriate and more comfortable because of climate conditions. Again, a little research will help you determine what supplies you can count on picking up during the course of your travels.

The biggest challenge in planning your first expedition is determining how much is enough. After you've gone once, things will get easier, especially if you keep detailed lists of everything you brought and how it was used. On your first go-round, get advice, seek items that serve more than one purpose, and don't cut corners to save money. In the long run, when your plastic poncho from Walmart disintegrates and you are faced with hiking out in monsoon rains, you'll be very sorry you saved $100 by passing up high-quality rain gear.

9 | FOOD AND FUEL

At NOLS there is an expression known as HALT, which stands for hungry, angry, lonely, tired. The idea is that before you attempt to resolve a conflict, make a decision, or address an issue, you need to make sure no one in the group is HALTing. It's no surprise that hunger comes first on the list. Most of us have bonked in our lives, and we know that our rationality disappears when our stomach is rumbling. For parents, this is one of the earliest lessons. Children have no filters, and when you find yourself with a hungry child and no snacks, you know you are in trouble.

Food is integral to our happiness and, therefore, integral to the success of any expedition. Stories of people running out of food or bringing food requiring high-maintenance preparation are rampant, but the reverse is problematic too. Bringing too much food can result in burning or wasting extras because of the burdens of carrying it. Keep in mind factors such as altitude, mode of transportation, and age of team members as you plan your rations.

Planning a ration for an expedition can also be a thankless task. People always have special needs, desires, or dislikes. You have to balance these factors with weight considerations, caloric requirements, climatic conditions, altitude, length of your trip, and any number of other issues that affect your decision. For long expeditions, greater than 30 days, you also need adequate long-term nutrition (see *NOLS Backcountry Nutrition*). So try to make the meal planning a team effort, or at least make sure everyone has ample opportunity to voice his or her opinions before you hit the road.

Molly Tells of Food in Good Times and in Bad

The first time I went backpacking in the canyons of the Southwest, I envisioned smooth slabs of warm slickrock; waterfalls cascading past maidenhair ferns and monkey flowers into deep, clear pools; hot sun, tall cactus, red cliffs, and dark slot canyons. I did not think about snow. And here we were, postholing.

Snow blanketed the mesa tops, and the pools hidden deep in the canyons were frozen. A yellow crust, buried about five inches below the snow surface, was our nemesis. Sometimes it held you up; most times it didn't. We would take two steps, delicately balanced on top, and then crash through up to our knees in sugary, faceted snow. At times it was easier to crawl than walk. Wallowing along on our hands and knees, we pushed our packs in front of us.

To compound the problem, we had very little food. On the morning before our re-ration, I'd eaten one small pancake, plain. No butter, no syrup, nothing. Hungry and tired, when I saw the crawl marks in the snow from my teammates ahead of me, I sat down on my pack and cried before dropping onto my knees to follow.

Food had become an issue over the past week as the temperatures dropped and we ate more than we'd calculated. We were all hungry and protective of what little food was left. Before leaving camp one morning, one of the members of our expedition came into our kitchen area: "I know Bob has to eat because of his diabetes, but how much does he have to eat?"

Apparently Bob's cook group had each had a handful of Grape-Nuts for breakfast, while Bob ate the last of the granola with milk. Watching him hungrily, they stared as he swallowed each mouthful; finally he picked up his bowl and disappeared to eat on his own. We did not know how much Bob had to eat, we just knew he could not go without food. The rest of us could. It was unpleasant but not life threatening.

The next morning, we rose and broke camp without bothering to light our stoves. Bob ate some energy bars he saved for such an emergency. We began hiking, moving slowly over the snow. The person out front would step forward tentatively, balancing on the yellow skim hidden underneath. We'd watch from behind, waiting to see if he or she would break through. It didn't really matter. If the leader stayed on top, the next person would crash down, falling into the snow up to his or her crotch. It was tedious going. Stopping for a break, we sipped water. There

Molly Tells of Food in Good Times and in Bad

was nothing to eat. Bob sat away from the group. He had food, but was reluctant to eat in front of our accusing eyes.

Finally we hit an old two-track road where the snow had melted, allowing us to walk unimpeded for the first time in a week. Our group spread out, each of us silently plodding forward, head down, dreaming of food. I thought about sandwiches: big, thick deli sandwiches with cheese, turkey, lettuce, tomatoes, avocados—the works. I thought of ice cream: mint chocolate chip, Oreo, even vanilla.

It was late in the afternoon; as the sun was sinking and the shadows were beginning to spread across our path, I saw him: Kay, our re-rationer. He looked clean and happy. His smile was wide under his big blond mustache and he wore a ball cap pulled down over his eyes. His first words when he saw us were, "Hungry?" And out of his pack he pulled a bag full of chocolate bars. We all laughed gleefully as we tore into our candy. It was like manna from heaven. Suddenly we were human again. Suddenly we had food. ■

Planning

There are many ways to plan meals for an expedition. Each has its supporters and detractors, and some techniques are better suited for certain types of expeditions than others, but all work. You can plan each meal, you can buy freeze-dried prepared meals, you can follow a bulk ration plan, you can divide up days and leave it to the individual team member to plan food for that particular time period, or you can even have each team member bring a complete individual ration. The critical thing is to make sure the entire team has weighed in and agreed upon the plan.

It may help to devise some kind of food preferences questionnaire to guide the ration planner. The more specific your answers, the less likely you are to be surprised with a month's worth of instant oatmeal packets for every meal. Convenient, yes. Tasty? Palatable? That's questionable.

Food Likes, Dislikes, and Must-Haves Questionnaire

1. Do you have any food allergies?
2. Are you on any kind of specific diet (i.e., vegan, gluten-free, etc.)?
3. Do you eat meat?
4. List your five favorite backcountry meals.
5. List your five favorite backcountry snacks.
6. What foods do you refuse to eat?
7. What foods do you tolerate in limited quantities?
8. What food could you eat nonstop for the entire trip?
9. Do you enjoy cooking in the field or would you rather just boil water?
10. Is baking appropriate for your expedition? If so, do you want to bake?
11. Do you prefer something easy to prepare over flavorful food?
12. What drinks do you like?
13. How does altitude affect your appetite?
14. What special treats do you like?

For years, NOLS has used a bulk ration meal planning system that gives students and instructors a great deal of freedom to be creative and elaborate in their field cooking. Many students come home from their courses thrilled to have learned how to make yeast bread, cinnamon rolls, pizzas, and countless other tasty treats from scratch. The bulk ration system is great for a NOLS-type expedition where you are in the wilderness for long periods of time without a specific objective like a mountain summit dictating the flow of your trip. NOLS courses are about living in the outdoors, and cooking is one of the living skills we teach. That said, this technique is time-consuming, and often cooking is not going to be a priority on a technical expedition. If your goal is to climb Mount Waddington, for example, your food is probably going to be pretty utilitarian: calories for fuel, not for a four-course meal. We'll go into some detail about bulk rationing later in this chapter, but first we want to offer a few ideas for other systems that may be more appropriate for your trip.

MENU PLANNING

As the name implies, menu planning is simple: Figure out how many dinners, breakfasts and lunches you will need and come up with a menu for each of those meals. This system works well for short trips. You can even pack the food for a given meal in a single bag with everything premeasured and ready to go. Then if you are on cook duty for Monday night, you just pull out the Monday dinner bag and follow instructions.

Pack animals can be a great resource for resupplies in the mountains during long expeditions.

Meals in this system can be as elaborate or simple as you like. Some people dry their own food beforehand, so all you have to do is add water. Boaters will often freeze meals and carry them in coolers. The frozen meals keep the beer and butter cold, and by the time you are ready to eat them, they've thawed, and all you need to do is heat the food in a bag. This method is less useful in the mountains when you are carrying food on your back, but sometimes it can be timed with resupplies on horseback or when using pack animals.

With meal planning, you can divide up the days among your group so one person is not in charge of the entire ration plan. If there are three of you on a six-day trip, each of you would plan for two dinners, two breakfasts, and two lunches. Confer with each other if you go this route, or you risk ending up with pancakes for breakfast every morning. Check out *NOLS Backcountry Cooking* for more ideas and menu planning how-tos.

PREPARED FOOD

Today's freeze-dried food options are tastier than those available in the past, and nothing beats them in terms of ease and convenience. With little more than a few cups of water and a stove, you can dine on anything from beef teriyaki to oriental spiced chicken or pasta primavera as you sit on your portaledge thousands of feet off the ground.

One word of caution, however, is that the portion sizes for freeze-dried food are often very small. Most NOLS instructors find that a packet that claims it contains two servings is usually only enough for one, and at approximately $7 a pop, freeze-dried meals get expensive fast. Furthermore, undercooked freeze-dried food can still make you—and your tent mates—very uncomfortable, so make sure you hydrate the meal thoroughly before consuming it.

That said, if your trip entails a week on a big wall or multiple days above 15,000 feet, freeze-dried food may be just what you want: It's quick, nutritious, and easy to prepare.

BULK RATION PLANNING

The NOLS bulk ration planning method can seem complicated, but if you break it down into steps, you'll see it is really pretty straight-

NOLS Instructor Jared Spaulding repackages rations for the field in Patagonia.

forward and leaves plenty of room for personalizing your food options according to the specific desires of your group. Before you get started, you'll need a calculator, a scale, and the following information about your expedition:

- Group size and ages
- Duration of trip
- Purpose of trip
- Exertion level
- Weather
- Altitude
- Individual appetites and food preferences
- Nutritional needs and dietary limitations
- Expense, availability, and spoilage potential of desired menu

Step One: Determine how many total pounds of food per person per day (pppd) you expect to use (this includes everything from snacks to drinks). See the guidelines below that NOLS has found useful in helping to determine the appropriate food amounts.

Before and after: NOLS' bulk ration method involves calculating and weighing a variety of dry foods that can then be mixed and matched for a wide assortment of meal options.

Determining Food Amount Per Person Per Day

- **1.5 pounds per person per day:** 1.5 pounds per day is appropriate for trips where you expect hot days and warm nights, where the participants include children or older adults, and the activities are of relatively low intensity. 1.5 pounds per person per day equates to approximately 2,500-3,000 calories per person.

- **1.75 to 2 pounds per person per day:** When you expect warm days and cool nights, or when you will be hiking with full packs for longer than seven days, 1.75 to 2 pounds per person per day is more appropriate. Appetites often kick in after a week, and more strenuous activity will require more calories. 1.75 to 2 pounds per person gives you approximately 3,000 to 3,500 calories per person per day.

- **2 to 2.25 pounds per person per day:** When you are hiking, climbing, or skiing with full packs during cool days and cold nights such as in the fall or spring, you may want to up your ration to 2 to 2.25 pounds per person per day. This gives you between 3,500 and 4,500 calories per person per day.

- **2.5 pounds per person per day:** For cold days and cold nights, strenuous trips in mountain environments, or winter conditions, 2.5 pounds of food per person per day gives you approximately 4,000 to 5,000 calories per person, enough to provide energy for staying warm and energized for heavy activity.

Step Two: Use the following formula and your per person per day amount to calculate the total amount of food you will need for the entire expedition:

no. people × no. days × pounds per person per day
= total amount of food

For example, if you have five people out for seven days at 1.75 pounds per day, the total amount of food for the trip will be 61.25 pounds.

Step Three: Break your per person per day amount of food into the different food categories outlined below. These food groups are designed to provide you with both adequate nutrition and variety. More than 45 years of ration planning at NOLS have proven this system to be effective. You can't keep everyone happy all the time, and you can run short if you miscalculate, but in general this formula gives you enough food and variety to keep you well fed throughout your trip. Note that the need for baking ingredients is lower in winter conditions when only quick pan baking is feasible. Also, high-fat and high-preservative meats are added in the winter to meet higher fuel needs.

Food category	1.5 lbs. pppd	1.75 lbs. pppd	2 lbs. pppd	2.25 lbs. pppd	2.5 lbs. pppd
Breakfast	.24	.28	.33	.35	.38
Dinner	.27	.32	.35	.37	.40
Cheese	.19	.22	.24	.26	.28
Trail foods	.32	.35	.37	.45	.49
Flour and baking	.11	.13	.16	.09	.10
Sugar and fruit drinks	.10	.12	.14	.15	.18
Soups, bases, desserts	.06	.09	.13	.15	.19
Milk, eggs, butter, cocoa	.21	.24	.28	.31	.33
Meats and substitutes				.12	.15

Step Four: Calculate the total pounds of each food category needed for the trip by using the following formula:

Food category amount × no. people × no. days
= amount of food type needed

Using the table above, our five people on a seven-day trip at 1.75 pounds per person per day need .32 pounds of dinner foods per person per day, and .32 x 5 people x 7 days = 11.2 pounds. If you calculate the amounts needed for all the different food categories for this particular trip, you end up with a total of 61.25 pounds of food, as in step two. That means each participant will start with 12.25 pounds of food in his pack.

Step Five: Now it's time to make modifications to the meal planning according to the specific needs of your group. For example, if you don't plan to bake, you can drop the baking items and move that poundage to another category, such as breakfasts or dinners. If you don't eat cheese, remove the cheese and replace it with nuts or nut butters. Remember to make exchanges with similar types of food to maintain balance among carbohydrates, proteins, and fats. Also, if you make changes, the adjusted totals should still add up to the total amount determined in step two.

Shopping for a Bulk Ration

What does it mean that you need 11.2 pounds of dinner foods? Well, once you have totals for each of your food categories, you can use your imagination to decide what specific foods to include. For dinner, this total amount can be made up of pasta, rice, and dried beans to supply the group with plenty of hearty food for their evening meals. You may like chocolate cake for breakfast, or you may be able to live on ramen noodles for the duration of your trip. NOLS has some well-tested ideas about what types of food work best in the bulk-ration system. Following are some guidelines, and *NOLS Backcountry Nutrition* is also a great reference for the nutritional considerations for expeditions in many different environments and for special diets.

Breakfast

- Cereals: Cream of wheat, oatmeal, grits, and granola are good sources of carbohydrates and are high in protein when mixed with milk. Adding margarine, nuts, and dried fruit provides fats and additional proteins.
- Hash brown potatoes: Hash browns come dried or shredded and are a good source of carbohydrates and fats if served with cheese and fried in butter.
- Pancake mix/baking mix: Make your own baking mix or use a quick add-water-only commercial brand. You can serve pancakes with brown sugar and butter or margarine, or indulge yourself with a small container of maple syrup.
- Bagels, English muffins, quick breads, tortillas, or biscuits: Bread products are available commercially, or you can bake

your own in the field. They make a great quick breakfast food.

Dinner

- Pasta: Pastas are a good source of carbohydrates. Serving pasta with beans or dairy products makes a complete protein, enhancing its nutritional value and flavor.
- Instant beans: Pinto and black beans are available dried or refried in most grocery stores or natural food shops. Beans are great with tortillas or rice or in combination with pasta and are an important source of protein in the field.
- Instant lentils: Dehydrated lentils can be found in most natural food stores. They are a good source of protein and can be used to make veggie burgers, soups, or curries.
- Instant falafel: Instant falafel is a spicy food made from chickpeas that can add flavor and variety to your backcountry menu. Make falafel balls and serve over rice or fried in a patty to make a veggie burger. Falafel is also a good source of protein.
- Hummus: You can find powdered hummus—a spread made from chickpeas and tahini—in most natural food stores. Hummus is an excellent dip with crackers.
- Couscous: By itself, couscous is a rather bland pastalike grain product, but it is very versatile as a base for many backcountry meals and it cooks up in minutes, making it perfect for a quick hot meal at the end of a long day.
- Instant potato pearls or flakes: Instant potatoes make a good thickener for soups and gravies. They are also an excellent quick pick-me-up meal that many NOLS instructors and students use after a long, hard day. All you need is hot water, some cheese, spices, and a cup, and you have a hearty mini meal that provides a great energy boost.
- Rice: Whether white, brown, or parboiled, rice is a versatile mainstay for many backcountry meals. Instant rice is preferable because it cooks faster so you use less fuel.
- Textured vegetable protein (TVP): Made from soybeans and mixed with other ingredients to make veggie burger or chili mix, TVP is a good source of protein.

Cheese

Cheese is a good source of protein and fats. For winter expeditions, it helps to cut your cheese into cubes to expedite melting. Purchase cheese in vacuum-sealed blocks and open one at a time to ensure freshness.

Trail Food

- Nuts: Nuts are a good source of protein and fat, and make a great concentrated source of energy. You can eat your nuts alone, or in a nut mix, or make your own gorp using nuts, dried fruit, and chocolate or candy.
- Seeds: Pumpkin, sunflower, sesame, and piñon seeds are popular and can be eaten plain or added to breakfasts, dinners, and baked goods. Seeds, like nuts, are a good source of protein and fats.
- Dried fruits: Dried fruits are an expensive but concentrated form of calories easily found in grocery and natural food stores. For trips that require large quantities of trail food, try purchasing fresh fruit at a fraction of the cost and drying it on your own using a food dryer. This system also works well for vegetables such as tomatoes, zucchini, and mushrooms. Dried fruit options include individual fruits and berries, mixed fruit combinations, and fruit leathers.
- Crackers: Crackers come in countless varieties and are available everywhere. Pack them in plastic containers with peel-off lids for protection. Occasional crunchy foods are usually welcome on long trips, and crackers are great with cheese and dips.
- Corn nuts and soy nuts: Corn nuts and soy nuts are salty, crunchy, cheap, and pack a strong flavor you either love or hate, so test them before you go! Soybeans are an excellent source of protein.
- Cookies: Fig Newtons, fruit bars, animal crackers, granola bars, and Pop-Tarts hold up well in a backpack.
- Energy bars: Numerous varieties of energy and high-protein bars can be found in grocery stores or natural food shops. These make a good, quick snack or meal replacement. Make sure they are edible in cold weather conditions,

and remember to have some variety in your selection—their flavor tends to get old after too many days without variation.

- Candy: Candy can be a great pick-me-up snack, so while you don't want to overdo it, it is nice to have some in your rations for those rainy days when you really need a treat. Backpacking favorites include candy bars, chocolate- or yogurt-covered nuts or raisins, and hard candies.

Baking Items
- Flours/meal: Choose from white, whole wheat, and other flours; cornmeal; and various commercial baking mixes.
- Baking powder or yeast

Sugar and Powdered Fruit Drinks
- Brown or white sugar
- Lemonade, Tang, apple cider, and other powdered drink mixes
- Tea

Soups, Bases, Dried Vegetables, and Desserts
- Soups: Cup-of-soups, ramen soups, or other instant soups are available in grocery and natural food stores and are a great quick minimeal on a cold day. They also make a good instant dinner when you are on a climb. Add cheese and potato pearls to make the soup more hearty and filling. Instant tomato soup is good for making tomato sauces. Pure tomato base is best, because it is a complete tomato product in a powdered form. Soups often have milk or sugar added, so if you want to use your tomato soup mix for sauces, check the ingredient list and look for a pure tomato product when you are shopping.
- Bases, broth packets, broth cubes: Beef, chicken, or vegetable bases make a good broth for meals. But watch out—they can be salty!
- Packaged sauce mixes: These days you can find innumerable instant sauce packages—pesto, white, alfredo, clam, spaghetti, and many more—in grocery stores. These mixes add

variety to your menu and can bring gourmet flair to almost any meal.

- Desserts: Desserts are high in carbohydrates, easy to digest, and a welcome treat on any extended expedition. The easiest option is to buy premade dessert mixes that require only water, such as cheesecake, gingerbread, brownie, carrot cake, or instant pudding.

Milk, Eggs, Margarine, and Cocoa

Powdered milk and eggs are a good source of complete proteins. Margarine (or butter) is a good source of fat, but watch how it is packaged. Squeeze tubes and containers can work well, but may open under pressure, so put the container in a plastic bag just in case. Cocoa is a favorite hot drink, and adding milk makes it a good source of protein and fat.

Meat and Meat Substitutes

Meat, soybean products, and nut butters are all excellent sources of fat and protein for the high-energy demands of the winter or alpine environment.

- Sliced pepperoni, cooked bacon bits, and sausage crumbles: These kinds of meat products work well when you are likely to encounter freeze-thaw conditions. They are precooked, very flavorful, and add some bulk to your meals.
- Beef jerky: Jerky is lightweight and tasty but does not have the high fat content that the meats listed above have, so it will stay fresh in summer and winter conditions.
- Tempeh: This is a soybean product that has the texture of meat and is used by many NOLS instructors as a meat or cheese substitute. Tempeh is perishable. Tempeh is available in many flavors and can be used on short trips or as a meat replacement in the winter. It's best to cube the tempeh prior to using it on winter trips, otherwise you'll find yourself sawing away at the frozen block.
- Nut butters: Peanut, almond, cashew, sesame, and sunflower butters are commonly used to replace cheese and meat for vegetarians in the winter months. They are high in fat and protein and work well in winter conditions.

Spices

Your spice kit can make or break your menu. A few key spices help add enough variety to your cooking to make everything, including 30 days of pasta, palatable. However, it is also easy to go overboard on spices; not everyone has the same tastes. For short trips, all you may need is salt, pepper, and a few sauce packages to ensure enough variety in your meals.

Consider including the following in your spice kit: salt, pepper, garlic powder, chili powder, curry, cinnamon, Spike, oregano, basil, baking powder, yeast, cumin, powdered mustard, dill weed, cayenne, oil, vinegar, soy sauce, vanilla, and hot sauce. Note that specific spices may be hard to purchase overseas, so even if you plan to do all your shopping at your destination, consider bringing a small spice kit from home to ensure you have the flavors you want.

Special Treats

On extended expeditions, it is nice to have a few special treats to break up the monotony of a field ration or perk you up on gloomy days. On big wall climbs, a can of peaches can really hit the spot, and hard candies are often great to suck on while trudging up a glacier. Maybe one bag of really good coffee is what you need to bring you out of the doldrums if the trip is hard or the weather bad. To make it fun and to maintain some element of surprise, consider having each team member bring one special delicacy to share with everyone during the trip. You don't want to be too extravagant and add unnecessary weight to your ration, so keep in mind the impact of the treat, not the quantity.

Packing

Once you've assembled all your food using one of the planning methods, it's time to repackage it. Cardboard, foil, paper, and cans are all excess weight and potential litter. At NOLS, we use commercial two-ply clear plastic bags to package most foods. The bags are lightweight, reusable, and allow you to see what is inside. You can identify items with a permanent marker. (White powders are notoriously frustrating for a new cook trying to find something in the dark. Milk looks like potato pearls or even flour at a glance.) For liquids, you can use small plastic bottles with screw-on lids.

If you are using a meal planning system, it helps to package each day's meals together. For the bulk ration system, it can make things simpler to separate breakfast, lunch, and dinner items when packing.

Always be careful when packing food to avoid any chance of contamination by soap, stove fuel, or a leaking lighter. Try to keep food above these items in your pack. Heavy items such as food should generally be packed high and close to your body, unless you'll be hiking through boulder fields or deadfall. In these conditions you might be more comfortable and stable with the weight a little lower for better balance when jumping or twisting.

Shopping Overseas

When traveling overseas, you'll probably buy most of your food once you've reached your destination. Remember, certain specialty items such as energy bars and powdered drink mixes may not be available in all places, so you should consider purchasing these items in the United States to ensure you can get them. Most standard bulk items—rice, beans, flour—are available just about anywhere, and many of the big cities around the world will have American-style supermarkets that cater to travelers, so you should have no trouble supplying your expedition.

When deciding whether to shop in the local market or at a western-style supermarket, you need to balance your desire for convenience and speed against cost. Shopping in most markets around the world requires bartering, and you will need to go to a number of different vendors to supply all your needs, so the process is slow. The upside is you'll have a cultural adventure and will probably save money. If you are in a hurry, go to a supermarket. It may cost more, but you'll be done shopping faster.

High-quality plastic bags and bottles for holding food and liquids may be harder to come by outside the United States, so bring these from home to ensure your food is not going to end up all over the inside of your pack as a result of burst bags or leaky bottles.

Shopping at local markets can be a great way to interact with residents (top right: Nepal) and to practice your language skills (top left: China). Not only that, you may end up trying some exotic fare, like dried rabbit (bottom: China).

Shopping requires some language expertise. If you don't have someone who speaks the language, use a dictionary to write out your shopping list in whatever language necessary before you go to the store. That will save you a lot of time guessing or looking things up as you go and will prevent mistakes such as substituting stewed cherries for stewed tomatoes because the picture on the can is confusing.

If you are going deep into remote parts of the world, remember food can be in short supply and your added needs may put a strain on the local food supply. On the other hand, you may provide some welcome money to the local economy by buying food en route. Check before you go. Do bring along some money. It can be nice to buy fresh vegetables or meat from villages you hike through.

Resupplies

You can comfortably carry enough food for a week to 10 or 12 days, depending on the amount per person per day you bring along, but even with the lightest food ration, if you plan to be out more than two weeks, it becomes challenging to carry all your food without either porters or some kind of resupply.

There are many ways to organize a resupply. In the United States, the easiest method is to hike to a road and either meet someone with fresh food or pick up a prearranged drop. On long through-hikes, such as the Appalachian Trail, many people mail food resupplies care of General Delivery to post offices along their route. Be sure to include a "to be picked up by" date on the package.

Caches can be used in some places, but in many parts of the United States they are illegal, so check regulations before planning to use this option. If you choose to leave a cache in the mountains, make sure you've packed it in waterproof, animalproof containers.

Finally, you can plan to have food brought to you by outfitters, guides, commercial packers, or bush pilots. Each of these resources has different weight and packing guidelines, so make sure you check with the supplier before you leave your ration. Also, write down everything to ensure you receive all your food at the appropriate time and in the appropriate place. No one wants to sit somewhere in the mountains hungrily waiting for a food resupply, wondering whether she has the time and place right as hours pass with no sign of her.

CRITICAL RE-RATION INFORMATION

- Mark the meeting place on a topographic map and make copies for both you and your resupplier.
- Make contingency plans with your resupplier in case either of you fail to make the meeting point on time.
- Package your resupply boxes so that the loss of one box does not mean the complete loss of one type of food.
- Pack matches in waterproof containers and in several places so they can't ignite by rubbing against each other or be destroyed if the box gets wet.

Cooking

NOLS Cookery provides a list of great backcountry recipes and instructions on basic cooking techniques, so it's a good resource for new backcountry cooks. The important topic for this book is deciding what type of stove and fuel you will use to cook.

Choosing a stove and fuel type for your expedition is dictated in part by your destination. If you are driving to the Rockies from the East Coast, your options are limitless; if you plan to get onto an airplane and fly overseas, you need to do some research. Transporting fuel in any form is not allowed, and if it is discovered, it will be confiscated. You may even find that you are not allowed to carry a stove or fuel bottle that smells like gas on board, so clean your stove and fuel bottles (or buy new ones) before attempting to take them on a plane.

These regulations mean that you have to buy your fuel at your destination, so the type of stove will depend on what is available where you are traveling. In some parts of the world, white gas, which is ubiquitous in the United States, is hard or impossible to find. Often the only fuel available overseas is kerosene. Fuel

Pros and Cons of Different Fuel Types

Fuel Type	Advantages	Disadvantages
Butane, propane, isobutane-butane blend canisters	• Convenient • Clean burning • Do not require priming, easy to light • Adjustable heat • Fuel cannot spill • Great for warm-weather camping, big walls, or high-altitude cooking where convenience is paramount	• More expensive than other fuel types • Canisters are bulky and disposal is problematic • Less flexibility in amount of fuel you bring, hard to calculate amounts in canisters • Performance may decrease in cold temperatures, especially for pure butane • Threads on different brand canisters do not fit all stoves
Kerosene	• Cheap and widely available worldwide • High heat output • Spilled fuel does not ignite easily	• Burns dirty, smelly • Priming required, easiest with priming gel or block • Tends to gum up stove parts requiring frequent cleaning
White gas	• Inexpensive • Clean, easy to light • Spilled fuel evaporates quickly • Reliable and efficient • Works in all weather conditions	• Volatile, spilled fuel ignites easily • Priming required • Hard to find outside United States and Canada
Denatured alcohol	• Renewable fuel resource, low volatility • Burns almost silently • Alcohol-burning stoves have fewer moving parts, lessening chance of malfunction • Viable, environmentally friendly option for quiet, slow-paced backpacking trips	• Lower heat output so cooking takes longer and requires more fuel • Hard to find outside United States and Canada
Solid fuel tabs	• Lightweight • No priming • Nonexplosive • No spill potential • Compact	• Most expensive fuel • Smelly (in spite of claims to the contrary) • Leaves sticky residue on bottom of pots
Unleaded gas	• Relatively inexpensive • Easy to find throughout the world	• Burns dirty, sooty, can lead to frequent stove clogs • Extremely volatile • Oxygenated gasoline used in winter months in United States can destroy rubber stove parts and seals
Paint thinner (solvent)	• Inexpensive, commonly used in parts of South America • Available at paint stores	• May have additives that affect its performance in stoves

Don't forget to enjoy yourself and get a little creative if you want to add some spice to your expedition.

canisters can also be hard to find in remote areas, so for international travel, you may want to go with a multifuel-burning stove. These stoves can be more expensive and more finicky to operate, but they are necessary if you are unsure what type of fuel will be available during your travels.

The bottom line in choosing your stove and fuel type is to know your equipment. Don't buy a brand-new stove type or use a different kind of fuel without some practice. You should know how to take your stove apart for cleaning and repair in the field, and you should carry a small repair kit containing critical replacement parts on any extended trip.

CALCULATING FUEL AMOUNTS

The amount of fuel you need depends on your stove and fuel, the temperature you may encounter, and type of cooking you will be doing. Winter camping, where you melt snow for water and consume large quantities of food for energy, requires the most fuel. In the summertime you will use less, unless you plan to bake every meal. There are some basic rules of thumb for determining fuel amounts, but you should give your stove a trial run to get a sense of how much fuel your individual model uses. Make notes and use that information to guide your fuel amounts for future trips.

To conserve fuel, always cook with a windscreen and prepare your ingredients before you light the stove. Use lids on pots and turn the stove off immediately after you finish cooking.

At NOLS, we use white-gas stoves, typically the MSR Whisperlite. These stoves have proven to be reliable, they are repairable in the field, and the fuel is cheap. They are not the lightest option available, however. If weight is your primary concern, check out fuel canisters, alcohol, or a solid-fuel-tab stove.

When calculating fuel for a white-gas stove, on average, one person will use $1/6$ liter of fuel per day in the summer, while a three-person cook group will use approximately $1/3$ liter of fuel per day. In the winter, a solo camper can expect to use approximately $1/4$ liter of fuel every day, while a group of three will average $3/4$ liter per day.

Integrated-fuel canister stoves, such as the Jetboil, are the most efficient stoves available in terms of fuel use. The downside is the Jetboil is a single-person stove and is relatively heavy, so unless you are doing a solo trip, it is not the best option for an expedition. Top-mount canisters aren't far behind in their efficiency, however, and they are light and easy to use. A top-mount stove will boil approximately 33 pints of water from a single 8-ounce canister. If you boil an average of 5 pints of water per day, an 8-ounce canister will last 6.7 days. Top-mount canister stoves are usually the stove of choice for big walls, technical mountaineering, or any time you want food fast.

NOLS Books on Backcountry Food, Cooking, and Nutrition

NOLS Cookery by Claudia Pearson
NOLS Cookery: Field Edition by Claudia Pearson
NOLS Backcountry Cooking: Creative Menu Planning for Short Trips
    by Claudia Pearson and Joanne Kuntz
NOLS Backcountry Nutrition by Mary Howley Ryan

10 | TRAINING

Prior preparation prevents piss-poor performance.
—NOLS FOUNDER PAUL PETZOLDT

Preparing for an expedition requires careful evaluation of the expedition's objective and your own physical and mental abilities. We all have lofty dreams, but not all of them are well suited to our real-life capacity. Being prepared for the demands of your expedition requires research, work, time, and a commitment to being ready for just about everything and anything you may encounter. In addition to travel and gear logistics, this also means launching a training program months before you depart. Training means getting fit physically, but to perform at your best, your training must also include emotional preparation. Expeditions require incredible mental toughness. You must be able to handle uncertainty, adversity, discomfort, stress, and even fear. Ultimately your brain is what allows your body to succeed in overcoming challenges and achieving your goal.

Mental Preparation

Before signing up for an expedition you should do some careful introspection. It helps to write up a checklist of potential mental challenges and to consider how you have responded to such challenges in the past in order to predict how they may affect you on your trip. Of course, there is always a first time for everything, and just because you've never been to altitude, does not mean you should not go to the Himalaya or Andes. It does mean you may want to consider a moderate objective or perhaps a warm-up climb to test yourself a bit before tackling a first ascent of an 8,000-meter peak.

Sport psychologists have found that mental toughness is what separates good athletes from great ones. What mental toughness means is somewhat nebulous, but in general it is the capacity to maintain focus and push through adversity to accomplish a task. It's the ability to keep climbing when your fingers are numb and darkness is coming. It's the ability to keep hiking when your body is exhausted and in pain.

Developing your mental toughness begins with developing confidence in your capacity to succeed. This confidence stems in part from understanding your physical ability, but even more, you need to be able to visualize yourself succeeding in accomplishing your goal, whether that goal is red-pointing a sport route at your local crag or climbing Mount Everest. Too often we undermine our potential by focusing on our weaknesses or our potential for failure. You do not want to be unrealistic about your abilities, but you also do not want to shortchange yourself by negative thinking. The clichéd expression "Never underestimate the power of positive thinking" has its basis in truth. Successful people, be they athletes, climbers, or businessmen and businesswomen, believe in themselves. So as you prepare for your expedition, think about your strengths, focus on your accomplishments, and surround yourself with successful people to enhance your chances of success.

With that said, behind the positive thinking and the mental toughness there is something more fundamental: the question of why. Why are you going on this expedition? Why are you exposing yourself to the discomfort and uncertainty of such a committing endeavor? Sports gurus have found that external motivators such as fame and fortune are, in the end, limited in how effectively they push people toward success. The most influential motivators it turns out are your internal drives: your passions, dreams, and desires. These are the things that will keep you moving when your body longs to stop.

To help figure out your internal motivators, ask yourself the following questions:

- What are you willing to fight for?
- What are your values?

- If you could only achieve one thing in your life, what would it be, and what would it take to make all your hard work worthwhile?
- If you had 30 seconds to live, what would you tell your children were the three most important things you learned about how to live a happy life?
- How does this expedition fulfill these dreams or desires?

The answers to these questions will tell you a lot about what drives you emotionally and will help you understand how your expedition fits into your larger dreams. This understanding can, in turn, help you persevere.

Mental Preparation Checklist

EXPEDITION GOAL

- Have you done something like this before? If so, what were the most difficult aspects for you?
- What will be new for you about this objective? Is there any relevant experience in your past that you can draw from (e.g., you've never been to the Himalaya, but have climbed Denali)?
- What skills will the expedition demand? How do you rate your competency for these skills? Do you need further training?
- What is your biggest fear or concern about the expedition? Is this a subjective or objective concern? Can you control it?

PERSONAL PREPARATION

- Have you spent this much time away from home and loved ones before? Can you be comfortable without daily contact with home?
- Do you have any unfulfilled obligations or business that conflict with this expedition? Can you take care of these obligations before you depart?
- How do you respond to stress? Boredom? Fear? Discomfort? How do you anticipate handling those factors on the expedition?
- Why are you doing this? Does your reason stand up to the potential risks?
- What will it mean to you if you fail to achieve your goal?

COPING WITH FAILURE

Unfortunately, there is a very real possibility that you will fail to achieve your goal in spite of all your preparation. Summiting a peak or successfully traversing a mountain range demands that a lot of uncontrollable factors fall into place: the weather holds, the snow conditions are good, everyone stays healthy, your equipment works, and so on. Anyone who heads into the mountains frequently will ultimately be faced with the need to turn around, to give up. For someone used to success, used to bullying his or her way to the top, failure can be pretty hard to deal with. It helps, therefore, to consider this possibility before you depart, and to be patient with yourself and conditions once you are on the expedition. You cannot force your body to adapt to altitude and you cannot change the weather, so give yourself room to accept the inevitable and recognize that the decision to abandon your goal is courageous and often wise.

Physical Preparation

There's nothing worse than being physically unfit for an expedition. You can't enjoy the journey when you are suffering the whole time. And the lack of physical preparedness affects your confidence and ability to remain composed under pressure. Self-doubt and fear begin to creep in when your body weakens, undermining your ability to succeed at your objective, regardless of whether that goal is climbing a hard route near home or summiting an 8,000-meter peak overseas.

The goal of a training regime is simply to make yourself as strong as possible. There are all sorts of training philosophies to choose from but all have one underlying premise: You need to work hard, change up your routine, add difficulty, and believe in yourself to see changes and make improvements. Use the following guidelines as you create a training program:

Training should support the physical demands of your sport or activity. The main challenge of training for an expedition is that our normal fitness regimes don't prepare us for the main activity of most trips into the mountains, which is trudging over rugged terrain

Running, long hikes, calisthenics, and yoga are all good options to get your body in shape for the rigors of an expedition.

carrying a heavy pack for long periods of time or paddling in a way that doesn't mimic the rowing machine in the gym. Basic cardiovascular capacity is part of the equation, but only part. So while riding your bicycle improves your overall fitness, it will not improve your strength and power in the areas you need, specifically the muscles required to carry a pack up steep hills, over boulder fields, and through deadfall. You need to figure out ways to mimic the stresses you anticipate encountering on your journey. Load up your pack and get moving. You can use full water bottles for weight to allow you to change the load as the day progresses: Carry a heavy load uphill, and then dump out some water to save your knees on the downhill. Try to go for long hikes—10 miles or more—to build up your endurance and tolerance for the pack. If you are in a city and can't get out to the mountains, wear a loaded backpack on a stair machine or VersaClimber. You can also string together a bunch of activities—biking, running, swimming—to get in enough time exercising to build up your endurance.

Just as marathon runners build up their mileage slowly to avoid injury, you'll want to pace yourself and give your body time to adapt. Ultimately aim to have at least a few full days—days that approximate expedition days—under your belt before you go on your trip.

Strength training improves your efficiency and performance. Training in the gym definitely has its limitations, but adding some weightlifting to your fitness regime can improve your power and strength. A study by the Norwegian University of Science and Technology found that competitive amateur athletes ran 21 percent longer at their maximum aerobic speed after doing half-squats for eight weeks at the gym. This shows that you can improve your overall performance by hitting the weights a couple of times a week. Start with light loads and lots of repetitions and build up as your strength improves. Remember, staying in the same place does nothing to make you fitter. Consult a professional to ensure your weight routine is balanced and targeted toward your expedition goals.

Add intervals or speed training to your workouts. In the past you may have been encouraged to train in the "fat-burning zone," which translated into lots of long, low-intensity workouts that were supposed to maximize your fat-loss potential. Recent studies have shown training in the fat-burning zone is not particularly effective, and athletes who add high-intensity intervals to their workouts actually burned more fat than those who stayed in the zone. They also improved their power, speed, tolerance for pain, and recovery rates. Intervals mimic real-life activities. Think about it: Climbing is really all about intervals. You push hard, pump yourself out, and then rest before going again. Train for this. You can do high-intensity weight circuits at the gym, run hills, or even push yourself for short spurts of speed on the skin track next time you are out backcountry skiing. As you improve, decrease your resting time and increase the length of your intervals.

Keep a training log. If you really want to improve your performance, you should keep a training log. Track your daily workouts, making notes on times and distances. Try to build on these milestones. If it takes you an hour and a half to bike up a nearby mountain one week, see if you can cut a minute or two off that time the next week. It's all too easy to fall into a training rut—and run your regular loop at the same easy pace day in and day out—but such ruts do little to help you get better. You can still run the same loop, just keep track of your time next go-round and see if you can beat it when you repeat the route. Tracking your progress can help keep you motivated as well.

Watch for overtraining. When you start underperforming after weeks of training, it's time for a break. Rest is an integral part of any effective training regime. Most trainers build a rest week into their athletes' schedules: Workouts are scaled back 20 to 30 percent or more to ensure adequate recovery. Where this rest week fits into your schedule depends on your body and the intensity level of your training, but it should usually occur once every five or six weeks. Adequate sleep and good nutrition are also integral to maintaining steady progress.

Find a training partner. Working out with someone else can be motivating. It's hard to go back to sleep after the alarm goes off if you know your buddy is waiting at the corner for an early morning run. You may also find taking a class can keep you inspired. Training with others helps you push yourself harder and inspires you to keep going when you would really rather stop. Sports psychologists also find that training with people who are positive and have lofty goals pushes athletes to excel beyond their expectations. If you can't find someone to train with, another motivational trick is to start telling people about your goal. It's kind of like telling people you are on a diet: Once the word is out that you are training for an expedition, you feel a certain obligation to see through your stated goal or risk having to explain yourself to your questioning public.

Molly on Pace Reflecting Preparation

By the end of the first week of our expedition in Nepal, it was obvious Paul was physically unable to keep up with us. He struggled to maintain our pace while ferociously defending his right to carry what he considered his fair share of the weight. We debated our options in his absence. Our route traversed the Khumbu Valley over three high passes before dropping into the Barun River drainage below Makalu. From there we would head downstream for 10 days, ending up in Tumlingtar and flying back to Kathmandu. There was no easy way to shorten the route. Somehow we had to find a way for Paul to keep up, but his stubborn pride, while understandable, made coming up with a creative solution challenging.

The situation came to a head the day we moved up and over Mingbo La, a technical pass near Ama Dablam. Here we left our porters behind and continued forward, ferrying our gear with the assistance of one sirdar, a Sherpa named Danu. We scrambled over broken ice, short roping or soloing up short vertical fins to get off the moraine and onto the glacier. Then Pete and Danu moved ahead to fix lines up the 50-degree slope leading to the low point in the ridge of rocks 800 feet above, while I guided the others in our group back to ferry the last of our gear forward. Paul was stumbling, tripping on his crampons, unused to walking on ice, and fatigued by the elevation and exertion. He never fell, but each misstep caused me to shudder. Finally I convinced him that he should wait with our cache while the rest of us moved loads.

When it was Paul's turn to head up the fixed lines, he continued to move slowly. At the top, the rest of us watched him inch his way up the rope, the minutes dragging, the sun sinking. Pete, Danu, and I were planning to head back down the rope for another load, but we did not want too many people on the fixed line at the same time, so we were forced to sit, watching the slow-motion drama unfurl below.

Molly on Pace Reflecting Preparation

Paul moved up a step, and then stopped to breathe, bent over and hanging on the rope; Barney stood below him, waiting patiently. Paul moved again and stopped again. Barney moved and waited. Finally, Paul dragged himself over the edge and lay in a crumpled heap at the top, breathing heavily, his face red from exertion. No one said anything. Pete, Danu, and I hurried down the ropes to bring up the rest of our gear.

The next day was a planned rest day, and we all slept in. It was midmorning before we began emerging from our tents. We were camped on the edge of a flat bench surrounded by high peaks. The glacier tumbled away to the east, and to the west Ama Dablam jutted upward. The sky above was cloudless, an intense blue against which the mountains were sharply etched. We were where we wanted to be and the scenery was stunning, but the air was heavy in camp. Travel promised to continue to be difficult: technical off-trail hiking over glaciers, unstable moraines, and two more fourth-class passes before we hit the main trade route in the Makalu-Barun Valley. We were unsure how our team would fare after the previous day's showing.

Paul had been thinking, however. He was not stupid and recognized that his pace was jeopardizing the success of the expedition. When we were seated around the camp stove, he broached the subject.

"I have come up with a plan that I hope will prevent me from slowing the group," he said. The plan, as he proceeded to outline it, would be for him to leave camp with Danu two hours ahead of the rest of the group. He also said he was willing to lighten his load and hike with the bare minimum to enable him to move more quickly.

We all sighed with relief. Paul had saved us from the difficult situation of confronting him and his weakness by coming up with his own plan, and we were grateful for his sacrifice. For the rest of the expedition, he would get up before the sun rose, eat a quick breakfast, and set off with Danu patiently walking along his side. We'd usually catch up with him in time for lunch, and then continue on ahead. He'd wander into camp an hour or two after we arrived.

I don't think it was the trip Paul imagined, and I know he was disappointed with his physical performance. He was in his early 60s, more than 25 years older than the next oldest on the team. He'd always been an amazing athlete and was a strong hiker, but he'd never been to altitude. He underestimated the challenges of the route, elevation, and loads we'd be carrying while overestimating his physical ability. ■

Skill Development

One final aspect of your preparation may involve new skill development or enhancement. You may want to take a course or a short test trip to improve your competency and build up your experience base on everything from climbing technique and avalanche awareness to first aid and navigation. Many mountaineering schools offer training trips (and most require them before allowing you to sign up for guided trips on major peaks such as Denali or Everest). You can also take courses from local outfitters, shops, clubs, or schools like NOLS.

Getting out into the elements and practicing your technical skills is an obvious necessity before committing to an expedition.

Determining whether you need to take this step is up to you. Look closely at your goals for the expedition and compare them with your past experience and knowledge. It can't hurt to brush up on areas where you may be rusty or to benefit from some professional training to see how things have changed if you've been out of the game for a while.

Resources for Skills Training

Avalanche training

American Avalanche Institute (www.americanavalancheinstitute.com)
American Institute for Avalanche Research and Education (www.avtraining.org)

Rock climbing, ice climbing, guiding, mountaineering, ski mountaineering, backpacking

National Outdoor Leadership School (www.nols.edu)
American Mountain Guides Association (www.amga.com)
Alaska Mountaineering School (www.climbalaska.org)
Exum Mountain Guides (www.exumguides.com)
Alpine Ascents International (www.alpineascents.com)
Jackson Hole Mountain Guides (www.jhmg.com)

River rescue, river rafting and kayaking, sea kayaking

National Outdoor Leadership School (www.nols.edu)
Wilderness Rescue International (www.wilderness-rescue.com)
American Canoe Association (www.americancanoe.org)

First aid and wilderness medicine

Wilderness Medicine Institute of NOLS (www.nols.edu/wmi)

Brush up on your navigation skills before leaving home!

Altitude

There is one glitch that can derail even the best-laid training plans: altitude illness. Unfortunately, you cannot train against altitude illness, and some people appear to acclimate to altitude better than others. All of us must go through some adjustment as we go up higher and the air pressure decreases. Twenty percent of those who ascend to 8,000 feet experience some signs of altitude illness, while 40 percent of us get sick at 10,000 feet and above. Almost all of us feel something: shortness of breath, headaches, lethargy. In some cases, altitude illness is lethal, so it should not be taken lightly.

The general method for reducing the likelihood of high altitude illness is to ascend slowly. Usually you don't want to sleep more than 1,500 feet above your last camp to help your body adjust to changing conditions. In most cases, symptoms will abate as your body acclimates. Some people do not acclimate, however. A certain number of individuals cannot go to high elevations without succumbing to sickness. There are no clear predictors for who will be

It remains unclear whether you can train for altitude. There are no clear predictors for who will be affected by altitude illness, and having been to altitude before with no problems doesn't mean you won't be affected the next time. Pay attention to signs and symptoms as you travel.

affected this way—age, sex, and fitness levels do not seem to be good indicators—so if your expedition will be the first time you go up high, take it slow and do not ignore any symptoms of altitude illness. (See the next chapter for more information.)

Resources

You can find plenty of resources on training on the Internet, at your local gym, or in the library. Check out climber Mark Twight's Gym Jones (www.gymjones.com), visit the Mountain Athlete (www.mtn athlete.com), or talk to Steve Bechtel at Elemental Training Center (elementaltraining.com) in NOLS' hometown of Lander, Wyoming, to glean some ideas from gyms catering specifically to climbers and mountaineers. If you decide to work with a trainer, ask around, but remember that not all trainers are created equal. It helps to find someone who is at least familiar with your activity of choice before committing time and money to his or her program. In the end, training for your expedition should be one of the more enjoyable aspects of your preparation. So get out there and move.

CHAPTER 11 | HEALTH CONSIDERATIONS

You've been planning for months, dreaming, scheming, and saving your pennies for a monthlong trek in the Himalaya, and then on the airplane you are seated next to someone who sniffles and coughs for the entire 14-hour flight to Bangkok. A week later, you are hacking up phlegm, spiking a fever, and unable to move. Or you've trained relentlessly for your attempt to hike the entire Pacific Crest Trail: running, biking, lifting weights, exercising day in and day out to ensure you are fit and strong; and then suddenly you feel a twinge in your lower back and the next thing you know you can't get out of bed.

An injury or illness can mean the end of your expedition dreams in an instant, leaving behind a bitter sense of disappointment. There are ways to minimize your chances of falling ill or getting hurt, however. Much of it is simple common sense: Take care of yourself, listen to your body, and plan ahead to deal with problems before they escalate and disrupt your entire expedition. Here are a few specifics to help.

Before You Go

Look up your destination on the Centers for Disease Control's Web site (wwwnc.cdc.gov/travel/destinations/list.aspx). Here you will find information on health concerns throughout the world, as well as suggestions for travelers including recommended vaccinations, useful medications, and other preventive measures for maintaining your health while overseas.

Schedule a visit with your physician, and make sure to allow yourself plenty of time. Many vaccines must be administered in a series with time between shots, so you should plan to visit your doctor at least six weeks before your departure date.

In addition to receiving immunizations and medications such as antimalaria drugs, get a full physical checkup at your doctor's visit. Make sure you are honest with your physician about your body to avoid any surprises on your expedition.

You should also discuss the details of your plans with a doctor who specializes in infectious diseases because the information provided by the CDC is usually pretty broad. Are you going to be above 10,000 feet? In malaria-prone jungle? Will you be away from medical care for extended periods of time? Talk directly with a doctor to make sure you are getting the most up-to-date advice about risks and precautions for your particular expedition.

Ask your doctor which prescriptions might be useful during your travels, such as antibiotics or painkillers. Traveling internationally with drugs—both prescription and nonprescription medications—can be tricky. Look into the regulations for the country you are visiting to see if there are any restrictions on bringing medications in with you. Most likely if the meds are prescribed to you, you should be okay. If you run out of meds while you're away, however, you may not be able to replace them in the country you're in. The American embassy or consulate for your destination should be able to provide this information.

To minimize problems in transit, carry all medications in their original bottles. Bring copies of your prescriptions and ask your doctor to write a note on notarized letterhead describing and explaining the use of all the drugs he or she has prescribed for your expedition. Include generic and chemical names for medications, as they may be known by different names in different places.

You should also visit your dentist to make sure you have no new cavities or other dental issues that could cause problems while you are in the field. If you wear glasses or contact lenses, see your eye doctor before you go to check your prescription. Bring an extra pair of glasses or set of lenses along on your expedition in case of breakage or loss. Altitude can be hard on contact lens wearers because of the dry, cold air. Bring extra wetting solution to help ease problems with dry eyes.

HEALTH INSURANCE

Before leaving on your expedition, contact your health insurance provider to find out what your policy covers and where. You may need to buy supplemental traveler's insurance to cover all contingencies. Be honest about where you are going and what you will be doing once you get there. Otherwise you may find yourself denied reimbursement for injuries or illnesses occurring during activities and in places that your plan does not cover.

Many health insurance providers do not cover you overseas or are slow to provide payment for services incurred out of the United States. Some travel insurance policies offer assistance in making payments overseas, but consider traveling with a credit card that has a high credit limit just in case a clinic or hospital in another country requires payment immediately. Your premium credit card may also offer other protections under the label "travel insurance," but these rarely include trip cancellation or medical evacuation. For example, American Express offers a platinum card that reimburses cardholders for many medical services (although its less exclusive "green" card doesn't). Additionally, some credit cards offer baggage delay insurance but not reimbursement for permanently lost luggage. Be sure to read your card's terms and conditions, or call your credit card provider's toll-free line for guidance.

International SOS, a nontraditional, high-end insurer, operates 21 health clinics and 24 help centers overseas and costs $60 (with no extra fees). It is just one example of a medical plan that can be used by travelers in western Europe. You receive access to a phone number for medical advice and local medical referrals, plus medical evacuation coverage and assistance. But expenses due to preexisting medical conditions are not covered and can't be waived. Medical evacuation is included up to a maximum of $1,000,000. Coverage that includes trip cancellation insurance costs $189 (with no extra fees).

EMERGENCY EVACUATION

Ask your insurance provider about emergency evacuations, either out of the wilderness or back to the United States. Travelers occasionally need to be evacuated to treat an illness or injury. In such cases, the cost can be astronomical. Many HMOs and insurance providers cap their evacuation coverage at about $1,000. Blue Cross of California, for instance, reimburses medical evacuation costs on a case-by-case basis but generally covers the full cost of a medical evacuation to the United States only when an injury or illness threatens the life of a policyholder.

You can buy a travel policy that will pay for assistance and evacuation up to a maximum amount. Depending on the terms, that amount can range from about $10,000 to $1,000,000. Travel Guard's ProtectAssist covers up to $500,000 in expenses for evacuation and transportation to the nearest adequate medical facility. Plan for these contingencies before you leave.

American Alpine Club (AAC) and Global Rescue

The AAC has contracted with Global Rescue, a leading worldwide rescue and evacuation service provider, to offer rescue service as a benefit of AAC membership. Global Rescue's mission is to provide high-quality medical, transport, and other critical services to members anytime and anywhere in the world. Global Rescue's evacuation service has no deductible and no altitude limitation or back-country activity exclusions (eligibility for rescue begins and ends at the trailhead). The group provides its services to the U.S. Adventure Racing Association and the U.S. Ski and Snowboard Teams, among others. AAC members also receive a 5 percent discount on Global Rescue's comprehensive rescue plans; these plans offer additional benefits and can be purchased annually or for a short-term trip. The following services are included in these plans:

- Medical advice and support from physicians, 24/7
- Medical evacuations from anywhere in the world to your choice of home-country hospital, anytime you are more than 160 miles from home and need hospitalization

- Field rescues for medical emergencies requiring hospitalization in the event you are in a remote location and cannot get to a hospital on your own
- Lost medication, visa, and passport assistance; legal referrals; and more

Enhanced security coverage includes:

- Emergency evacuations for nonmedical reasons, including war, civil unrest, natural disasters, or other causes
- Evacuation in the event you are more than 160 miles from home and there is a government declaration to leave the area, or you are facing imminent grievous bodily harm
- Deployment of security teams and transport on fixed- and rotary-wing aircraft as necessary

Global Rescue coverage can be purchased for short trips (7, 14, or 30 days) or per year. Annual costs for Global Rescue's basic coverage in 2009 were $329 per individual for medical and $655 for the additional security benefits.

En Route

The spread of H1N1 and SARS around the world raised public awareness of the potential for illnesses to travel rapidly on our increasingly interconnected planet. Airplanes in particular can act as a kind of disease incubator, so take precautions while you travel to avoid exposure. Some people go so far as to carry antibacterial wipes to wipe down airplane armrests and food trays, door handles, and other surfaces that come in contact with many human hands. You may not go to such extremes, but should make sure to wash your hands frequently and thoroughly, which means lathering up with soap and rubbing your hands together vigorously for a minimum of 20 seconds. Make sure to get under your nails and any jewelry you may be wearing. Dry your hands and use a paper towel to turn off faucets and open or close doors. If you do not have access to water and soap, hand sanitizer gel helps kill germs. Remember, hand washing is the single most effective way to prevent the spread of disease, so take your time and be thorough.

Get plenty of sleep and stay hydrated while traveling. And you've heard it before: Avoid excessive alcohol and sugar to help your body stand up to the stresses of long hours en route to your final destination.

During the Expedition

COMMON PROBLEMS, ILLNESSES, AND INJURIES

The key to a successful expedition is to stay healthy. We all know what that takes: Drink plenty of fluids; eat a well-balanced diet; get enough sleep. We also know that can be challenging, especially on an expedition. Therefore, there are a number of common illnesses and injuries for which you should be prepared. (See *NOLS Wilderness Medicine* for a more in-depth discussion on prevention and treatment of the following conditions.)

Dehydration

Dehydration is not an illness, but an underlying condition that can exacerbate other physiological problems such as altitude illness, diarrhea, headaches, and cold injuries. Dehydration is, unfortunately, difficult to avoid when traveling unless you make a concerted effort to drink plenty of fluids. This doesn't mean lots of soda or juice. You need water and other nonsugary beverages such as tea or specially formulated electrolyte replacement drinks to maintain adequate hydration.

Beware, you can drink *too* much water. Hyponatremia is a condition caused by an imbalance in your electrolytes exacerbated by excessive fluid. This condition has caused problems in places like the Grand Canyon where hikers attempting to maintain hydration in extreme heat drink too much water without eating or consuming salts. Hyponatremia is serious, even deadly, but can usually be avoided if you eat salty snacks and drink weak electrolyte solutions at the same time you maintain hydration.

Traveler's Diarrhea

Diarrhea is the most common illness affecting travelers. Each year, according to the Centers for Disease Control, between 20 to 50 percent of international travelers, or an estimated 10 million people, experience some form of diarrhea during their overseas journeys.

Boiled goat head in Mongolia during Dave's "Long Walk" expedition. If you're not used to boiled goat, be careful what you eat out there to avoid a potential bout of traveler's diarrhea.

Developing nations in Latin America, Africa, the Middle East, and Asia are the highest risk destinations, with the primary source of infection being the ingestion of fecally contaminated food or water (80 percent of all cases are caused by bacterial pathogens, with *E. coli* being the most common causative agent). Other causes of diarrhea include parasites and viruses.

Motion Sickness
Caused by a "disagreement" between the movement you actually see (bouncing horizon lines, flashing trees) and your brain's sense of movement, motion sickness causes nausea, headaches, and general misery, often leaving its sufferers totally incapacitated. Most people know if they are prone to motion sickness and have developed tricks over the years for coping. They sit up front in vehicles, avoid closed-in spaces on boats, stare at a still spot on the horizon, avoid reading while in transit, and stay near fresh air if possible. Behavior modification doesn't always do the trick, however, and some people must resort to medications or natural or homeopathic remedies to deal with the problem. If you know you are prone to

motion sickness, you may want to experiment with different treatments to see what works best for you.

Altitude Illness

There is less oxygen available to breathe at higher elevations, which makes it harder for our bodies to function. People begin to show the effects of altitude above 8,000 feet, with symptoms becoming more common and more severe the higher you go. Each of our bodies need to adjust to the changes; some of us do this better than others. Unfortunately, there are no good predictors for who will acclimatize and who will not.

Normal physiologic changes that occur at altitude include hyperventilation, shortness of breath during exertion, changed breathing patterns at night, wakefulness, and increased urination. As our bodies adjust to the lower levels of oxygen, these symptoms abate and our "zone of tolerance" or the elevation where we can perform effectively goes up. One common sign of our body's process of adjustment to elevation is periodic or Cheyne-Stokes breathing. Typically, periodic breathing is characterized by a slowing respiration rate, followed by a period where the sufferer actually holds his or her breath, and then he or she gasps and begins breathing rapidly again for a few moments before gradually falling back into the same cycle. Periodic breathing is alarming, but is usually not a problem except for the fact that it may disrupt everyone's sleep, even those not suffering from the condition but disturbed by their tent mate's strange breath noises.

More concerning are symptoms of acute mountain sickness (AMS), high altitude cerebral edema (HACE), and high altitude pulmonary edema (HAPE), which indicate your body is not acclimating to conditions. These altitude illnesses can be fatal if not treated.

What is High Altitude?		
High	2,500 to 4,200 meters	8,000 to 14,000 feet
Very High	4,200 to 5,500 meters	14,000 to 18,000 feet
Extreme Altitude	over 5,500 meters	over 18,000 feet

Wounds and Burns

Skin is an amazingly effective barrier against bacterial infections; however, once the skin is broken, bacteria can get in and cause infections that range from harmless to life threatening. The most common bacterial infections are due to either *staphylococcus* or *streptococcus*. However, other nasty bugs can cause serious problems if they are introduced to your system. These bugs can be found in hospitals, nursing homes, or dirt, and in lakes, ponds, and oceans. Blisters from hiking, gobies from climbing, cuts and scrapes from a fall, sunburn, fire or stove burns, and wounds made by aggressive scratching all can make a break in the skin's barrier and provide an entrance for nasty invaders, so your number one goal in the wilderness is to keep your skin whole. You don't always know when or where you may come in contact with infection-causing bacteria, but you should know how to take care of your skin to prevent potential problems. Animal bites; large wounds that need stitching; jagged, open wounds that are impossible to close; dirty wounds that are difficult to clean; wounds or burns to the face or hands that may cause severe scarring or loss of function—all of these injuries should be seen by a medical professional.

This is a pretty minor scratch, but if it's not taken care of over a long period of time, it can turn into a more serious infection. Make sure you have the supplies and the know-how to deal with injuries.

Rabies and Tetanus
Rabies and tetanus are common in many parts of the world. Both can be deadly if introduced to your body. Be sure to get a tetanus booster before you travel, and consider getting a rabies vaccine as well after talking to your doctor about the potential for exposure in the area you will be spending most of your time. A rabies vaccine reduces the number of shots required after exposure and allows you more time to get medical help. With both rabies and tetanus, good wound management is imperative.

Urinary Tract Infections
Women get UTIs more commonly than men, and some women are more prone to UTIs than others. Often you know if you are susceptible. The leading cause of UTIs is *E. coli*. Typically the bacteria are transmitted from the anus to the opening of the urethra either as a result of poor hygiene or through sexual intercourse. Follow basic hygiene routines to prevent UTIs on expedition.

Vaginal Yeast Infections
Yeast, or *candida albicans*, is commonly present on human skin, particularly in moist areas such as the mouth or genitals. In fact, an estimated 20 to 50 percent of healthy women carry yeast in their vaginal area. This is not a problem unless it gets out of balance, which can happen when either your protective bacteria are removed (say after taking antibiotics) or if a new form of yeast is introduced. Either way, the result is an inflammation or vaginitis that causes soreness, itching, discharge, and pain during intercourse. Men can also get penile yeast infections, although this is much less common. Some women have recurring problems with yeast infections. Most yeast infections are easily treated by over-the-counter antifungal creams, so for an expedition's purposes, it may be worth carrying a tube as a precautionary measure.

Malaria
Malaria is one of the most common mosquito-borne illnesses present in many parts of the world, specifically parts of Asia, Africa, and South America. Malaria can be fatal, though illness and death from the disease is preventable. Public health measures in the United

States and Europe have succeeded in eliminating malaria; however, both the United States and Europe continue to have populations of *Anopheles* mosquitoes that are capable of transmitting the disease, so the risk of malaria being reintroduced is always present.

All clinical symptoms associated with malaria are caused by asexual erythrocytic or blood-stage parasites of the malarial organism. During this stage, the parasite gives off waste products and other toxic factors that accumulate in the infected red blood cells. These toxins are then dumped into the bloodstream, triggering the body's reaction, specifically a high fever and other symptoms. Malaria symptoms usually show up 7 to 30 days after the infective bite, longer in some cases, so if you return to the United States and begin showing symptoms of the disease, seek medical attention.

Sprains, Strains, and Tendonitis

Athletic injuries are common on expeditions: you are working hard, using your body constantly, demanding high levels of performance of yourself, and often not receiving adequate rest, nutrition, or hydration. Taken all together, these factors make you prone to overuse and traumatic injuries.

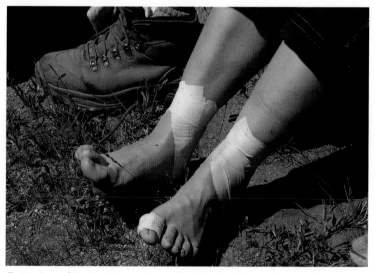

Taping is good for both prevention and treatment of minor ankle sprains and strains.

Your best bet is to be aware of the potential for injury. Make sure you have trained wisely before your expedition. That means you need to do activities that mimic what you'll be doing on the trip: Six weeks of swimming everyday is certainly good cardio, but make sure you include a few trips on the trail with your pack, too, if you're training for a backpacking expedition.

Once you are in the field, try to work rest days into your schedule, particularly early in the trip when your body is adjusting to the workloads and new environment. Make sure you are eating a good, balanced diet and staying well hydrated. Try to get plenty of sleep. If your objective demands long sustained pushes with little sleep, make sure you allow yourself a rest day between efforts to recover.

Give yourself time to warm up before any sustained effort. Do some jumping jacks, jog in place, strike some yoga poses—anything to get your blood moving and your muscles warm. An adequate warm-up helps prevent injury, as does stretching after exercise. Again, you can't always do this on an expedition, but when you find yourself sitting around camp, it's worth pulling out your sleeping mat to stretch a bit. Anything but a mild athletic injury won't heal sufficiently within your expedition time frame; most injuries of this type will need to be managed with rest, ice, compression, elevation (RICE), and tape or braces, and will probably lead to an early end to your expedition.

HEALTHCARE ABROAD

It can be difficult to find healthcare providers when you travel, regardless of your destination. Your best bet is to get a reference from a friend or trusted local contact. In the absence of such help, you can use the Internet to do some research. Overseas, the U.S. embassy or consulate may be able to recommend a physician.

The International Society of Travel Medicine (ISTM) is a member organization committed to promoting healthy, safe travel. Most of its members are healthcare providers, and the organization's Web site (www.istm.org) provides a Global Travel Clinic Directory that lists healthcare clinics around the world geared to providing travelers with care before, after, and during their journeys. You can look up clinics in the directory without being an ISTM member.

Dave running a fever while in India.

The American Society of Tropical Medicine and Hygiene is a worldwide organization of scientists, clinicians, and program professionals dedicated to promoting global health through the prevention and control of infectious diseases. ASTMH has published a book *Health Hints for the Tropics* that provides essential information for travelers, including sections on travel preparation, immunizations, malaria prevention, and much more. The current edition was printed in December 2005 and is available on the society's Web page (www.astmh.org/Health_Hints_for_the_Tropics.htm).

BUYING MEDICATIONS OVERSEAS

In some parts of the world, you can buy almost any drug over the counter without a prescription; in others it's difficult or even impossible to find standard medications. Your best bet is to bring meds from home—particularly if you take any drug routinely. The only problem with this strategy is that some countries will not allow you to bring medications across their borders, so check before you go. If you choose to buy medications in developing countries, exercise caution. Drug quality may not be well regulated. Medications may be expired or doses inconsistent. Try to talk to expatriates or

Western healthcare professionals about where to buy good quality medications.

EMERGENCY CARE

The World Health Organization's 2001–2002 Global Database on Blood Safety reported that 40 countries around the world do not test all donated blood for HIV, hepatitis B and C, and syphilis. This information is alarming if you happen to be in one of those places and end up needing blood. Check into the details about healthcare in the country you plan to visit before you go. You never know if you may need emergency treatment, and some knowledge can help you—and your team—know what to look for, who to talk to, and what to worry about. Even if you are traveling in the States, it's worth doing a little bit of research into some basic information, such as locations of nearest hospitals and clinics and numbers for local search and rescue organizations.

First-aid kits and skills can also come in handy before you get to the backcountry.

TRANSPORTATION AND LODGING

It's easy to forget while planning for a big trip in the mountains that first you have to get to the trailhead. Travel logistics are usually less exciting than looking at topographic maps of distant peaks and dreaming about the things you'll see once you get there: glaciers, snow-capped mountains, meadows blanketed in alpine flowers, sparkling lakes, the perfect climbing line, blue-ribbon trout streams. That's the stuff that gets your adrenaline going. But nailing your logistics down is vital to ensuring you arrive at the start of the exciting part of your journey—the actual expedition part—well rested, happy, and with everything you need.

Some trips don't take much effort: You get into your car and drive a few hours or days to the mountains with your gear loaded up in the back. You just need a road map and cash or credit for gas. As your destination gets farther removed from home, things get a bit more complicated. Veteran travelers have learned through experience that there are definitely right and wrong ways to go about your planning. The wrong way leaves you separated from your team, sleeping in some dive with bedbugs and creepy patrons, paying excess baggage fees, and taking an inordinate amount of time to get to your actual starting point.

Getting There

AIR TRAVEL
Assuming you are traveling a long way to begin your expedition, you'll probably need to fly to get there. Plane travel can be pretty straightforward: A two-week backpacking trip in the Rocky Moun-

Air travel doesn't always mean airplanes. You may find yourself needing a helicopter ride to get all the way to your expedition starting point.

tains could be as simple as taking a domestic flight into Denver and then a rental car or shuttle to transport you to the mountains. But flying overseas is a little more complicated.

Here are a few considerations:

- Does your destination involve multiple stops? If so, your entire team may want to book your flights together to ensure you all end up in the same place at the same time. Multiple connections also increase the chance that your luggage won't make it to your destination at the same time you do.
- Are the cheaper tickets cheaper because they take a circuitous route? Is saving $500 worth an extra two days of travel or five flights instead of two? Be wary of a "great deal." Travel is exhausting. Sometimes it's worth booking a direct flight to help cut down on travel stress.

- Can a travel agent help? If your plans are complicated or involve obscure destinations, you may want to consider working with a travel agent who is familiar with the type of logistics your trip entails. Talk to guiding organizations that conduct overseas expeditions in the area you are visiting to see who books their tickets. Those travel agents will know the ropes and will probably prove to be well worth the $30 fee they tack on to your ticket, especially if the ticket comes with a 24-hour help line in case you get stranded.

- Can you get a package deal? Some Internet travel agencies allow you to include a hotel or rental car with your flight. These kinds of deals may save you money, and they will definitely expedite your transition from plane to ground travel, so it's worth checking to see what kind of rates you can get if you book everything together.

All About Baggage

Most airline carriers now charge for checking bags on domestic flights. Baggage fees may range $15 for your first bag and $25 or more for a second, unless you are traveling first or business class, in which case checked bags may be free. Some mileage programs also include free baggage, so be sure to ask if that's included in your program.

International flights usually allow two checked bags under 50 pounds per person with no charge. Bags between 50 and 70 pounds will probably cost you around $50 dollars each, while the fee for bags between 70 and 100 pounds may jump to as much as a whopping $450. The lesson? Travel light and make sure your bags don't weigh over 70 pounds. (These fees are subject to change and are just included to give you an idea of what you might expect.)

In addition to weight restrictions, most airline carriers have size guidelines for the checked luggage they will or will not accept, and some may even limit the number of carry-on bags. Look up the numbers and dimensions allowed for checked and carry-on bags on your airlines' Web site, and make sure your baggage fits within these limits. Checking particularly large items, such as whitewater kayaks, can be a considerable dilemma because it often has more to do with who checks you in at the counter and not what the written policy is. Arrive at the airport a few hours in advance to give yourself time to negotiate or problem-solve if necessary. Even better, arrange for that large piece of gear through renting, buying, or borrowing at your final destination.

Some ways to help cut down the weight of your checked baggage include:

- Traveling in your hiking or mountaineering boots (put a pair of flip flops or slippers in your carry-on bag to put on once you are in the air).
- Putting heavy gear like your climbing rack or photography equipment in your carry-on baggage.
- Shipping gear in advance. Check with guiding agencies that conduct business in the area you are traveling. They may send a container of gear over once a year, and sometimes will include yours for a small fee.

 ## Dave Just Trying to Get There

"Jesus," I gulped, trying to swallow my stomach as a wave of turbulence slammed against the Twin Otter I was flying in. As I glanced around the small aluminum fuselage, I noticed the other 15 passengers were all staring out the windows at the snow-covered Himalaya undulating dangerously close to the underbelly of the plane. The cockpit door was open, and I had an intimate view of the pilots' actions. Another sudden downdraft had the pilot and copilot grabbing levers and flipping switches, trying to stabilize the small craft.

"Hey, Dave," yelled my traveling companion. "Do you see the flashing yellow light on the control panel? Can you read the sign underneath it?" Straining forward against my tightly cinched seatbelt, I squinted hard, trying to bring the seven letters underneath the blinking gauge into focus.

"Low . . . low fuel," I yelled back, fighting not to be drowned out by the propellers.

Our luck up until that moment had been amazing. We had spent the month of January (not the typical trekking or climbing season) traveling through the mountains of the Khumbu region of Nepal. Although nighttime temperatures sometimes dipped below zero, we had experienced 28 days of cloudless skies and no wind. As our expedition drew to a close, we hiked down to the village of Lukla to catch a small plane back to civilization. The night before our flight, the high-pressure weather system crumbled, and we woke to blizzardlike conditions.

Dave Just Trying to Get There

Peering through the windows of a teahouse, we could see the runway was covered with a thick layer of snow and ice. We knew we would not be leaving anytime soon. The runway itself was a testament to modern engineering. Carved into the side of a mountain, it had an unusual 10 percent grade. The uphill slope helped landing planes decelerate before they slammed into the rock wall at the end of the very short runway. Conversely, on takeoff, planes raced down the tilted runway and literally dropped off the edge of the mountain. Eventually, they gained enough elevation to clear the cirque of the surrounding peaks.

In Lukla, we spent time taste-testing different batches of Rakshi, the local homemade liquor, with some porter friends as the weather slowly improved. After two days of waiting, we boarded a small twin-engine plane and under the windy skies of the Himalaya, we took off toward Kathmandu.

"Yup, it definitely says low fuel," I reiterated. The roar of the engines prevented any thoughtful conversation, and I looked around the plane to see if anyone else had noticed the potential crisis. The rest of the travelers, however, were either still glued to the windows or in a hunched position with airsickness bags wrapped tightly around their mouths.

Just as thoughts of fastening my rain gear together into some sort of homemade parachute began to creep into my brain, the green fields of the Kathmandu Valley appeared before us and we were soon taxiing safely down the runway toward the terminal. Was the fuel gauge faulty, or was the pilot trying to push the limit of a tank of aviation fuel? I had no idea, but I did know the solid tarmac sure felt good underneath my feet. ■

BUSES AND TRAINS

Once you're in the country, the type of transport you use will depend on your destination. Most of the world has well-developed rail and bus systems for travel within the country, and often your best option for getting to your trailhead will be to catch a bus or train. Some places require reservations and advance booking; others allow you to show up with cash on the day you want to travel. It pays to know the system beforehand so you don't end up stuck someplace waiting for the next transport out of town.

Buses can come in all
shapes and sizes.

In most places, trains and buses have different classes. You'll find a variety of options from first-class, air-conditioned sleepers to third-class open-sided buses complete with elaborately painted decorations, fringe, and nonstop horn honking. Traveling third class can be an interesting cultural experience; it can also be exhausting. Not many of us can sleep on a bus with squawking chickens, bawling

Though the views from a train may be the same as from a bus, the ride is definitely faster.

babies, and overcrowded conditions. Third-class travel is also often slower, as the buses or trains stop in every town, village, or station along the way to load and unload passengers. Furthermore, you may find the bathroom facilities are nothing more than a bush by the side of the road. (Women can wear a long skirt when taking the local form of transportation. The flowing material can help give you some degree of privacy if you have to go to the bathroom by the side of the road.)

First- and second-class buses and trains are usually a big step up in what you can expect and what you pay. On buses in India, you may find yourself watching Bollywood movies and reclining your chair almost to horizontal on many long-distance routes. Likewise, Chile is renown for its luxurious long-distance buses. Trains usually have dining cars and sleepers to help make you comfortable on long journeys.

Before you make any decisions about the type of transport you want to use, ask yourself the following:
- How long will it take?
- When do I need to arrive at my destination?
- What's the temperature? (Can we survive without air-conditioning?)
- Do I need sleep?
- What can I afford?

Once you have an accurate sense of your own tolerances and resources, check the train and bus schedules. Be thorough. Compare prices. Ask what kind of accommodations you can expect for any given class. Check into safety standards. Don't skimp unless you are completely aware of what you are getting yourself into.

CARS, VANS, OR BUSES FOR HIRE

If you have a large expedition with mounds of gear, you may want to consider hiring a private car, van, or bus to take you to your destination. You could rent a car, but most of us find driving in some parts of the world unnerving. At the very least you may need to get used to driving on the opposite side of the road, and at the worst you're likely to find yourself having to veer your way through mazes of traffic, dodging animals, motorbikes, and pedestrians with no visible system for traffic control to guide you. Your best bet is to hire a car and driver. You can investigate options online, but beware of false advertising. Ask for recommendations—preferably from foreign travelers like yourself—and make sure you have all the

If you are using a private vehicle to get to your expedition destination and parking it for a period of time in the wilderness, it might be a good idea to safeguard against animals. This little fence is supposed to keep porcupine out while Dave climbs in the Canadian Bugaboos.

details outlined in a contract before you get into the vehicle. If you are working through a local agency—for example, you are using a local guiding service to hire porters or base camp support staff— have them secure your transportation.

Lastly, make sure that you understand the customs with regard to tipping. In many parts of the world, you are expected to leave your driver with a gratuity.

TAXIS AND RICKSHAWS

While you are in town, the best way to get around is probably by taxi or, in Asia, auto rickshaw. Ask your driver how much the fare will be before you get into the vehicle. Drivers often hang around waiting for customers, so you can compare prices to find the best rate. Some of the vehicles have meters, but in many cases the meters aren't used, so be sure you have an understanding of the cost before you commit to the ride.

Taxis often have fixed rates for specific routes, say from the airport into town, and your best option, if possible, is to secure one

Transportation options can be unique depending on where you travel.

of these rides inside the airport or bus terminal rather than expose yourself to the melee that often greets visitors when they step outside the confines of the terminal. Often you'll find yourself bombarded with offers to carry your bags, drive you places, take you to a "very nice" hotel, and so forth. These offers may be legitimate, and then again, they may not. If you are jet-lagged and don't speak the language, you'll probably find it easier to prepay inside with the taxi service rather than fend for yourself. A few rules of thumb work everywhere:

- Set the price before you get into a taxi, car, bus, or motel room.
- Ask your hotel to secure a cab for you.
- If you stick with a driver over time, make sure you continue to discuss costs. Don't assume he will continue to give you the cheapest deal based on yesterday's services.
- Ask around. If one rickshaw driver quotes a price, check with the next one to see what kind of deal he is offering. Sometimes they'll all give you the same figure; other times someone will lowball the rate. Once you get in the taxi or rickshaw, you may find your driver offering more services. Just smile and say, "No, thank you."

TRAVEL SAFETY

While American roads and airways are not without their hazards, there are laws that help assure some degree of attention to safety. This is not true in all parts of the world. Driving in parts of Asia can be confusing, chaotic, and dangerous, particularly for those of us who aren't used to it, while some small airlines in remote regions have been known to have dubious maintenance and safety records.

It's worth taking a few precautions to increase the chance you'll arrive at your destination in one piece. Do a little investigation. If you know you will be flying on an obscure airline, look up its safety record online. If you are hiring a car, ask to inspect the vehicle, look for safety belts, check to see if seats are bolted to the floor (they aren't always!), and request to see maintenance records. Consider hiring a driver rather than attempting to negotiate confusing, chaotic traffic patterns yourself. You can take similar measures with buses, trains, or other forms of public transportation if you have concerns.

Where to Stay

Accommodations on expeditions can range from simply camping for the entire duration of the trip to staying in hotels, teahouses, or hostels for all or part of the journey. Most likely, your trip will include a little of both. You'll probably end up staying in some kind of hotel en route to your destination and may even end up staying in teahouses or huts while you move through the mountains, so it helps to know a few things about your options before you go.

HOSTELS
The United States is not known for its hostels, and so many Americans grow up with little more knowledge of their existence than a postcollege Euro-Rail tour. Youth hostels have gotten a reputation for being grungy, loud, and not very private, but times have changed. A 2009 article in *The New York Times* expounded on the new face of international hostels: They are reputedly hipper, cleaner, and offer perks like WiFi, cafes, bars, private rooms and bathrooms, convenient locations, diverse clientele, and good prices. The other new development is that hostels no longer cater only to young, independent travelers. Now, according to the article, families, businessmen and businesswomen, and even older solo travelers are welcome.

Hostels are ubiquitous around the world, and the new image touted in the *New York Times* can hardly be considered universal. There are undoubtedly still plenty of dirty, loud, unsafe hostels out there, so just as with hotels and campgrounds, it helps to do some research and ask around. You can check hostels out at numerous sites online, and talk to fellow travelers if you are concerned with specific issues. If you have a lot of gear for your expedition, it can be tricky to stay in a dormitory room. You don't want to have to lug your climbing rack around the grocery store, so having a place to lock stuff up can be important. Many hostels offer private or semi-private rooms or may have storage lockers where you can leave your gear safely.

HOTELS
You can find budget hotels everywhere in the world, ranging from great to awful, and in fact, many travel companies offer flight/hotel

packages, especially to popular areas. In some places, Western travelers are required to stay in specific hotels that cater to tourists. This used to be true everywhere in Russia and China, as well as some other countries. Restrictions have loosened up since the breakup of the Soviet Union and the westernization of China, but the farther you get off the main travel routes, the more restrictive accommodations may be, so make sure you've researched your destination before you go. In general, be wary of arriving anywhere late, tired, and in desperate need of a place to stay. It's when you are vulnerable that you are most likely to fall prey to thieves or others looking to take advantage of an ignorant tourist and make some quick money. You don't want to be suspicious of everyone, but you also don't want to be unprepared.

CAMPGROUNDS

You undoubtedly know how to plan a camping trip if you're going on an expedition, and camping will most likely be a bulk of your accommodations once your expedition has begun. Once you hit the trail, the sleeping arrangements are relatively predictable regardless of your destination: a tent or fly and a sleeping bag and pad. The variation is usually limited to the style of your shelter, the weight and materials of your bag, and the type of pad you choose to use. But finding camping accommodations en route to your destination can be more daunting, especially if you are traveling to a part of the world where you've never been or if your understanding of the language is limited.

Internationally, most public campgrounds offer a wide range of services beyond a tent or camper site: They provide laundry facilities, showers, restaurants, playgrounds, and many other amenities for guests. They also can be a bit pricey, at least compared with forest service or state park campgrounds in the United States. In the United States, your cheapest bet is to car camp in a national forest or on other public lands, and some small towns in the West even offer free camping in their city parks. The upside to camping is the privacy and the known condition of your accommodations. The downside is often campgrounds are located away from city centers and, without your own transportation, can be inconvenient.

COUCH SURFING

Couch surfing is an Internet-age phenomenon that links travelers with people around the world willing to take guests into their homes. Couch-surfing Web sites have details about where and with whom you can stay, and the trend seems to have created a close-knit community of international travelers who bounce from home to home as they make their way around the world. These sites include a variety of safety nets to prevent surfers from ending up with a psycho somewhere far from home, so you can feel reasonably assured the hosts are legit, but you should expect a certain lack of privacy if you go this route. Couch surfing is about the cultural experience of living with people in their homes and, therefore, may not be the best option for someone intent on getting to his or her destination quickly and easily.

AIRPORTS

Sometimes the easiest option for travelers is to camp out at the airport during long layovers. Unfortunately, not all airports are created equal. To help endure a long airport stay, it helps to pack a small pad to lie on and a sleeping bag, blanket, shawl, or beach towel to

Consider yourself warned: Trying to overnight in the airport is not going to be comfortable.

use for a cover. A toothbrush, headphones or earplugs, and a sleeping mask can help make your stay more enjoyable as well.

The benefits of sleeping in the airport are it's cheap, you can usually leave your luggage checked through to your destination, and you don't have to deal with the hassle of finding transportation and a nearby motel after long hours on a plane. Some airports cater to long-distance travelers and offer lounges with couches for sleeping. Others are bright, loud, and uncomfortable, making it just about impossible to get any sleep. If you have a long layover, it may be worth going to a motel for a shower and bed. This is one time when using a well-established travel site or travel agent can be very beneficial. If you've just flown halfway around the world, finding a hotel, dealing with your luggage, and securing transportation—especially if you don't speak the language—can be enough to put you over the edge. Making a reservation before you go, even if only for the first night, simplifies your arrival. Many airport motels are very expensive and usually not worth the price, so wading through the marketing hype with help from someone who has been there before or is a travel professional can save you a lot of heartache in the long run.

HUTS AND TEAHOUSES

Many mountainous regions of the world have hut systems that provide shelter for backcountry travelers. The nature of these huts varies: You may literally be sleeping in a lean-to with a woodstove, or you may find yourself in a hotel-like accommodation with a full-service restaurant and bar. The prices will also reflect this range of possibilities. Sometimes you will be asked simply to make a donation, other times the cost will be comparable to a midrange inn.

Europe, New Zealand, Canada, Japan, and parts of the United States have well-established hut systems that allow hikers to travel for days, even weeks, at a time with little more on their backs than a change of clothes and a wallet to cover expenses. Huts can also provide you with a welcome respite at the end of a strenuous expedition. It's nice to be pampered a bit after working hard. Again, there's a plethora of information on huts available online. You can also check with mountaineering associations around the world about how the hut system in a particular country works. You may need reservations or to arrive early in the day to secure a place. You may need sleeping bags and your own cooking gear or a simple sheet may fill all your needs. Each hut is different.

Molly's Home Sweet Hut

After graduating from college, I went trekking in the Kita Alps of Japan for two weeks. Here, rather than lug around tents, sleeping bags, and pads on their backs, most hikers stay in the mountain huts that are sprinkled throughout the high peaks. These accommodations varied from huge ramshackle buildings sleeping 600 people to small shelters that could accommodate a dozen or so. One of the places we stayed allocated 21 inches of sleeping space to each guest. A number was painted on the eaves overhead to delineate your spot on the futon below. I drew the short straw that night and slept on the end of our group, shoulder-to-shoulder with a stranger.

Some huts offered semiprivate rooms, but most featured these long rows of futons laid out along the walls to create one big bed where everyone slept side-by-side throughout the night. We were woken each morning at 4:30 a.m. by the crinkling of plastic bags as people gathered their belongings in the predawn darkness. This was followed by a rush for the communal bathrooms. I quickly learned the proper etiquette was to ignore people as they performed their morning rituals. An acknowledgement meant you recognized someone's existence and suddenly were not alone. The practice made sense: when hacking, primping, and brushing, most of us prefer privacy. Breakfast followed the bathroom routine and generally consisted of rice, miso soup, a strip of seaweed, one raw egg, and the ubiquitous cup of tea.

There were very few Westerners traveling through the Japanese Alps, and we were often asked to pose in photos or to chat for a while so a fellow traveler could practice his or her English. The Japanese hiked in groups and dressed alike: brightly colored button-down shirts, wool trousers, and umbrellas seemed to be the norm. In places, we stood in line to scramble across more challenging terrain, and chains and ladders had been installed to provide access up what would be technical climbs in other parts of the world.

Molly's Home Sweet Hut

For the first few days of our two-week excursion, I found the strange contrast between the crowds of people and the rugged scenery disorienting. Most of my mountain experience had been in North American wilderness, so staying in huts, standing in lines, eating in shifts, and dealing with crowds while hiking through the mountains was not at all what I had envisioned when planning the trip.

That trip was the only time I've gotten up before dawn to catch sunrise on a peak, only to reach the summit and find there was no room for me on top because of all the people. On another mountaintop, we stood in line for a blessing at a Shinto shrine and were treated to a beautiful ceremony involving chanting, bells, and feathered fans. Gradually my attitude changed as I shifted from expecting a wilderness experience to enjoying the cultural adventure.

In the long run, that adventure ended up being all about the accommodations, the people, the food, and the Japanese culture of mountain travel. The alpine scenery, while lovely, has faded into the blur of my mountain experiences over the years, but those huts and the busy social scene they hosted remain vividly imprinted on my mind. ∎

Researching and Booking Online

The Internet has changed the world for travelers. Now you can find hotels, campgrounds, hostels, even private homes that take paying guests with the click of a button. However, the Internet can also mask many flaws with the careful use of camera angles and romantic lighting. Fortunately, more and more Web sites provide places for customer feedback, allowing you to get some sense of what to expect from accommodations just about anywhere. You can Google hotels in Timbuktu, Bariloche, Kathmandu, or Twentynine Palms and find a variety of sites with choices in all price ranges. Trip Advisor (www.tripadvisor.com) is an easy-to-navigate site that includes detailed comments from past guests about their experience at different hotels throughout the world. Of course, these comments come without much context, and undoubtedly hotels often get reviewed by disgruntled travelers more frequently than by those who had a neutral or even a nice stay, but still you can recognize general themes—dirty, loud, friendly, clean—pretty quickly. Bear in mind that major travel sites such as Expedia, Travelocity, Orbitz, and others usually drop hotels after they receive too many negative comments from travelers, so while this is no guarantee against mediocrity, it does serve to weed out the really bad places.

The Lonely Planet Web site has a forum called Thorn Tree (www.lonelyplanet.com/thorntree/index.jspa) for travelers where you can post questions about places to stay and things to do all over the world. You can get advice on lodging, camping, traveling with children, crime, nightlife, gay/lesbian travel, food, and just about anything else you may want to know. It is worth reading different posts by one individual to get a sense of his or her take on things. Often individual commentators show up several times in the forum, so it doesn't take too much effort to figure out if the person is writing thoughtful posts that contain legitimate insights.

In addition to the Lonely Planet Web site, another good spot for travel advice online is BootsnAll (www.bootsnall.com). BootsnAll has articles, travel information, and an open message board where you can post questions and find advice. It also offers advice from so-called insiders. To qualify as an insider, people have to fill out an application demonstrating their credentials. The questions posted on the insiders' page are similar to those you find on forums elsewhere, but the answers seem to be a bit more specific and detailed, so it might be a good place to get reliable information. At least you know the answers come from someone who has demonstrated a degree of knowledge and credibility regarding the country he or she writes about in order to qualify as an insider.

INTERNET VERSUS GUIDEBOOKS

It can be nice to flip through a paper guidebook to get a sense of a country, but specific details change quickly. A hotel may have gone out of business or changed ownership since the guidebook went to press, and restaurants often disappear overnight, making the information available in your book obsolete. For these reasons, the Internet is often the best place to gather the most up-to-date information available. However, once you leave home, you won't always have Internet service available and you may not want to lug around your computer. So for these situations, guidebooks can fill in the gaps. These days you can often download specific chapters from guidebooks online and print them at home, so it isn't necessary to bring the entire book for southern India when you are only planning to visit parts of Kerala.

TRAVEL AGENTS

When the airlines cut travel agency commissions, and the dot-coms began to offer airfares on the Internet, many people thought the end of the travel agency industry had come. However, U.S. travel agents' total annual sales are between $120 and $130 billion and rising. Despite all of the online travel sites, travel agents still sell 51 percent of all airline tickets, 87 percent of all cruises, 81 percent of all tours and packages, 45 percent of all car rentals, and about 47 percent of all hotels. These numbers demonstrate that travel agents still have power, and that power is customer loyalty.

There are a host of compelling reasons to use a travel agent. Travel agents can find the best rate available, and they save you time as well as money. A travel agent has information at her fingertips, saving you a few hours in front of a computer screen. If you have a problem with a particular part of your travel experience, the agent acts on your behalf to see that restitution is made. Travel agents are experts in understanding and deciphering the myriad travel information and codes often found online. Instead of an impersonal voice thousand of miles away, travel agents are your neighbors. They know what you want and what you value in your travel experience; they work for their clients, not for a travel supplier. All that said, one of the only negative aspects of using a local travel agent is that she usually works during regular business hours, leaving you on your own when your flight in cancelled at 11:00 p.m., although larger agencies or firms that cater to international travel often have a 24-hour hotline for stranded travelers.

CHAPTER 13 | INTERNATIONAL LOGISTICS

The logistics involved in traveling vary according to your expedition's destination, and there are specific things to consider should your destination be international. Details ranging from tipping etiquette to key phrases in the local language are things that shouldn't be overlooked even if the majority of your expedition will be spent in the backcountry.

Local History and Culture

Your trip will be richer and more rewarding if you know more about the area than the number of miles you need to hike and the amount of money you should carry. Guidebooks often have a section on local history and customs and are, therefore, a good place to start for a general overview. You can also go to the library or research online. Gathering this information will enable you to appreciate everything from the architecture you pass to the food you eat. You will also have more understanding of the significance of place names and the legends behind special places. In the Grand Canyon, for example, Separation Rapid marks the spot where three members of the first John Wesley Powell expedition left the trip, convinced they were doomed. Their fears were misplaced, and Powell and the rest of the expedition reached the end of the canyon successfully just a few days after the men departed. The men, however, were never seen or heard from again. This kind of story adds significance to the site and enhances your appreciation for the people who have come before you.

Understanding a bit about local customs also ensures that you do not perform any cultural faux pas by accident. In Nepal,

Zanskar, India.

it is considered virtuous and respectful to pass mani walls (which contain Buddhist mantras carved into flat rocks and are often found at significant points along the trail such as the tops of passes or near holy places) on the left, with the wall to your right. You should walk around stupas, or Buddhist temples, clockwise. In many parts of Asia, it is considered unclean to eat with your left hand, while some Native American tribes consider it disrespectful to look directly into a stranger's eyes. Understanding these kinds of cultural norms can help you navigate an unfamiliar place without inadvertently offending your hosts and, keep you from being put off by unfamiliar customs as well.

Appropriate Attire and Behavior

In some parts of the world, men in shorts and women in pants are totally unacceptable. In others, nude bathing goes unnoticed. Before you go, find out the cultural norms regarding dress and behavior that you should be aware of. It may simply mean women hike in skirts and cover their hair, while men wear long pants. Or it may be more complicated, dictating where people sit, what people say, and who talks to whom. The big questions often revolve around the role of women in a particular society, but religion, caste, and wealth can also dictate behavior.

Women travelers, unfortunately, do need to take some added precautions in many parts of the world. Even in the United States, a single woman on the road is often subject to unwanted attention and hassles. If you are a woman and opt to travel alone or without a male companion, make sure you have investigated what precautions are recommended in the country you plan to visit. You may want to avoid picking up hitchhikers or hitchhiking yourself. You may not want to camp alone or wear revealing clothing. You should not feel as if these precautions are intended to put you off, but rather to remind you not to be complacent about your safety.

Regardless of your sex, when you are traveling in a foreign land, be smart and show respect. You'll gain much more from your experience and avoid problems as well.

Dave Remembers His Table Manners

"Dude, there is no way that I can eat all this," I said to my expedition mate, Tom, while staring down at the huge plate of food in front of me.

Tom, an expert on local customs, replied, "Refusing food would be showing great disrespect to the family."

Seated on the floor of the kitchen of a tiny home in Bhaktapur, Nepal, breakfast had started out slow and pleasurable, with an orange accompanied by two fried eggs. I was just getting up to leave when Tom said, "Hold on, that was just the appetizer."

Amma (the mother) of the Nehwar household was smiling with pride as she gave me plate of perfectly prepared steaming *dal bhat*—lentils with rice, chicken, and chutney.

Normally I enjoy dal bhat, the most common meal in Nepal, but during the past two days my stomach had felt like a big bloated pancake, full of angry new bacteria, being flipped back and forth by the hot subtropical temperatures here at the 28th parallel.

While utensils are widely available in Nepal, the most common method of eating food is with your right hand. The first thing I did was sit on my left hand to eliminate any chance that I might accidentally use it during any part of the meal. In most of Asia and the Middle East the left hand is reserved for one specific task, wiping, and I don't mean your mouth or nose.

Dave Remembers His Table Manners

Although eating with your hands sounds simple enough, actually getting the food in your mouth without wearing it on your face or in your lap takes some practice. I was feeling fairly confident in my finger scooping technique when Amma started talking with Tom in Nepali, and after a few sentences they both burst out in laughter.

Apparently, after observing my difficulty in getting the dal bhat into my mouth, Amma asked Tom if there was a reason for my inferior table manners. Tom told her I had only eaten with my hands three or four times before, so the technique was rather new to me.

"How old is he? Why has he not eaten with his fingers? Did his mother always hand-feed him at home?" Amma asked incredulously.

Tom stylishly finished consuming his meal leaving just the shiny plate and was busy packing his pack in the next room. I felt like I was at one of those barbecue joints in the States where if you can eat the whole rack of ribs, your meal is free or, in this case, you gain the good will of the household. Eventually, I scooped up the last handful of dal bhat and stuffed it into my bulging cheeks.

When I glanced up at the hostess, I was greeted by the sight of a large ladle overflowing with rice, making a beeline for my now empty plate. Feeling that I might actually explode if I ate one more grain of rice, I racked my threadbare Nepali vocabulary for the right word. Just as the ladle was about to drop its payload I remembered. "Ah, ah, *pugcha, pugcha*. I'm full, that's enough," I said, smiling while patting my distended midriff. ■

The Rich Westerner

In many developing countries, Western tourists are considered rich regardless of the reality of their situation. And when you compare the living conditions of many places—slums in India, remote villages in the Himalaya and Andes, small towns on American Indian reservations—our living standards are remarkably high. For someone who has never left his or her village, the fact that we can travel halfway around the world to hike or climb a mountain is inconceivable. From their perspective, we are extravagantly wealthy, even if we scraped and saved to make our expedition a reality.

Foreign guests often intrigue youngsters. Islamabad, Pakistan.

Given this, you are likely to be surrounded by children begging for money or candy and vendors who push aggressively for your business. Some people carry handfuls of change or pencils to give out to children; others believe giving things to them just encourages begging. Talk to people who have traveled in the place you are visiting before you go, or ask a local what he or she recommends. Read guidebooks or talk to social service nongovernmental agencies working in the area to find out what to do when surrounded by a swarm of pleading children. It can feel hard-hearted to walk away, ignoring their calls and the hands grabbing at you, but in truth, you just make the situation worse by capitulating. Your best bet if you really want to do something is to seek out a local charity, go to a school or church, or find someone who is working to make a difference in the lives of these children and ask if there is something you can do to contribute to their effort.

Crime

Unfortunately, crime is everywhere, and tourists are always good targets. Typically you are carrying valuable gear, documents, and at least a certain amount of cash, and often you are in crowded places

Take time to interact with people and
share your cultures in a positive way.

where pickpockets or thieves can operate without detection. Be alert and smart.

Carry a rubber doorstop. Cheap and lightweight, a doorstop can help you get a good night sleep when you stay in hotels with flimsy doors or insufficient locks. On public transportation, keep your luggage in sight. Watch as people get on and off to make sure they don't grab one of your bags along with their own. Carry your valuables on the front of your body, preferably around your neck or waist where you can see and feel them at all times. It's all too easy for someone to slit open your backpack with a knife and remove your wallet while you stand in line, oblivious of their presence. There are stories of people drugging and robbing travelers on buses and trains, so be wary of accepting food and drink from people you don't know.

Don't be paranoid, but too many travelers have been taken advantage of when they were too trusting. If you take adequate precautions, you should be fine.

Petty crime is one thing, but in some places in the world you may be confronted by more than pickpockets in your travels. Before you go, double-check the U.S. State Department Web site to see if there are any travel advisories for the country you are visiting. Think carefully before ignoring these advisories. Pirates, armed robbers, terrorists, and other desperate criminals are real and can be extremely dangerous. It's not worth risking your life if such threats exist. Find another mountain to climb.

Language

Learning a few key phrases in the language of the country you visit can help you win friends. Most people are grateful if you make an effort to communicate with them in their language, even if your pronunciation is preposterous and your grammar idiosyncratic. So take time to learn the basics: Hello, good-bye, please, excuse me, where's the bathroom, what's your name, how much is this, do you speak English, and so forth, are some of the key expressions you'll need to know. In addition, it helps to familiarize yourself with numbers so you can understand prices and count out money. If nothing else, bring a small pocket calculator to help determine the price of goods or services; numbers are more or less universal if you're struggling with the language, not to mention it's also a great tool for converting foreign currency prices into dollars.

Carry a phrase book, preferably one that has both English to the other language and vice versa. That way if you find yourself trying to understand someone who does not know any English, you can take turns pointing to the words you are trying to communicate.

Many popular tourist destinations around the world have language schools lasting from a few days to weeks or months. If you expect to spend a long time in a foreign land, sign up for language classes. Your experience of that culture will be much deeper if you have some understanding of the language.

Knowing at least a little of the local language will enrich your experience through interaction and understanding of the people you meet.

Hiring Staff

Many large-scale expeditions in the Himalaya need support staff: Porters, cooks, and guides may be part of your entourage as you head into the mountains. South American mountaineering trips also occasionally use pack animals as support. Having staff along to serve you can be an interesting experience if you are used to carrying your own weight and doing your own cooking. It's a luxury: There's something about being roused in the morning by a gentle knock on your tent and a warm bowl of washing water that is very easy to get used to. But it also requires management to ensure your staff is happy. If you've read much mountaineering literature, you've probably heard about porter strikes where support staff refuse to move unless they are paid more.

To avoid problems with your support staff, make sure that you negotiate salaries and loads before you start off. You may have a liaison officer along who makes these arrangements, but you should have at least one team member present at the discussion to represent your interests. Once the two sides have agreed to terms, you must uphold them. Changes in pace, load weights, and distances all require renegotiating wages. The difference between $4 and $5 a day may seem petty to you, but it's a big deal for many people. Remember, money is a weird commodity. It always adds tension to relationships—even married couples argue over finances—so make sure you are operating well within the accepted norms (salaries are fair and loads reasonable, for example) and that your terms are agreeable to everyone involved. This is not the place to cut corners and save pennies.

In some places, not only will you be expected to pay your support staff, you will also be required to provide them with equipment such as sleeping bags, boots, and food. Make sure you understand what is expected before you go. It can be pricey to outfit a whole group of porters at the roadhead, especially when you can often purchase used gear in the city that will suffice.

Tipping is appropriate in some places and not in others. Find out from a disinterested third party whether you should expect to tip your support staff at the end of the trip. Or check in guidebooks before you leave: Often there will be a section on tipping guidelines.

Packers, cooks, and porters are all staff whom you may need or consider hiring for the duration of your expedition.

If tips are not considered appropriate but you would like to reward someone's effort, consider giving him or her a piece of equipment that is difficult or expensive to find, such as a headlamp or a pair of sunglasses.

Porters are employed by the thousands throughout the world's mountainous regions where the lack of roads and other forms of transportation require loads be moved by people or animals. Unfortunately, porters often have insufficient clothing, food, equipment, and shelter, and as a result, many of them suffer from illnesses and incur debilitating injuries. Porters carry monstrous loads and are often paid miserable wages. To prevent this mistreatment, the International Porter Protection Group has come up with guidelines to help trekkers when hiring porters. These guidelines include the following:

- Ensure that all porters have clothing appropriate to season and altitude. This may mean windproof jacket and trousers, fleece jacket, long johns, suitable footwear (leather boots in snow), socks, hat, gloves, and sunglasses.
- Ensure porters have a dedicated shelter, either a room in a lodge or a tent, and a sleeping pad and blanket (or sleeping bag). They should have food and warm drinks, or cooking equipment and fuel.
- Provide porters with the same standard of medical care as you expect for yourself.
- Ensure loads are manageable (maximum weights: 20 kg on Kilimanjaro, 25 kg in Peru and Pakistan, 30 kg in Nepal). Weight limits may need to be adjusted for altitude and trail and weather conditions; experience is needed to make this decision.

You can use these guidelines to dictate your own practices with your support staff. If you are using a trekking agency to handle your logistics, make sure to ask if they abide by the International Porter Protection Group guidelines. If they do not, take your business elsewhere.

Terms

Liaison Officer: Some countries, such as Pakistan, require expeditions have a liaison officer, or LO, along to communicate and coordinate between the team and the government or military.

Sirdar: The name given to the lead Sherpa or mountain guide on an expedition.

Sherpa: Literally means "people from the East" and refers to an ethnic group in the mountainous regions of Nepal. The Sherpas are often employed as guides on expeditions, and their climbing and mountaineering skills are highly regarded. The term is sometimes used incorrectly to refer to porters in general.

Porters: Men and women hired to carry loads. Usually these laborers are not expected to climb or travel in technical terrain.

Approaching the Mount Fitzroy base camp in Argentina. Horse packers are ubiquitous in Patagonia as support for expeditions.

Other organizations working with the people most directly affected by mountain expeditions include the Alex Lowe Charitable Foundation, which has a mission to preserve Lowe's legacy by providing support programs designed to help people in remote regions of the world. One of these programs is a climbing school for training Sherpas to become mountain guides for expeditions. In addition, the nonprofit organization The Mountain Institute is dedicated to empowering mountain communities and conserving mountain environments throughout the world. Both organizations are good resources for travelers seeking to minimize their impact on the cultures they encounter during their expeditions.

Securing Money Overseas

Twenty years ago, a trip out of the United States meant buying a stack of traveler's checks to see you through your adventure. Nowadays, it's almost impossible to find or use traveler's checks. Most international travelers rely on a combination of debit cards, credit cards, and cash to cover expenses while they travel. This combination seems to work well, but there are a few tips to bear in mind to avoid finding yourself stranded without money in the middle of nowhere.

DEBIT CARDS

For the most part, if your bank card is part of one of the major networking services—such as Cirrus, PLUS, or STAR—you should be able to use your card almost anywhere in the world. Using a debit card to secure cash means you don't have to carry a lot of money with you. If you have a good PIN, your card is quite secure. You'll automatically get local currencies, so you don't have to bother changing money (although you may be able to get a better exchange rate on the street).

ATMs are all over the place in most cities, but outside of town, you may have a hard time finding one. Make sure you have enough cash to last until you return to an urban area. Some cards can be problematic at times, so consider carrying two cards from two different accounts. That way if you run into trouble, you have a backup. It is also a good idea to carry the cards in separate places so if one is stolen or lost you have a spare.

Make sure you contact your bank before you go to tell them of your travel plans. If you neglect to do this, you may find your bank putting a security hold on your card when it encounters an unexpected transaction from overseas. When you talk to the bank, find out about any fees you may incur pulling money out of an ATM while traveling. Some banks have both a finance charge and a charge for a foreign exchange. If your bank has too many fees, shop around. You may find a better deal elsewhere.

If you encounter problems with your ATM card while traveling—such as an error message when attempting to secure funds—make note of the time, date, and content of the message. You may also want to keep track of your receipts from the trip just in case when you return you discover you have unexpected withdrawals on your account. There are stories of people attempting and failing to get money on their debit card, and then returning home to discover their account had been debited even though they did not receive any funds.

Write down bank phone numbers as well as your account number and carry them in a safe place, such as with your passport.

That way if you run into trouble, you have a way of contacting your financial institution for help.

Finally, check with your bank to make sure your PIN will work in foreign ATMs. Some ATMs do not allow you to use zeros, others do not accept PINs with more than four numbers, so make sure yours will work wherever you plan to go.

CREDIT CARDS

In urban areas you can use a credit card (at least major credit cards such as Visa or MasterCard) to cover most expenses, especially big ones like hotel rooms, car rentals, and restaurant meals. Credit cards are more secure than a wad of cash, and some come with travel insurance (read the fine print outlining the services included with your card).

On the other hand, again like debit cards, your credit card is not going to be very useful in rural areas and for inexpensive items such as rickshaw rides or a cup of tea. For these services you will need a supply of cash.

The magnetic strips on credit cards can wear out, so consider carrying two cards (maybe even cards from different accounts) to cover you if one card stops working. As with a debit card, you need to contact your credit card company about your travel plans to ensure you don't trigger an automatic fraud alert by suddenly using your card 1,000 miles away from your home.

Write down the phone numbers on the back of your card for reporting a lost or stolen card or for customer service, and keep the information separate from the card itself. That way, if you do lose your card, you know whom to call for assistance.

CASH

The nicest thing about cash is that it is accepted everywhere by everyone. However, cash can be bulky and take up a lot of space. Furthermore, cash is totally insecure: If you misplace your money, it's gone.

Don't convert a lot of cash to the local currency at home before you go, and try to avoid changing large amounts at the airport. You'll always find better rates in country. If you anticipate needing money to get from the airport to your hotel, convert $100 or so American dollars. That amount should be plenty to cover your initial expenses until you have access to better exchange rates. In many parts of the world, you can use American dollars in local shops or restaurants (in fact, in some countries, crisp U.S currency is so highly valued that a small stash for emergencies is a good idea), but in other places you will need to go to a bank or currency exchange. Beware, banking hours vary around the world. Midday siestas in Latin America mean many banks and businesses shut down from 1–4 p.m. Banks may also be closed unexpectedly for holidays. Ask around to see what kinds of exchange rates are available from different vendors. The difference can be noticeable, particularly when you are changing large amounts of money.

FINANCIAL EMERGENCIES

If you are robbed and have no cash or way to access cash, the U.S. Department of State's Overseas Citizens Services (OCS) Office of American Citizens Services and Crisis Management (www.travel .state.gov/travel/tips/emergencies/emergencies_1198.html) can establish a trust account in your name in order to transfer funds overseas. Upon receipt of funds, OCS will transfer the money to the appropriate U.S. embassy or consulate for disbursement to you. There is a processing fee—$30 in 2010—to set up the trust account. The OCS trust funds are a onetime service. For more information, call the OCS at 1-202-647-5225.

There are three methods for transmitting funds to OCS. Western Union is the fastest method: Funds sent via Western Union are usually available for disbursement overseas within 24 hours during the business week.

Call 1-800-634-4322 or log on to www.westernunion.com to use Western Union's Quick Collect service. You will need a major credit card. In addition, you can ask someone to go to any Western Union agent and use cash to transfer funds to an OCS trust fund. This is the least expensive way to send money. Call 1-800-325-6000 to locate the nearest agent or look online for a listing. The State Department's processing fee must be included in the total amount sent by Western Union; failure to do so will result in the money being deducted from the amount intended for the U.S. citizen recipient.

You can arrange to have your bank wire money to an OCS account; however, this method can take up to seven days to process. Tell your bank that you want to transfer the desired amount plus the $30 processing fee to:

Bank of America
Department of State Branch
2201 C St. NW, Washington, D.C. 20520
ABA number: 114000653
Account number: 7476363838
Account name: PUPID State Department

(Include the recipient's full name and overseas location, and the sender's name, address, and telephone number.)

Finally, you can have someone send a cashier's check or money order via U.S. mail or courier service to Overseas Citizens Services, Department of State, SA-29, 4th Floor, 2201 C St. NW, Washington, D.C. 20520. Include the recipient's full name and overseas location, and the sender's name, address, and telephone number. Again, failure to include the $30 processing fee will result in the money being deducted from the amount intended for the U.S. citizen. Delivery of overnight/courier mail to OCS may take three to four days. Regular mail can take three to four weeks to reach OCS due to ongoing irradiation procedures. We strongly discourage this method for emergency use.

14 LEADERSHIP

An Expedition Leadership Case Study

The rocks were black and slippery, wet with the spray of pounding waves that came crashing onto the shore, over and over again, noisily mocking Anne, Mark, Nicole, and Sam's need to launch, to paddle, to leave the island and head for home. The four of them had been traveling along the coast of Chile for a month. The previous day was supposed to have been the last day of the trip, and they all had places to go, things to do. But they were trapped, winded in on a beach a day's paddle from their destination. For four days, they'd walked out to the rocky point to stare at the waves, to see if things were calming down, to decide if they could paddle; and for four days they had returned to their tent, stymied by the storm.

Finally, Mark ran out of patience. He was antsy and needed to move and had convinced himself the waves looked smaller. If nothing else, he felt it was worth getting on the water to see how the conditions actually felt in a boat as opposed to how they thought they would feel watching from their vantage point on shore. The kayaks were packed and ready to go in hopeful anticipation of a break in the weather, so why not take them out and try something? Mark thought they could experiment with tying their boats together into a raft and seeing how it performed in the rough seas.

Nicole remembers thinking Mark was crazy, although his suggestion was not without precedent. Kayakers do routinely raft together for rescues because the larger surface area of the raft makes a more stable platform than a single, tippy kayak. But Nicole had never heard of anyone traveling with their kayaks tied together, certainly not anyone trying to cross seas like those that lay before them.

"The waves are at least six feet high," she said, hoping that would be enough to discredit Mark's idea and send them back to their tents for another round of cards. But the group's tensions were beginning to rise. Sam had been the naysayer for the entire trip, and he was sick of being the one to call a stop to things, so he unexpectedly announced that he thought Mark had made a great suggestion. Anne, the most experienced kayaker in the group, could usually be counted on to be the voice of reason. But she was finding it hard to say anything that might contradict or insult Mark. They had begun the trip as friends but over the course of the expedition, her feelings had shifted and now she found herself falling in love with him. Everything he said sounded good to her in her distracted state.

Nicole felt rather betrayed to have both Anne and Sam abdicate when it seemed so clear to her that Mark's idea was utterly insane, but she said nothing more and just shrugged and followed the group as they hurried back to the beach where the kayaks were pulled up on the shore. Quickly everyone, including Nicole, became immersed in the intellectual challenge of designing and building a workable raft. They tied the two singles on either side of the double, and then experimented, moving the boats back and forth to see how they meshed. They tied elaborate knots, all with quick release systems to ensure they had the ability to separate quickly if necessary. Finally they decided they were satisfied with the construction. It was time to test the craft on the water.

In the shelter of the cove, the raft felt surprisingly stable and maneuverable. Gradually their confidence grew and they began pushing their way farther out into the larger waves to see how the raft responded as conditions worsened. Somewhere along the way, they crossed an invisible line. A line that demarcated the haven of the cove where they retained the possibility of returning to shore from the teeming turmoil of the open water and the reality that turning back was no longer possible. Suddenly the four of them realized they had inadvertently made a decision to attempt the crossing without ever having a conversation about the wisdom of this course of action.

The raft continued to perform surprisingly well, however, and Anne, Mark, and Sam gradually gained confidence, sensing that they could manage the mounting seas and make their way safely to the haven of a distant island. But Nicole felt differently. She was seated in the front of the double kayak and the configuration of the raft had left her positioned so she could not paddle. She was a passenger and as such felt none of the confidence the others experienced as they grew more comfortable maneuvering the boat. Sam, in the back of the double, had assumed the role of captain and was responsible for steering. Anne and Mark, in singles alongside, provided forward momentum with their paddles. Their focus and effort allowed them to get out of their heads, to forget about the potential risk of their situation as they worked to control the raft and propel themselves forward. Nicole's job was to watch for incoming waves. With no physical activity to diffuse her anxiety, she was more open to the real threat of their predicament.

They continued like this for an hour or more, making their way across the passage that separated their camp from the island they decided would be a logical place to stop. Nicole said even she began to believe they were going to make it in spite of her apprehensions. Then the wave hit. They were caught off guard and struck broadside by a wall of water that lifted the kayak up and folded it back over itself. Anne recalls looking down at Mark below her. He seemed very far away, and she was momentarily amazed, sure the raft would right itself, and thrilled at its seaworthiness. But then she was plunged into the 50-degree waters of the Pacific Ocean.

The four of them quickly exited from the kayaks and thrashed their way to the surface. They scrambled onto the overturned raft and automatically began to figure out how to cope with their new situation. They were well trained. No one panicked. The kayak raft proved to be even more stable upside down, but when they tried to maneuver it, they found it unresponsive and sluggish. It lumbered its way laboriously over the waves like a great beast, slowly getting nudged toward the shore by the relentless pressure of the current. It was obvious they were not going to be able to land the beast safely and the last place they wanted to be was in the surf between the beach and the raft. So once they came in close enough to shore, they abandoned ship and swam.

All four made it to the island safely, and soon the kayaks came in as well. They quickly fell to work, two of them dismantling the raft, retrieving gear, and stashing equipment above the high-tide line, while the others started a stove and got food and water heating. They changed out of their wet clothes and within an hour were sitting down to a meal. But they had a hard time looking into each other's eyes, a hard time confronting the raw fact that they had come perilously close to dying because of a rash experiment and a subsequent nondecision.

DO YOU NEED A DESIGNATED LEADER ON YOUR EXPEDITION?

If you asked Anne, Mark, Nicole, and Sam, the four of them would all say yes. Even in that team, where their friendships were long-standing (Nicole and Sam were married), and they had worked together both leading wilderness expeditions and doing administrative work; where they had spent dozens of weeks exploring the Patagonian coast in kayaks; and where Anne was midway through a master's program in organizational leadership—even in that highly qualified team, when it came time to make a hard, potentially risky decision without a leader, they bumbled into a hazardous situation from which they narrowly escaped. Blinded by love, pride, boredom, anxiety, stress, and countless other nebulous emotions that clouded their judgment, they failed to make a well-thought-out decision.

HOW WOULD A DESIGNATED LEADER HAVE HELPED?

These four believed that, if nothing else, if one of them had been picked to lead the group, that person would have kept them from slipping across that unseen line into the dangerous open water without stopping to evaluate the decision, assess its pros and cons, and weigh their alternatives. Without the formal structure of a designated leader, they found their desire to protect the relationships that bound them together overcame their internal doubts about the wisdom of what they were doing. No one was willing to rock the proverbial boat.

Their story is a classic example of the Abilene Paradox, a psychological phenomenon identified and labeled by Jerry Harvey in 1974 that concludes groups and individuals frequently take actions contradicting their internal desires because they do not want to counter what they perceive the rest of the group wants. Harvey says we experience intense anxiety when we believe our convictions contradict those of the group, and our fear of being ostracized often leads us to go along with what we think others want simply to be included, to be part of the team, to maintain our relationships. The catch is that often what we believe the group wants is totally inaccurate.

Anne, Mark, Nicole, and Sam had consciously decided not to have a designated leader on their expedition. They believed they had the tools and experience that would allow them to make decisions as a group, reaching some kind of consensus through their discussions. And the system worked well initially, but gradually it began to break down and the four fell into predictable roles—roles that the others grew to rely on. Sam served as the check, the conservative voice. Mark—the least experienced boater but one who liked to push himself and was comfortable in potentially risky situations—had assumed the role of the experimenter who pressured the group to test their limits. Anne and Nicole fell in the middle, balancing the two extremes. When these roles broke down, the group's understanding of how they made decisions also broke down. When Sam sided with Mark on the wisdom of building the raft, Nicole found herself questioning her own reluctance, wondering if she was being too conservative; while Anne says she had lost all perspective because of her emotional attachment to Mark—an attachment that was unspoken and, therefore, unknown to the rest of the group, making its effect on their decision-making somewhat insidious.

There are countless stories that parallel this one, as well as numerous tales of expeditions where the team divides into factions and returns not speaking to one another. Hindsight helps analyze these failures, and often it boils down to a lack of leadership.

Not all teams need the structure of a designated leader, of course. A small expedition where everyone sleeps in the same tent, eats meals together, and travels in close proximity to each other, may be able to do without any kind of rigid leadership model, but as the complexity of your objective grows, the size of your team expands, and the challenges and risks you face increase, the difficulty of working without a formal leader grows. If nothing else, your team should sit down and talk about leadership and decision-making before you leave home to ensure you understand each other and have a system in place should you need to act quickly and decisively.

What Is Leadership?

NOLS defines leadership as timely, appropriate actions that guide and support a group to set and achieve realistic goals. Great leaders create an environment that inspires individuals and groups to achieve their highest potential. Great leaders are defined by the success of their team, rather than by their own personal achievements.

Leadership is a skill that can be learned and refined, but someone planning an expedition needs to know what to look for in a leader and how to implement an effective leadership model.

NOLS uses a framework of four leadership roles, seven leadership skills, and one signature style to teach leadership to students. Leadership roles are the ways leaders apply leadership to help their group set and attain goals. Leadership skills are attributes that history has shown enhance a leader's effectiveness with his or her followers. Signature style is an individual's most comfortable approach to guiding or leading a group.

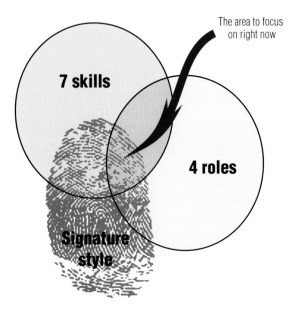

Leadership Roles

Simply naming someone the leader does not make him or her effective. The team must also concede power to that individual, and what that power entails will vary. As you prepare for your expedition, bring your team together to discuss leadership before you are faced with the challenges and discomfort you will inevitably encounter on your expedition.

At NOLS, this discussion extends beyond outlining the responsibilities of the designated leader. All team members have a leadership role to play in the ultimate success of any endeavor. These roles include the designated leader, as well as active followers, peer leaders, and self leaders. These roles should be defined and valued by the team.

Taking the lead while route-finding is an example of designated leadership in an expedition team. The other three leadership roles are still at play here, however: active followership (not following the leader blindly), self leadership (making sure your basic needs are met so you're able to keep up with the group), and peer leadership (lending a hand to a teammate who might be struggling under his load).

Four Expedition Leadership Roles

Designated leadership: Having a head architect or guardian of the group process. He or she can delegate and collaborate when possible but cannot abdicate responsibility and accountability. Complex, potentially risky or tough activities and decisions are best handled with a designated leader guiding or monitoring the process.

Active followership: Expedition members show good leadership by following the leadership of others. They seek clarity, give input, respect the plan, help out, and work for the betterment of the group and its goals.

Peer leadership: Leadership without hierarchy. Team members see what needs to be done and do it. All members assure quality completion of group tasks, functions, and goals. Peer leadership works best when members clarify who is responsible for what. Peer leadership is less effective during high-risk or emergency situations.

Self leadership: Every member of a team is a leader by virtue of who he or she is and how he or she influences others.

Situational Leadership

Practically, what may end up being more important for your expedition than knowing the leadership roles is to establish an agreed-upon leadership model. Obviously the easiest kind of leadership situation is a guide with a group of clients or a NOLS instructor with students. Here the leadership role is clearly defined. The guide or instructor is a designated leader with ultimate control of the decisions and actions of the group. He or she is both legally and ethically responsible for everyone's safety and for the achievement of the group's goals. Whether a designated leader incorporates the group into the decision-making process ultimately depends on the nature of the trip. On a three-day guided climb of the Grand Teton, there probably isn't a lot of collaboration going on. On a three-month NOLS semester, the students will be assuming much of the leadership for the course by its conclusion.

On a personal expedition, your leader's role can fall anywhere along a continuum ranging from directing all action to delegating

Group Decision-Making Styles

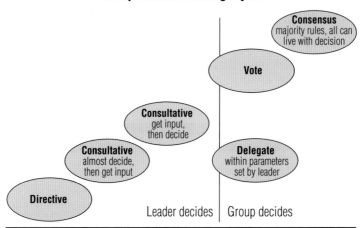

Level of group ownership and time to make decision

Situational Leadership

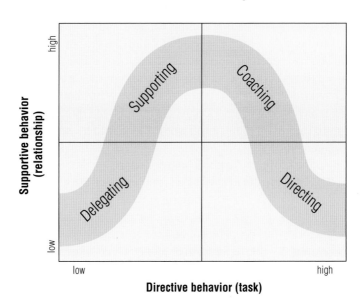

most of it. Direct leadership is most effective with inexperienced groups. It is also often the best strategy for quick, decisive action in an emergency. Delegating and collaborating are more appropriate on an expedition comprising team members with comparable experience. The key is to have one person who is ultimately responsible for determining a course of action so that decisions aren't made by default.

Leadership Skills

As a team, your expedition may comprise individuals with varying levels of experience. You may be close friends or new acquaintances. Your group may have a wide range of ages, different nationalities, different sexes, and very different backgrounds. These factors all play into how an individual performs in a leadership role. So how do you pick your team leader? And how do you manage yourself as a good peer or self leader and as an active follower?

Your most effective designated leader may not be the best climber in the group or the oldest member of your team. Rather you are looking for someone who is able to consider the opinions, skills, and makeup of your group and find ways to meld those components together into a functioning, capable, and compatible team. That can be a big order, especially toward the end of a long trip when you have been stormed in and the clock is ticking, when people need to get back to work or catch a plane, or they are longing to see loved ones, enjoy a good meal, or have a hot bath. At these times, many people can no longer see through the filters that have begun to color their view of the world. Good leaders, while empathetic, are able to step outside the siren call of the unwise solution and help the group make good, safe decisions.

NOLS has identified seven skills that enhance the effectiveness of group members and the different leadership roles they take throughout an expedition. Some things are obvious. Leaders need to have the technical competence required to achieve your objective; and they must be able to function as part of a team effectively. Other skills are less evident but equally important: judgment, calmness in the face of adversity, and the ability to communicate effectively. The

A team discusses the planned route for the day. Good communication, solid judgment and decision-making, and clear vision and action are among the leadership skills vital for everyone to aim for the same goal.

breakdown of these leadership skills can help you identify attributes that are sometimes hard to define or pinpoint in great leaders and can provide you with a useful tool for identifying what you are looking for in your team members and what you should work on yourself as a high-functioning member of the team.

Seven Leadership Skills

Expedition Behavior

- Serve the mission and goals of the group.
- Be as concerned for others as you are for yourself.
- Treat everyone with dignity and respect.
- Support leadership and growth in your teams.
- Respect the cultures you encounter.
- Be kind and openhearted.
- Do your share and stay organized.
- Help others, but don't routinely do their work.

- Model integrity by being honest and accountable.
- Say yes and deliver or say no clearly if you cannot.
- Resolve conflict in a productive manner.

Competence
- Display basic competence and actively work to improve your knowledge, organization, and management skills and technical and physical abilities.
- Set goals, make action plans, and follow through.

Communication
- Speak up when appropriate, and be silent when appropriate.
- Help create a positive team environment.
- Let your group know what is expected of the team and the leadership.
- Keep people informed as situations change.
- Listen actively, paraphrase, and ask questions to clarify.
- Have the courage to state what you think, feel, and want.
- Be empathetic during conflicts.
- Give timely, growth-oriented, specific, and clear feedback.
- Be open to feedback.

Judgment and Decision-Making
- Consider all available experiences, resources, and information to make decisions and achieve positive results.
- Give your group choices that have acceptable consequences.
- Set clear limits and boundaries when letting people make choices.
- Use the strengths and knowledge of other group members to solve problems.
- Help others see how choices fit into the big picture.
- Question norms and challenge assumptions.

Tolerance for Adversity and Uncertainty
- Turn challenging situations into opportunities.
- Learn to endure, even enjoy, hard work and challenge.
- Use humor and keep things in perspective.
- Function effectively under difficult circumstances, making focused decisions and remaining connected with others. Don't panic.
- Work effectively with different types of people.
- Be patient with less-competent team members.

Self-Awareness

- Understand your abilities and limitations.
- Learn from experience and take steps to improve.
- Work at being authentic.
- Be clear with others about your personal values and goals.
- Find a healthy balance between work, play, reflection, and rest.
- Seek feedback from others.

Vision and Action

- Create an environment that inspires individuals and groups to achieve their full potential.
- Assess what needs to be done and do it.
- Motivate others through your own actions and attitude.
- Have empathy for others, yet be decisive.
- Help create what you want to see.
- Use group goals and values to guide your actions.
- Take risks at an appropriate level for you and your group.
- Seek creative ways to move the group forward.
- Stay open and flexible to change.
- Lead by example.

Your Signature Style

All of us have a natural leadership style. You may be the directive type who likes to assert your authority over others, or you may be a nurturer who wants to make sure everyone in the group is happy. Over time, many of us learn to modify our natural style to be more effective or acceptable as leaders, but under stress we are likely to revert to our old ways, leaving our teammates wondering what happened to us. It is important to be aware of our own tendencies as well as alert to the styles of our teammates.

You can think of leadership styles as a four-square matrix with intersecting lines that represent two continuums. One continuum is between individuals who hesitate to express themselves in group situations and those who state their opinion freely and openly. The intersecting continuum represents the calm, cool rational individuals versus the fiery, emotional types. This matrix generates four

Knowing your personal style of leadership is important before becoming part of an expedition team. Are you a driver or a spontaneous motivator? An analyst architect or a relationship master?

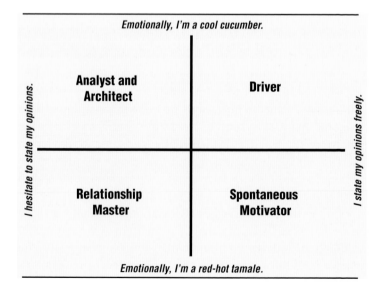

quadrants representing four general leadership styles that NOLS has come to define as analyst architects, drivers, relationship masters, and spontaneous motivators.

Each of these leadership styles has strengths and weaknesses, and each plays an important role in a functioning team. Recognizing your own style, as well as the styles of your teammates, can help you understand the character traits of your group, its strengths and weaknesses, and how it may function under stress. This knowledge may be enough to help you recognize that when a quiet voice in the background is mumbling something about running out of gas, you'd better listen, or if you're that mumbling voice, you'd better speak up.

ANALYSTS and ARCHITECTS
Emphasize meaning and conceptual functions

Advantages

+ information and opinion seekers

+ good at analysis and process observation

+ prefer to make decisions based on facts

+ prefer as much information as possible before deciding

+ can come out with totally off-the-wall solutions that work

+ translate feelings and experiences into ideas

Disadvantages

− can be slow in making decisions or bogged in the facts

− can happily leave most decisions to others and focus on only one decision

− can become uninvolved or have unrealistic ideas

Some Effects on the Group

Analysts and architects are often in the minority but their function is essential. If a group doesn't pay attention to them, it will miss out on significant learning that comes from observation and analysis. The group may also be missing important process steps or other ways to view a situation. Too much of this style in a group may stall movement because the discussion, laissez-faire attitude, and analysis allow opportunities to pass. If a leader has this style, honor his need for information while also requesting that he tell you how and when he will decide or delegate.

DRIVERS
Emphasize action and directing

Advantages

+ are information and opinion givers

+ have an easy time making decisions

+ often are the keepers of the vision in a group

+ great at taking a stand, being direct, and making things happen

+ usually not too shaken by critical feedback

Disadvantages

−sometimes decide without input from others and urge quick decision-making

− make mistakes when moving too quickly without adequate info

− can come across as too impersonal and lose connection with their group

− have to be careful not to overlead

Some Effects on the Group

If a group does not have drivers, it must pick up driver functions or it can fail to meet far-reaching goals. Mature drivers are nonreactionary individuals with a wide range of ability in the other leadership-style quadrants, and they help ground a group. Drivers who are not mature may place too much value on individuality and structure, resulting in turf battles or a lack of member autonomy and collaboration. If a leader has this style, be as direct as possible when dealing with her. Bring problems and opinions to her: She expects this.

RELATIONSHIP MASTERS
Emphasize caring

Advantages

+ excellent at building and sustaining community

+ work well on a team

+ great at building rapport, consensus, commitment, seeking feedback

+ provide support and praise and show concern

+ display high regard for others' wishes, viewpoints, and actions

Disadvantages

– may not take an unpopular stance if it puts a relationship at risk

– can put so much emphasis on relationships that tasks and decision-making fall behind

– can forget or downplay their own needs, to their detriment

Some Effects on the Group

You cannot have too much caring and respect as part of your capacity—it is the glue that's essential for a group to function. As a leader, these attributes are powerful when combined with other leadership-style functions.

If this is the only style a group has, however, the group may not take enough risks or make enough decisions to move forward significantly. The group may also avoid conflict so much that genuine connection and innovation suffer. If a leader has this style, you may need to ask him to be more specific in outlining his expectations. Encourage critical feedback from him and tell him when you want to know what he thinks and wants.

SPONTANEOUS MOTIVATORS
Emphasize emotional stimulation

Advantages

+ often voice their ideas and supply passion to follow those ideas

+ great at motivating people because of their sense of mission or vision

+ good at energetic dialogues with other group members

Disadvantages

– can be emotionally bound to their ideas; objectivity can be their biggest challenge

– can create a highly emotionally charged climate if they put too much emphasis on challenging others and confronting assumptions

Some Effects on the Group

Spontaneous motivators are often like lightbulbs: Groups need them to sparkle, create, prod, stir the pot, and impassion. A group without this style may be functional but somewhat lackluster.

When mature people with this style are detached and monitor their emotional involvement, they are highly effective. But if they are not mature, a group of such people can be overly reactive or so impassioned about their ideals that they lose touch with other realities. Many charismatic leaders and cult leaders are spontaneous motivators. If a leader has this style, know your own position and don't be afraid to voice it. Ask her to give concrete examples to back up her viewpoints.

Leadership Checklist

Pre-Expedition

1. Choose your team leader.
   a. Assess leadership skills of team members including their personal desire to assume the role.
   b. Discuss how the team leader will be selected and implement that decision.
   c. Identify your leader's style and experience and clarify if there are areas where further training or shared responsibility is required.
   d. Discuss roles and responsibilities of the remaining team members and identify individual personality traits that may influence the group's ability to function effectively as a team.
2. Determine the leadership model you will use.
   a. Discuss the team's needs and desires for its leader.
   b. Define the decision-making model the leader will use.
   c. Clarify individual roles (i.e., if leadership is going to be divided between, say, a technical leader and an overall logistics leader, identify areas of overlap and establish some kind of hierarchy for decision-making).

On-Expedition

1. Implement periodic check-ins to assess the team's leadership and make adjustments if necessary.
2. Debrief challenging communications or decisions and determine effectiveness of leadership. Make adjustments if necessary.

Post-Expedition

1. Debrief the trip by highlighting successes and challenges, analyzing leadership, and identifying areas for improvement on future trips.

EXPEDITION BEHAVIOR AND COMMUNICATION

Expedition behavior and communication are two of the seven leadership skills explored in the previous chapter. They bear further attention and more detailed analysis here because of their relevance on the success of your expedition.

Expedition Behavior

NOLS founder Paul Petzoldt believed what he called *expedition behavior* was critical to the success of any wilderness venture. The ability to communicate effectively, participate fully, and tolerate adversity and uncertainty on an expedition were, he said, almost more important than technical skills and experience in determining an individual's ability to be a successful team member. But predicting who has "good" expedition behavior (or EB) can be hard. Expeditions have a way of bringing out both the best and the worst in people; and no matter how many questionnaires your team has filled out, how many pretrip meetings you've held, or how many years you've all known each other, sometimes things don't turn out the way you expect them to.

Paul Petzoldt also reportedly said that if everyone on an expedition felt as if he or she was doing 110 percent of the work, each was probably doing just enough. Expeditions require a lot of effort. There are logistical chores, long hard days moving from one camp to another, technical obstacles to overcome, camp tasks to perform, and sheer emotional endurance involved in going on a wilderness trip of any length of time. Even a weekend excursion can deteriorate into a screaming match when one person feels as if he or she is bearing an unfair share of the load. And most of us think we are doing 110 percent of the work long before we reach that threshold.

SHARING THE LOAD

So what is your load? Is the team doing its own cooking? Are you carrying all the gear and setting up camp? Do you have porters and cooks to help? What chores need to be done before you can safely retreat to your sleeping bag each night? What needs to be done to get going in the morning? What is your objective and how do you plan to achieve it? Does everyone understand his or her responsibility toward that goal?

On trips where the team is self-supported, it works well to divvy up tasks at the onset of the expedition. You can always change the schedule if necessary, and the system does not have to be so rigid that it precludes someone from taking a time-out every now and then, but having a place to start ensures that you begin with a routine that is equitable *before* tensions arise over who is doing—or not doing—what.

Your system may be as simple as having one person cook while other team members set up camp, take care of equipment, clean the dishes, fetch water, or make preparations for the next day's activities. These tasks can rotate on a daily basis or, in larger teams, it may work best to change after every meal. Such a system allows you to rest when it is not your turn to work, something that can be pretty rare on a challenging expedition.

So before you head out on your trip, it's worth talking to your teammates about how they would like to divvy up chores. Be wary of the suggestion to do everything together all the time. Not that it isn't fun to cook a meal as a team sometimes, but if you are out for an extended expedition, you may find the downtime you gain while someone else prepares a meal is precious and critical to your mental health. You can use that extra hour to nap, write, fish, tinker with gear, play cards, pack up for the next day, or do any number of leisure activities that are impossible to accomplish when you are climbing, traveling, moving, or working toward your expedition goals.

Dividing up tasks can be equally important when it comes to your actual expedition objective. You may want to designate a leader

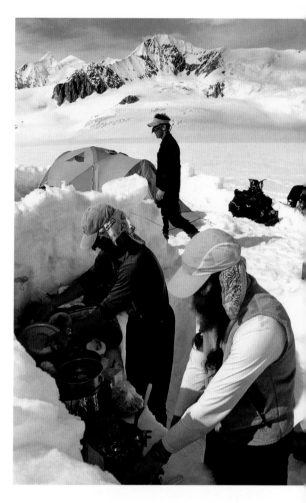

Expedition mates finding their way around their snow kitchen, dividing up tasks so all expedition chores are completed.

of the day or come up with a clear system for making decisions (see chapter 14) so that everyone on the team feels heard. On technical rock routes, make sure you've talked about how you'll determine who leads what, so no one feels gypped or frustrated. Basically the bottom line is to communicate before you find yourself yelling at each other on a glacier.

ATTITUDE AND EGO: BEING A GOOD TEAM MEMBER

Sharing the load is really not that difficult especially when you've devised a system that allows for equality. Obviously the system needs to be flexible enough to accommodate changing needs, but starting with an outline goes a long way toward ensuring a smooth, functioning team. The other aspects of good expedition behavior are more nebulous and basically boil down to personality and attitude. It's tricky to know who is going to get along with whom especially when things deteriorate and you find yourself stormbound, lost, dealing with logistical nightmares, or in a dangerous predicament.

Ultimately the personalities of the members on your team play a critical role in successful expedition behavior. William Felps, who is a professor at the Rotterdam School of Management, studied the effect one person can have on workplace productivity. His dissertation— *How, When, Why Bad Apples Spoil the Barrel: A Theory of Destructive Group Members*—found that one negative individual *can* destroy group dynamics and result in team dysfunction. The trick is figuring out what a bad apple looks like before you put it into the barrel.

The basic "bad behaviors" Felps identified were: interpersonal deviants or individuals who are essentially jerks: abusive and insulting; slackers or individuals who do not contribute to the group or withhold effort from the common goal; and finally, depressives, whose negativity and pessimism bring down the entire team's morale and belief in itself. Conventional wisdom has held that groups usually overcome the power of individual personalities, but Felps' study revealed the opposite. In nearly all cases, he found teams that included a bad apple performed 30 to 40 percent worse than teams without, regardless of the makeup of the other individuals. Furthermore, Felps said that he was surprised to see that often the other team members began to assume many of the character traits of the so-called bad apple. He concluded that the best predictor of a team's performance is not its highest performing members, but its worst ones.

This information can be helpful when you are pulling together an expedition team. Being sensitive to the types of destructive behavior can help expedition leaders identify potential bad apples and prevent them from joining your team. These behaviors include things like teasing or insulting others; withdrawing from activity by sending text messages or reading during group functions; demonstrating negative body language like putting one's head down, sighing, or generally displaying a pessimistic attitude; and finding

Lending a helping hand goes a long way in being a good team member.

excuses for not participating or avoiding work. Often these bad apple behaviors can be funny or attractive in social settings at home—who hasn't teased someone or laughed at another's expense? Felps' findings, however, are striking in their insight into what may or may not allow a group to succeed. That one bad apple on your trip, especially if he or she is one of the most technically proficient or is a natural leader with a forceful personality, can bring everyone down.

Thinking back on all the weeks we've spent in the field on NOLS courses, we can pinpoint some bad apples who ruined both their experience and the experience of their course mates. There was the student who was too cool to show any enthusiasm, thereby making it uncool for everyone else to be excited; another whose sense of humor focused on insulting others, ultimately setting a cynical, sarcastic tone that pervaded all course communications; the girl who couldn't or wouldn't do her share around camp; and countless others who for whatever reason refused to give themselves fully to the expedition, thereby dooming its ultimate success. And the courses that succeeded? They were the ones where everyone wanted to be there, wanted to learn, and was willing to be open to the experience; the ones where people tried hard, laughed, and helped each other out.

Mike Lilygren, a Lander, Wyoming–based climber, went on a couple of climbing expeditions with the late Todd Skinner, a renowned rock climber who led expeditions around the world to free climb big walls. Mike says that what made Todd's leadership so effective was his ability to pull together teams that functioned well and had fun even when stuck for days by inclement weather, travel snafus, or other obstacles that slowed things down or stopped them altogether. Mike said that Todd sought people who were positive, hard workers and who believed in their ability to succeed. And they usually did, often against seemingly insurmountable odds.

"I remember the classic example of one of Todd's teams was on our Nameless Tower expedition in Pakistan," says Mike. "We were a fairly unimpressive lot, really, and then one of our key members, Steve Bechtel, got sick and had to go home because he wasn't getting better. Steve's brother had come along as a camp manager. He wasn't a climber, but he was really strong and had an incredible attitude. He ended up joining the climbing team up on the wall. At first he just hauled some loads, but then after watching us lead, he decided he wanted to do that as well. Jeff did his first lead ever 1,500 feet off the ground on a granite spire in Pakistan.

"You would never have picked Jeff to be part of the climbing team based on his technical skills, but he ended up being invaluable to us because of his attitude, work ethic, and selflessness. Those were the things Todd could see in people. Those were the things that made his teams work."

So it all comes back around to picking your team. Use the preexpedition questionnaire to find people's quirks, watch them at a party, go on a camping trip together, talk about personal goals and objectives, make sure your team comprises people with the personalities that lend themselves to success. And once you are on the expedition and the team is set, it's time to dig deep and practice good expedition behavior: work hard, collaborate, laugh, be there.

Molly Points Out Dangers Greater than a Crevasse Fall

We stopped on the glacier below a steep face that rose up above us for a thousand feet to the summit. Separated by 75 feet of rope, we had to yell to hear each other as we assessed the lines above. A narrow snow couloir that tapered into a thin line of ice looked appealing. The path was straightforward, and the snow free of divots or debris from rockfall. Aileen and I began debating the pros and cons, discussing our gear, and pondering our confidence with the potential difficulty of the lead. We ignored Lisa.

The three of us had been in Canada's Waddington Range for more than a week now and had climbed a number of routes successfully, but we had also been turned back on others by Lisa's uncertainty. She would become frightened by the exposure, tearful and unsure of her movement, and then often fall into questioning why she was with us and not back home with her boyfriend. Aileen and I had both lost our composure on climbs in the past—I'd hung off the rope countless times screaming at my husband for getting me into a scary predicament. So at first we were sympathetic to Lisa's plight. But at some point our patience had worn out and with it, our respect. We felt she was too often blinded by her fear, too unsure on snow and ice, too out of her element, so we no longer even bothered to ask her opinion.

Lisa had had enough. She yelled from the back of the rope, "I'm here too. Don't you even care what I think?"

We were silenced by her voice, embarrassed to answer her honestly, to say that no, we did not care what she thought. In fact, if we did say what was on our minds, we'd probably have to tell her that, at that point, we would prefer her to stay in camp the next day rather than to hamper our climb. Aileen managed to come up with some sort of answer, some tactful way of saying that of course we cared, but since Lisa hadn't been leading on snow or ice so far, we did not really expect her to have much of an opinion. I'm not sure where the conversation went from there. I know there were tears, raised voices, and awkward silences. I know the conversation quickly dove down into the murky depths of our friendship, our lives back home, our histories. All those fuzzy factors affect everyone's communication, judgment, and courage, and they color the way we view the world. All those factors are somewhat manageable in the comfort of our homes but can come out in surprising ways when we venture away from civilization in a small group of people.

Molly Points Out Dangers Greater than a Crevasse Fall

At some point in our quarreling we suddenly realized how ridiculous it was to stand there yelling at each other out on the ice separated by a long stretch of rope. We headed back to camp silently, dreading the inevitable conversation that was to come. Back at the tent, we dropped our packs and crowded into the snow kitchen. Aileen started the stove to boil water for hot drinks, and we sat quietly listening to the roar of the Whisperlite, waiting for someone to break the silence.

Finally Aileen asked if we wanted to talk. We spent most of the afternoon sipping tea and trying to sort through our conflicting emotions: ambition, guilt, anger, frustration, and hope. The three of us were friends, we had similar climbing abilities and experience, and we'd all been NOLS instructors for a number of years. Lisa was actually the best rock climber of the group, although she had less experience on snow and ice. But Aileen and I had seen her climb; seen her boldly lead hard sport routes and take lead falls with more composure than I, for one, ever managed to achieve on the sharp end. We assumed that boldness would translate well to the mountains.

And we knew the routine; we were NOLS course leaders after all. We sat down months before the expedition and talked about our goals, about how we were committed to starting slowly and building up our comfort level before tackling harder routes. We'd asked all the right questions of each other, said all the right things, and still, there we were, on the glacier at each other's throats.

As we talked, the tension eased, even though it was clear we needed to make significant changes in our agenda to bring the three of us to common ground. We realized our problem wasn't a failure to plan ahead, but simply a failure to implement a system for communicating effectively when things were not going as we hoped. Our silence came to a head for us that day, and we were forced to work through some tricky issues.

By evening we were joking again and had a plan to traverse a nearby, easy-looking peak the next day. We hoped this climb would allow us to have fun, work together, and reestablish our sense of team.

Ultimately, we succeeded. We spent another 10 days in the Waddington Range and climbed numerous named and unnamed peaks. We turned back on our ultimate objective—Mount Waddington—but only after reaching a consensus that we weren't up for going on. From camp we radioed our pilot to see about getting a lift out of the mountains. He asked if we could be ready in 20 minutes. We scrambled around frantically, breaking down camp and packing up hurriedly to be ready

---

Molly Points Out Dangers Greater than a Crevasse Fall

for his arrival. Then in a flurry of movement, the rushing roar of the helicopter, and a quick flight over the rugged, snow-capped mountains we were back down among trees, flowers, smells, water, and people. The trip was over and we were still friends. ■

Communication

Regardless of the care with which you pick your team, there is a very good chance that at some point on your expedition, some kind of conflict or tension will arise. It may be as simple as the escalating annoyance you feel over someone's quirky habits. It may be a misunderstanding over who was supposed to clean up the dishes. It may be as significant as a screaming argument over a route-finding decision. Your team, it is hoped, will have established some ground rules for conflict resolution well in advance of any all-out war. These rules—or better yet, tools—can help you take care of issues before they escalate into an expedition-threatening misunderstanding.

A crucial part of good expedition behavior is good communication among expedition members. There are thousands of gimmicks designed to help with effective communication. Some work, some don't, but one common denominator runs throughout: the critical importance of self-awareness. The most effective communicators—and the most effective team members—have a highly developed sense of themselves. They know their strengths and weaknesses; they are aware of their competencies and limitations; and they are able to critique themselves and accept feedback from others without feeling threatened.

That all sounds simple until you find yourself in a heated moment when it is all too easy to lose your temper and jump to conclusions. Or sometimes your perceptions are colored by boredom, homesickness, or a burning desire to get out of the tent and moving.

There are tricks to circumvent these kinds of emotional traps, and hokey as it may sound, you may want to share something called the Awareness Wheel with your teammates before you ever

Awareness Wheel

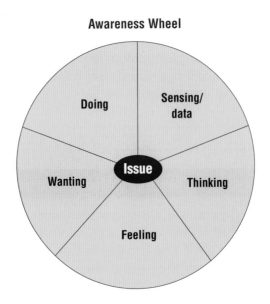

leave town. The Awareness Wheel is a system for dealing with an issue or conflict. It breaks down your reaction to an issue into five categories: sensing, thinking, feeling, wanting, doing. The key to looking at a problem through this lens is that is forces you to examine what is actually happening, what is real, and then to separate those facts from what is entirely in your head.

HOW TO TALK TO EACH OTHER

One key to initiating potentially challenging conversations—and a critical part of effective communication—is using "I" statements. Starting from your personal vantage point forces you to take ownership for your part of a conflict and helps avoid the finger pointing that can result in a defensive response from your teammates.

It also can help to establish a routine check-in time. This may be an informal conversation about the day that takes place over dinner, or if your team is big and you don't know each other well, you may choose to have a more structured debriefing time. Such conversations can feel awkward, especially at first, but they help put a structure into place that gives everyone a venue for sharing his or her feelings and thoughts when and if it becomes necessary to deal with interpersonal issues.

Molly Knows a Sigh Is Just a Sigh

By day five of waiting out a storm in a tent high on the mountain on an expedition to Mount Logan in Canada, I was sure my tent mate James was sighing heavily every few minutes just to annoy me. I found myself tensing up, waiting for his next deep breath, confident that he was timing it to set my nerves on edge. Of course, his sighs may have been in response to my constant fidgeting as I tried to make myself comfortable after hours of lying prone inside my clammy sleeping bag. I was convinced that James was sighing to get at me, not because he was bored, sick of being in the tent, ready to be home, or maybe just had something in his throat. Using the Awareness Wheel, I broke down my perceptions and came up with an appropriate action: What I *sensed* was simply the sound of James' sighing loudly and frequently. I *thought* James may have been making the noise on purpose to annoy me, and it made me *feel* angry and annoyed. I *wanted* James to stop. So what could I *do*?

I quickly realized that I was being absurd. James wasn't trying to make me crazy; I was just feeling crazy because I was bored. A solution isn't always that easy: People's feelings may be hurt; someone may be angry or upset for good reason; the expedition may be in jeopardy; and life-threatening hazards may be involved. In these situations, having an effective tool for communicating becomes even more important. ■

Summary

So what makes a good team member? Most successful expeditions say it is a combination of attitude and effort and an absence of ego. Effort is the easiest part of the equation, especially if you define each team member's roles and duties. Attitude and absence of ego are more subtle character traits, but in the end they are probably the more important factors in determining your ultimate success. Don't underestimate the power of personality on your experience; just because you know someone climbs 5.13 and can run for miles and miles does not mean he or she will be a better expedition

A successful expedition group comes together to check in and includes all participants in a group decision.

member than an individual like Jeff Bechtel, who went from base camp manager to climbing team member based on his selflessness, adaptability, and work ethic. And it may be fine to head out into the mountains with your spouse or longtime climbing partner without explicitly discussing expedition behavior or communication, but as the size of your team grows and the intimacy of the relationships between members decreases, it helps to create some kind of clear system for sharing the load and communicating effectively as well as to agree on what it means to have good EB.

16 | RISK MANAGEMENT

Many people find wilderness adventures exhilarating and enjoy pursuing outdoor activities in the natural world. Activities like climbing, whitewater boating, skiing, and expeditioning can enliven your experience and add an element of thrill and accomplishment. Part of the enjoyment comes from the challenge of managing risk, controlling fear, and succeeding at difficult tasks.

We seek out risk to test ourselves, to feel the adrenaline rush, to do something few others have done, to work with a team or partner to overcome odds, to have an exciting adventure, or simply because it is fun. We don't want the experience to be too easy or safe. The hazards we encounter in the wild present risks—risks that are inherent in the activities we are pursuing. These risks need to be managed because we don't want to find ourselves in situations where we might get hurt or die because we weren't prepared or aware. To face the risks of a wilderness expedition without forethought and preparation is irresponsible not only to yourself, but also to your teammates and your loved ones back home.

To be a responsible wilderness traveler, you need to identify hazards and understand the risks. Your team's survival comes first and foremost, but you must also continuously evaluate the situation and either manage or avoid danger in order to mitigate the potential for injury while attempting to achieve the expedition's goals. You may not be able to stop the lightning from striking in the high peaks on a summer afternoon, but you can mitigate the risk by getting off the mountain early enough in the day to avoid areas where lightning is most likely to strike.

Molly's Balancing Act

I stood waiting for an all-clear signal, leaning forward on my ski poles, relaxed, enjoying the winter scenery. Around me snow weighed down the fir trees with heavy blobs that fell off unexpectedly as the temperatures rose and the day warmed.

Pete had skied ahead of me. The slope rolled away steeply below, and I could not see him once he disappeared over the top. We'd skied the run once already that day and were back, looking for fresh lines.

Suddenly I heard Pete yell, "Avalanche!"

My stomach lurched. This was it. I'd trained for avalanche rescue, had practiced searching for victims with beacons, had probed through snow trying to locate buried bags meant to feel like people trapped in the debris, but I'd never actually searched for a real person in a real avalanche. I had never performed under the pressure of the ticking clock, driven by the desperate knowledge that each second that passed decreased someone's chances of surviving. And now that someone was my husband. It was up to me. I felt sick, weak with fear as I tried to remember how long you could live without oxygen. Four minutes until suffocation? Four minutes to save Pete's life?

I skied up to the rollover and looked down the slope. The powdery blanket of snow we'd been skiing was gone; below me was an icy base layer over which the avalanche had slid. The slide was small, maybe 40 feet across, but the snow had piled up in the creek bottom in a classic terrain trap. I turned my transceiver to search and started sliding down the ice, trying to control my panic, trying to focus on the blinking red numbers indicating Pete's position in relation to my own. Then I saw movement. Pete's gloved hand was exposed, sticking out above the snow below, moving. He was alive, and I knew where to go to dig him out. I felt like laughing with relief.

I had Pete's head out of the snow in a matter of seconds. The avalanche debris was relatively soft, so I was able to dig easily and he was close to the surface. It took us longer to get his feet and skis unburied, but within 10 minutes or so, the two of us were sitting in the debris, looking up at the slope above, wondering where we'd gone wrong.

It wasn't hard to pick out a few of our errors. Pete told me that he had been bummed when on the last run he'd missed out on precious turns because he'd

Molly's Balancing Act

been checking the snow's stability with ski cuts that traversed the fall line. He said it had annoyed him when, after making his way carefully and slowly to the bottom, I'd followed, enjoying a sweet run straight down the slope through untracked powder. He wanted some good turns as well, so on his second run, he dove into the heart of the slope and skied the fall line. He ignored the fact that we were more exposed on our second drop, skiing a steep but short line that faced slightly more west than our first run.

Pete had not mentioned his frustration to me before he took off for the second run, so I was oblivious that he'd felt a little gypped on his first descent. I assumed he was checking out the second slope as well. That was the role he usually took when we went out. I conferred with him and offered my opinion when it came to decisions, but he was the leader and I usually followed him without much question. I don't think we ever really thought much about the hierarchy of our relationship. It was just the way we operated.

As we made our way back to the car after the avalanche, the snow collapsed twice on us in great rippling whumps. We both knew that sound told of an unstable snowpack, but we had not felt any prior to the avalanche. Now the temperature was rising and the snowpack seemed to be heaving and sighing in response to the weight of the warming. We hadn't noticed the temperature change before we skied either.

We had done a few things right, however. Only one of us was on the slope at the time of the avalanche. We both carried the appropriate gear and were trained to use it. But we'd neglected the very real human component of our decision-making. We wanted to ski. We wanted to have fun. We'd driven a couple of hours that morning to reach the mountains; we'd skinned up 2,000 feet; we'd worked hard to put ourselves in position to ski. It was the weekend, our only chance to get out until next Saturday rolled around. We had already been turned away from one slope, not because of avalanche concerns but because the snow was crusty and heavy and the skiing more work than fun.

All these things came together to put extra pressure on our desire, allowing us to ignore the normal protocol, turn off our brains, and jump onto the slope when a more-thorough assessment of the conditions would have revealed the instability. ■

Understanding Risk

What exactly is risk? The definition we'll use is "exposure to hazard or danger." That seems pretty straightforward, but it becomes less clear when we have to evaluate what that exposure means to us individually or for the group and when we have to draw conclusions about how the risk may affect our expedition. Generally we think of risk as exposure to a hazard or danger that might result in a loss, but this exposure can also result in a gain, like obtaining your sought-after objective. We risk in order to gain, but with possibility of losing.

Hazards are the threats—the potentially dangerous or unsafe conditions—you can expect to encounter in the course of your expedition. There are two categories of hazards: Environmental or objective hazards are those elements of nature that we cannot change such as natural features and forces. Environmental hazards include obvious dangers such as rockfall, avalanches, steep terrain, snow and ice, unpredictable weather, moving water, and potentially harmful flora or fauna. The risks of these hazards are that they can hurt, maim, or even kill you.

Human or subjective hazards are more nebulous and include things like experiences, attitudes, habits, states of mind, and physical and cognitive abilities. Each of us has our own perceptions and understanding of what a hazard or danger is and how it may or may not affect us. We also have our own individual tolerance of hazards and dangers. The human factors influence how we see the world and the situations we're in and how we respond.

The interplay of natural hazards and our perception and personal tolerance of the risk are the basis of risk management. Simply put, a river is just a river until you decide you need to wade across. It then becomes a potential hazard that presents the risk of drowning, and you need to consider the characteristics of the river and the physical and emotional states of everyone in the group. This interplay between objective factors and subjective factors is referred to as the Risk Management Equation (see the Venn diagram). When the factors overlap, they create a potential for risk; in some cases the overlap is great and the potential for risk is great, and in others the overlap is small and the risk potential is low.

Risk management really boils down to making decisions based on your understanding and perceptions of the people you are with and environment you are in. This understanding and perception can often be uncertain, so risk management in its simplest form is the ability to make a decision when the outcome is uncertain. To manage risk effectively, you must recognize the hazards and understand their potential consequences and then make a decision based on your perception of the likelihood of harm. The uncertainty comes from the potential that you may not fully understand the situation; did you assess the risk fully and will you or your team execute the necessary technique properly to manage the risk?

A key element to expedition planning is to adequately prepare to manage risk. You need to research the objective hazards you may encounter and decide if the expedition has the gear—and if the team has the skills—to manage the risk. You also need to foster communication among all team members so they respect and understand one another's attitude toward risk. And you need to develop an emergency action plan to cope with emergencies. Together these elements form the basis of your risk management plan.

Possible Objective or Environmental Hazards

In many ways, objective hazards are the easiest part of the risk management equation to assess. Do your research before leaving on your expedition so you are prepared for the potential related hazards and risks. Here are some of the most likely hazards:

- Moving water
- Rockfall and icefall
- Glacier travel

- Avalanche
- Animals
- Funguses and parasites

Possible Subjective Hazards or Human Factors

Recognizing and understanding human emotions and their effects on judgment is one step in mitigating their impact on behavior, especially in association with risk management. The following human factors can affect your group:

- Complacency
- Overconfidence or hubris
- Distraction
- Differing perceptions of risk
- Risk tolerance
- Expectations and peer pressure
- Fatigue, stress
- Trying to adhere to a schedule
- Expedition culture
- Lack or loss of situational awareness

For more specifics on objective and subjective hazards, see *Risk Management for Outdoor Leaders*, by Drew Leemon and Tod Schimelpfenig, available at www.nols.edu/store.

Expedition Risk Management Plan

Preparing a risk management plan organizes and documents your research and preparation for managing risk on your expedition. The plan can be simple but should address the four elements of risk management talked about already: potential hazards, group skills, group tolerance, and emergency preparedness. A risk management plan can serve as a way for all team members to come to agreement on these issues.

1. *Research all objective hazards intrinsic to your objective.* This includes everything from understanding the terrain, weather,

There are many ways to reduce the risk of moving water: river crossing techniques, using natural and man-made bridges, finding a way around, or building a tyrolean traverse. All of these options are contingent upon your skill base and equipment, so choose wisely!

Like moving water, glacier crevasses require good judgment to navigate. Natural bridges or finding an alternate route are usually more ideal than simply jumping over a chasm.

and environmental conditions you will encounter on your route to knowing the resources you have available in the event of an accident.

- What are the hazards inherent in our objective? Can they be avoided?
- Do we have the equipment, experience, and training to manage the hazards?
- What weather patterns can we expect to encounter?

2. *As a team, discuss your attitude toward risk and come up with a "team culture" or unified approach toward hazards.* Make sure you have adequate experience and training to achieve your desired goals, and be sure that everyone agrees with what is and what is not acceptable. Since different people have different values/attitudes toward risk, someone who is not a risk taker would probably not do well on an expedition with someone who needs or likes a high degree of risk.

- Why are you on this trip and what is your number one goal?
- What is your perception of risk?
- Do you take pride in suffering and epics?
- Does the difficulty of the objective usurp your desire for enjoyment?
- Is there financial or public pressure to succeed?

3. *Take time prior to setting out on your expedition to discuss the tools you intend to use for assessing risk with your team.* Deciding *how* you plan to make the decision to turn around on a climb or portage around a rapid is best made in the comfort of your home, not when the sun is setting and you have nowhere to bivy. Rules provide a framework for making decisions. Keep in mind, though, that rules can also be limiting when context changes. For example, backcountry skiers conform to the notion that avalanches are most common during or after storms, so they avoid hazardous terrain following a big dump. When you are attempting to climb a mountain, however, the windows following storms are often the only time you can move upward, so the rule that says stay home until the snow stabilizes is not useful for guiding behavior in this situation.

At NOLS, many instructors use heuristics or rules of thumb to help them make decisions about hazards. A classic heuristic is to make an alpine start. Climbers around the world begin their ascents well before dawn to avoid being caught in afternoon thunderstorms high on an exposed peak and to be back to camp before dark. Heuristics can also be mnemonic devices that help you remember the various factors you need to consider when assessing any given situation. Whatever tools your team decides on, make sure everyone understands and agrees on the process.

4. *Develop protocols and procedures for dealing with emergency situations*, which include identifying leadership roles, planning for media coverage, and devising contingency plans. Clarify your decision-making process in the event of an accident.
- Do expedition members need to know specific rescue skills?
- Do you have first-aid training and supplies?
    First-aid kit contents: Are there prescription medications? Are there instructions for the medications? Is any specific

Be bear aware! No matter what area of the world you're traveling in, know the wildlife you may encounter and the risks associated with each.

training necessary, such as for injecting medications? Are specific treatment protocols necessary for treating injuries and illness specific to your destination?

First-aid/medical training: Is everyone trained in wilderness medicine? Is there an expedition doctor?

Evacuation guidelines: What criteria will be used for initiating an evacuation? (Evacuating for some illnesses and injuries is obvious, others less so.)

- Is outside help available? Where is it? What evacuation resources are available (e.g., private, military, land-managing agency)? Do they need to be notified in advance that you may need to call them for evacuation assistance?
- How strong is your team? Can you rescue yourselves? Is this your only evacuation option? Is any specific evacuation gear necessary (e.g., litters, backboards, etc.)?
- Who do you contact in the event of an emergency? What are your emergency communication/notification procedures? Who will you contact for help and how?
- Who talks to the media?

Planning for Emergencies

Awareness of the factors that can lead to accidents is an important step in preventing accidents from happening on your expedition, but the fact is, accidents can happen in spite of your preparation and training. Responsible expedition planning includes developing contingency plans that outline how you will respond if things go wrong. If an expedition member suffers a serious injury, say a broken leg, you will use your emergency plan to guide how you treat and evacuate the injured person. A contingency plan guides whether the expedition will continue, end, or seek another goal. Planning in advance helps the team make more effective decisions while in the field. The old saying, plan for the worst and hope for the best, has logic to it.

An emergency plan lays out the following considerations:

GROUP CAPACITY
- Do you have the technical and medical training necessary to stabilize and evacuate an injured team member?
- Do you have enough people to implement an evacuation?
- What individual skills and training do you have on your team that may prove helpful in an emergency?

OUTSIDE RESOURCES
- Who is responsible for rescue in the area?
- Are there helicopters, technical rescue teams, or paramedical support available?
- How do you get help?

COMMUNICATION
- How far are you from help?
- Do you have the technical ability to communicate with outside resources (satphones, cell phones)? If not, where is the nearest phone, dwelling, or town where you might find help?
- Do you have names, addresses, and telephone numbers for outside resources?

SOAP note template

Name_____ Date _____

Subjective (age, sex, chief complaint, OPQRST, MOI/HPI).

_____

_____

_____

Objective (Describe position found. Describe injuries).

_____

_____

_____

Patient Exam
  Vital Signs _____
  TIME _____   LOC _____
  HR _____   RR _____
  SCTM _____
  Pupils _____   Temp _____

History
  Symptoms _____
  Allergies_____
  Medications _____
  Pertinent medical history _____

  _____

  Last intake/output _____
  Events leading to the incident/illness _____

  _____

Assessment

_____

_____

_____

Plan
  Anticipated problems _____

  _____

Know how to use and report emergency medical situations with a
SOAP (subjective, objective, assessment, plan) note.

Calling out on a satellite phone in Mongolia. A communication plan and the necessary equipment to carry out that plan are vital to risk management in the event of an emergency while on an expedition.

CARING FOR YOUR TEAM AND THE INJURED PARTY

- How will you stabilize your patient, assess injuries, and develop a plan for caring for him or her until help comes? Do you have forms to help guide your treatment (see SOAP note template on page 232)?
- How will you get help? Are you sending someone out to fetch resources? Do you have a travel plan and supplies to support the team (food, water, extra clothing, marked maps)?

EVACUATION CONSIDERATIONS

- How badly is the injured party hurt? Does the injury threaten life or limb?
- What is the condition of the rest of the group? Was personal gear or team equipment lost or damaged?
- What are your evacuation options: walking, skiing, horses, helicopters, snow machines, vehicles, or boats?
- How far are you from vehicle transport? How long will it take for you to get there? Do you need to travel through the night?
- How difficult is the terrain? Are there obstacles that you need to overcome (river crossings, steep terrain) to reach your destination? Do you need special equipment?

- What's the weather like? Could it slow, stop, or delay your plan?
- How strong is your team? Do they have the physical and mental stamina and technical ability to implement your evacuation plan?
- If helicopter rescue is an option, is there a suitable landing zone? Could weather preclude flying? If so, what is your backup plan?

SERIOUS INJURY OR FATALITY PROTOCOL

- Who do you need to contact in the event of a serious injury or death? Who will notify the family?
- What documentation is required by law in the country you are in?
- Who will deal with the media?
- If expeditioning in a foreign country, do you have the phone number of the U.S. embassy or consulate? Their help will be critical in the event of a serious injury or death.

Serious injury, illnesses, and fatalities are emotionally stressful. Clear expectations, effective communication, and the delegation of tasks are essential to managing the crisis in the best interests of the victim, the family, and your team.

Summary

In some ways, risk management is simply a matter of common sense. Take precautions, don't rush into things, do your research, and use your judgment and you can avoid many of the dangers that lurk around the corner. But you can't avoid everything. Understanding risk and developing an emergency plan help you prepare and respond effectively when things go wrong. Unfortunately, all too often groups go out into the wilderness without giving any thought to problems and as a result get into even more trouble trying to deal with an unforeseen incident than the initial incident itself. Be prepared. Talk about the risks involved in your trip. Write up an emergency plan. And all your preparation, it is hoped, will be for nothing.

DEALING WITH ADVERSITY AND UNCERTAINTY

You plan your expedition for months. You buy or borrow all the necessary gear, study your maps, save your pennies, and talk to the right people. You dot all your i's and cross all your t's, but still, sometimes you fail. The weather doesn't cooperate; your team never coalesces; the hazard is too great; the route too hard; someone gets hurt; you get sick. The list goes on and on. Regardless of how well you plan, expeditions don't always turn out as you hope. Dealing with the unexpected—with adversity and failure—is a critical skill for anyone who ventures into the wilderness where situations are never within our control. Those who learn to tolerate or even thrive on challenge are the ones who succeed in the end, whether they salvage their expedition and manage to achieve their objective in spite of everything or they laugh off their failure and set it aside as fodder for their next adventure.

Traits of a Survivor

Adventurers who achieve the most success are tough, tenacious, and able to endure incredible hardship and discomfort. That said, there are many levels of adversity and uncertainty. You don't have to take on the extremes of Antarctica or the Himalaya to have a challenging wilderness experience. No matter how modest your objective, the fact is that in the wild you cannot control the weather, you are far from help, and there are objective hazards that are unavoidable almost anywhere you go. This means that if you choose to go to wild places routinely, at some point you will be faced with some kind of adversity. It's not a matter of if, but when.

Josh Beckner digging into thick brush while navigating the Piritas Valley, Argentina.

What enables someone to function in such difficult situations? Psychologists have identified several key attributes in people who have survived harrowing experiences. These attributes include:

Curiosity: Survivors look for new possibilities and seek to learn from their situation. They ask questions and consider options. Survivors believe they can learn from both the positive and negative experiences in life.

Optimism: Survivors are willing to appreciate and find humor in tough situations. They are optimists, and their attitude rubs off on those around them.

Mental and emotional flexibility: Survivors are both serious and playful, gentle and tough, unpredictable and consistent, proud and humble. In other words, they are not just one way. They can bend and change according to the demands of their situation.

Will: Survivors have tenacity. They believe they can and will endure difficult situations and look for ways to get out of danger when it arises. They are not paralyzed by fear when accidents happen or tragedy strikes, nor do they allow themselves to become helpless victims waiting for rescue from an outside source.

For expeditions, these attributes are useful to bear in mind. Attitudes have a profound effect on morale, so the positive influence of one or two people who exhibit survivor characteristics in the face of adversity can help salvage an expedition, especially one that hits a bump in the road. That said, negative behavior can be equally, if not more, influential (see chapter 15 for more on the "bad apple" theory), especially if there is no positive force to counter the drain.

When you choose to go forth into a challenging situation such as an expedition, part of your responsibility to your team is to be resilient, positive, and flexible. The New York Yankees longtime manager, Joe Torre, writes, "Competing at the highest level is not about winning. It is about preparation, courage, understanding, and nurturing your people. Winning is the result."

Right: Marilyn Funk embracing the rime on Mount Washington in New Hampshire.

Below: Dave bivying on Mount Hooker in the Wind River Range in Wyoming.

Tent-bound due to weather—a great way to test your threshold for adversity.

The same can be said for successful expeditions. There are too many unknowns, too many factors beyond your control in the wilderness to ever guarantee your success, but mental and physical tenacity and preparation can allow you to, at a minimum, survive and, at a maximum, succeed.

Molly Versus Mount Logan

Day six of the storm. I lay in my sleeping bag, staring at the checkered pattern in the yellow ripstop dome over my head. "How many squares are there?" I wondered listlessly, trying to figure out a way to calculate the total. Next to me, James sighed and rolled over.

"Is it time to eat yet?" he asked. I looked at my watch. We'd eaten a little over an hour ago, and given our dwindling supplies, we should probably hold off a while before eating again.

"Too soon. Shall we see if Deb and Phil want to play cribbage?"

Molly Versus Mount Logan

"Sure. I have to pee; I'll get up and ask them."

James struggled out of his sleeping bag and began piling on layers. The wind shook the tent, sending snow sliding down the sides like sand. We had to dig out every few hours to keep from being buried. I couldn't tell how much snow was coming from the clouds and how much was blowing over the glacier, pooling up behind our walls. We thought the walls would protect us from the force of the blast, but instead we'd created an eddy that filled up with snow as quickly as we emptied it. We experimented with the wall's height and shape, trying to build a wedge on the outside to act like a snow fence, forcing the wind to drop its load before it settled around the tents, but most of our efforts were futile. And anyway, the digging gave us something to do, some exercise, a reason to get out of our sleeping bags.

The trip had hit a series of bumps. We'd been stuck in Kluane Lake for a week waiting to fly into the mountains to begin the expedition. Every day, the pilot took off with two climbers who'd been waiting even longer, and every day they had returned—the passengers looking green and frightened. I was grateful they were the guinea pigs. Flying scared me enough as it was; I really did not want to go up with the pilot to "check things out" and see if we could slip through some risky weather window. Finally, however, there had been a break, and all the waiting expeditions had been able to fly into their separate peaks, including us. We were headed for Mount Logan, Canada's highest mountain.

We'd moved up slowly at first, working to get used to each other and to figure out our systems. Gradually things had been gelling, and for five days we made steady progress up the glacier. Then the storm struck, stranding us at King Col.

For the most part, we'd been doing okay with our forced layover. Food was our best diversion, and our cooking had grown increasingly elaborate as the hours passed. We'd played endless games of cribbage, hearts, and gin. We shared our books and read aloud to each other. We shoveled and built walls to protect our camp. And we lay in our bags silently, hour after hour, our bodies growing weary and sore from the lack of exercise.

On the sixth day of inactivity, the weather seemed to moderate. In places, the endless sea of white broke apart, giving us a glimpse of the surrounding peaks before closing up again. We were optimistic the breaks meant a change and staked out our clammy sleeping bags to dry. I'm not sure how long James' bag had been out, when suddenly Deb yelled.

"Your bag, James, quick it's flying away!"

Molly Versus Mount Logan

James looked up from his shoveling in time to see the red mummy bag lift off. The wind carried it a few feet, and then dropped it back down to the ground where is slid along the snow for a moment before a gust picked the bag up into the air and blew it out of sight. We stared at each other in disbelief.

"I'm sure we can find it," I said. "It's probably down the glacier a bit in some kind of natural eddy. Let's go look."

Visibility had lifted enough that leaving camp for a quick scout seemed reasonable. James and I roped up and headed out, full of hope that the bag would be discovered close to camp. We had not traveled far before our optimism faded. The glacier was vast and featureless. We were looking for a needle. After an hour, the weather began to close in on us, and we turned back to camp. Deb and Phil knew by our faces that we'd failed.

That night James wrapped himself in everyone's insulated jackets and slept the best he could, but the temperatures plummeted as the storm moved out and the skies cleared. I could hear him shivering most of the night.

The next morning the skies were blue and the white snow dazzling. Mountains and fields of snow and ice stretched away from us in all directions. After the claustrophobia of the storm's whiteout, the expansive view was overwhelming. We cooked in silence, until Deb finally broached the unspoken.

"What are we going to do?" she asked.

James admitted that the sleeping system he'd tried out the night before had not been adequate. He wasn't prepared to continue moving up if that was all he had for warmth. We tossed around ideas: Deb and Phil could share a bag and James could use one of theirs. We could try to find more layers for James. Maybe if three of us slept in one tent it would be warmer. But there wasn't a lot of enthusiasm in our voices. Finally Phil said it.

"We could just go down," he said.

We'd been planning this expedition for months. I remember flipping through old magazines and American Alpine Club journals looking at pictures of Mount Logan, reading descriptions of people's trips, dreaming of our own. There were many accounts of people turning back due to weather. In fact, I remember thinking more people failed than succeeded on the mountain, even those attempting the fairly straightforward King Trench route that we were on. But failure had not occurred to me. I believed we'd succeed. But now it became clear that we were heading home, defeated by the weather, the time, and a little bad luck. ∎

How Do You Decide to Turn Around?

If you ask some people what happened on Mount Everest in 1996 when eight climbers ended up dying high on the mountain, they will say the teams failed to turn around at their prescribed turn-around time. That's an easy answer that fails to include all the nuances that go into making such a decision, but there's something tangible about it that is attractive. We want concrete answers. It makes life much easier.

But face it, deciding to abort your expedition when the final objective is close is rarely a black-and-white call, especially when you consider all the factors that color our decision: money, sponsorships, time, honor, peer pressure. For these reasons, having something defined—such as a specific time—can make your decision easier, if you are able to abide by that guideline.

Morning coffee goes a long way in bracing yourself for adversity and uncertainty. God forbid if that uncertainty is whether or not you remembered to pack your coffee, though.

The story of Everest illustrates that a time guideline is no guarantee against tragedy, but if used correctly, it should force your team to stop and make a decision about the wisdom of continuing. It's never easy to quit. No one wants to decide to head home only to get partway down the mountain and have the weather clear, but you cannot second-guess yourself. A popular expression that we hear at NOLS captures the ambiguity of making the decision to quit: "Wimp to wimp again." No one wants to be a wimp, but we all understand that sometimes it is the wisest course of action.

When Should You Turn Around?

Considerations include:
- Time
- Weather
- Fatigue
- Food and water
- Hazards
- Willpower
- Consequences

Do We Jinx Ourselves by Considering Failure?

We seem to have some societal taboos against discussing the possibility of failure. Coaches rarely talk to their teams about how to lose graciously, and most of us don't enter a test having thought through how we will react if we do not pass. It's almost as if we think talking about bad things makes them more likely to happen.

We know rationally that this is not the case, but the stigma remains powerfully entrenched in our culture, so it takes some courage to sit down and talk to your expedition mates about how you plan to deal with failure should it happen. But make the effort. It may make your decision-making easier in the long run if you understand where people are coming from.

Embrace those moments when everything turns out as planned, and be determined to find the fun and silver lining during those moments when it does not.

Having Fun

Why do we go on expeditions? In the end, isn't it to have fun? We've demeaned the word fun so that it carries a note of frivolity, but in reality the adventure and the camaraderie of an expedition is rooted in the joy it brings you. So when the storm sets in and you are bored to tears by your book, remember to find humor in your predicament. Remember to laugh and not take yourself too seriously. Humor is a great way to endure, even thrive, in a challenging situation. It is also one of the best ways to deal with failure. If you can come back from a monthlong expedition where you spent most of your time tent-bound, having never seen the mountain you hoped to climb, and still say you had a good time, then your expedition succeeded.

18 | LEAVE NO TRACE

In the 1960s, America discovered backpacking. Several things happened to instigate the boom. Equipment had evolved so the experience was less physically painful; the recently signed Wilderness Act drew attention to the nation's wild places; and a growing number of people across the country had become enamored with the idea of rediscovering nature. Since 1965, wilderness use has exploded by more than 600 percent. But the natural world is not well suited to having hordes of people descend upon its fragile beauty. Impacts began to be seen in popular backcountry destinations early on: large stretches of bare ground surrounded campsites; trees were stripped of their lower branches as high as one could reach; toilet paper peeked out from under rocks; fire pits filled with trash dotted lakeshores; and multiple trails snaked their way across damp meadows in many of the nation's wild places.

The Forest Service began searching for ways to educate the public and minimize visitor impacts early in the 1970s, and gradually other federal land management agencies followed in its footsteps. NOLS had been practicing minimum-impact camping from its early days. For example, courses used to cook solely on fires while in the mountains. To mitigate the effect of these fires, we'd carefully remove the sod surface when we dug a pit, tend the displaced plants throughout our stay, and replace the vegetation plug when we departed to camouflage the site as well as possible. NOLS courses spread out their campsites and packed out their trash. We hiked in small groups. These practices were mainly based on intuition, so in 1986 the school began to collect scientific evidence of their efficacy.

NOLS Soft Paths: How to Enjoy the Wilderness without Harming It was a collaborative effort by NOLS and the Forest Service to back up minimum-impact camping practices with a scientific rationale. Written by Bruce Hampton and David Cole, the book was first published in 1988, and it quickly became a kind of backpacker's bible. Now going into its fourth edition, *Soft Paths* was one of the first efforts to provide backcountry users with a code of ethics to guide their camping practices.

This same time period was marked by the formation of Leave No Trace Inc., now the Leave No Trace Center for Outdoor Ethics. Originally a partnership between the federal land management agencies and NOLS, Leave No Trace has evolved into an independent nonprofit dedicated to spreading the minimum-impact message to outdoor recreationalists.

The idea behind Leave No Trace is to provide users with a set of principles—rather than rules and regulations—to guide their decision-making and prevent unnecessary impacts to the natural world and other backcountry visitors. The seven basic principles of Leave No Trace are:

PLAN AHEAD AND PREPARE
- Know the regulations and special concerns for the area you'll visit.
- Prepare for extreme weather, hazards, and emergencies.
- Schedule your trip to avoid times of high use.
- Visit in small groups when possible. Consider splitting larger groups into smaller groups.
- Repackage food to minimize waste.
- Use a map and compass to eliminate the use of marking paint, rock cairns, or flagging.

TRAVEL AND CAMP ON DURABLE SURFACES
- Durable surfaces include established trails and campsites, rock, gravel, dry grasses, or snow.
- Protect riparian areas by camping at least 200 feet from lakes and streams.
- Good campsites are found, not made. Altering a site is not necessary.

Both sand and snow are examples of durable terrain that bounces back quickly after human presence.

In popular areas:

- Concentrate use on existing trails and campsites.
- Walk single file in the middle of the trail, even when wet or muddy.
- Keep campsites small. Focus activity in areas where vegetation is absent.

In pristine areas:

- Disperse use to prevent the creation of campsites and trails.
- Avoid places where impacts are just beginning.

DISPOSE OF WASTE PROPERLY

- Pack it in, pack it out. Inspect your campsite and rest areas for trash or spilled foods. Pack out all trash, leftover food, and litter.
- Deposit solid human waste in catholes dug 6 to 8 inches deep at least 200 feet from water, camp, and trails. Cover and disguise the cathole when finished.
- Pack out toilet paper and hygiene products.
- To wash yourself or your dishes, carry water 200 feet away from streams or lakes and use small amounts of biodegradable soap. Scatter strained dishwater.

LEAVE WHAT YOU FIND

- Preserve the past: Examine, but do not touch, cultural or historic structures and artifacts.
- Leave rocks, plants, and other natural objects as you find them.
- Avoid introducing or transporting nonnative species.
- Do not build structures, furniture, or dig trenches.

Calafate berries in Patagonia, South America. Be mindful of how many you gather, others may rely on them as well.

MINIMIZE CAMPFIRE IMPACTS

- Campfires can cause lasting impacts to the backcountry. Use a lightweight stove for cooking and enjoy a candle lantern for light.
- Where fires are permitted, use established fire rings, fire pans, or mound fires.
- Keep fires small. Only use sticks from the ground that can be broken by hand.
- Burn all wood and coals to ash, put out campfires completely, and then scatter cool ashes.

RESPECT WILDLIFE

- Observe wildlife from a distance. Do not follow or approach them.
- Never feed animals. Feeding wildlife damages their health, alters natural behaviors, and exposes them to predators and other dangers.

Whether big or small, respect wildlife.

- Protect wildlife and your food by storing rations and trash securely.
- Control pets at all times, or leave them at home.
- Avoid wildlife during sensitive times: mating, nesting, raising young, or winter.

BE CONSIDERATE OF OTHER VISITORS

- Respect other visitors and protect the quality of their experience.
- Be courteous. Yield to other users on the trail.
- Step to the downhill side of the trail when encountering pack animals.
- Take breaks and camp away from trails and other visitors.
- Let nature's sounds prevail. Avoid loud voices and noises.

Molly's Reality Check

We had been hiking for several hours up a rough drainage in the Talkeetna Mountains of Alaska. It was my first NOLS course as an instructor, and I remember the thrill of discovery my hiking group felt as we worked our way up a narrow rock chasm. We could see no signs of people, no footprints or old trails, no trash, nothing but pristine tundra, and the rocky defile through which we sought a way.

We were three weeks into the course and deep in the mountains. None of us had heard any other NOLS courses hiking up this particular drainage. On the map it appeared to lead to a dead end. Steep peaks surrounded the top of the valley, and it was unclear whether we'd be able to cross the divide into the next drainage without climbing gear. Since we weren't carrying any equipment, we thought we might have to circle back and find another way to reach our destination; nonetheless, we were excited to try what seemed like a new route.

We talked ourselves into believing we were the first to visit the valley, and that belief added excitement to our exploration. The route included a third-class scramble through a narrow slot and over some rugged boulders, and then suddenly the

Molly's Reality Check

valley opened up before us into Shangri-la. A smooth, grassy meadow covered with cream-colored avens and white bell heather spread in front of us. The creek lazed its way through the meadow, meandering in great looping turns with sandy beaches in the inside of the curves. Above us, the mountains circled, covered with snow and jagged rocks, creating a formidable rampart against the outside.

We felt as if we'd discovered our own secret garden, and all of us were moved by the sense of wonder and awe the discovery generated. And then, as I was setting up my tent, I came upon a discarded cardboard toilet paper roll. The find brought the outside world crashing in on me. I hadn't realized how much of my excitement came from my belief that we were the first to stumble upon the hidden valley. I had convinced myself no one had been there before because we'd seen no sign of another's passing, and in the fragile tundra, masking your passage can be challenging. Now I stood with evidence that shattered my illusion. The valley was still beautiful, but my experience of it had shifted. ■

Adapting Leave No Trace to International Travel

The seven basic LNT principles were originally written for wilderness areas, or places with no human habitation, where, according to the U.S. Wilderness Act definition, people are visitors who do not remain. However, many of us travel overseas on expeditions, and most of the world's mountainous regions have been inhabited by humans for thousands of years. Therefore, Leave No Trace developed special considerations applicable to different settings.

SENSITIVITY TO OTHER CULTURES
As mentioned before, Leave No Trace is a set of principles, not rules; therefore you are free to be selective in the way you apply them, especially in a country with a long tradition of accommodating expeditions. Just do your homework, don't be rigid in your interpretation of the guidelines, and be open to different approaches.

Prayer flags in Nepal: Be respectful of cultural customs and sites.

That doesn't mean you should make a problem worse: There's no need to defecate on the outskirts of town without burying your feces just because that's what the locals do, and you probably don't have to camp 200 feet from water if the village is sited right along the river's edge.

TRASH

Leave No Trace advocates packing garbage out and disposing of it when you return to civilization. This practice is fine in the United States where there are municipal landfills and you can be reasonably assured your garbage will be managed appropriately, but it's not like that everywhere. Not all countries have established facilities to take care of garbage, and packing your stuff out of the mountains may simply mean it ends up on the outskirts of some town that has no other means of getting rid of it. It's worth taking this into consideration before you dump your garbage on someone else. This is not only an international problem. Arctic villages in Alaska cannot absorb the waste of all the visitors who pass through, and some small rural communities have serious waste disposal issues that are exacerbated by summer tourist traffic. So before you blithely toss your trash in the nearest waste bin, make sure you know where that stuff is going. If you discover there is no established waste management system, you should determine ways to minimize your trash and avoid overburdening your hosts.

Consider unwrapping bars and getting rid of excess packaging while you still have access to garbage disposal. Avoid lots of prepackaged meals, and plan your menus to avoid leftovers. Try to use containers that can be cleaned and reused; or, if possible, use containers that will break down if buried.

Once you are out in the mountains, consider burning your trash. It may be the best solution for preventing unsightly and unhygienic litter from being scattered across the countryside. Do this with care to avoid wildfires. That said, some cultures actually frown on burning garbage, believing the gods disapprove, so you may be faced with a conundrum. Just try to do what seems best.

FUEL

Many mountainous regions of the world have been denuded of vegetation by people seeking firewood for heat and cooking. In parts of the Himalaya, villagers often have to hike for a day to reach wood supplies. The problem becomes more acute the higher one goes and the less wood is naturally available. On your expedition, you are undoubtedly planning to cook on stoves and will have brought adequate fuel to supply your personal needs, but if you have porters helping you ferry loads to your base camp, you need to consider their needs as well. Often porters have very little besides the clothes on their back to keep warm, and, therefore, need a fire for their well-being as they head up in elevation. In some countries, you are required to provide porters with equipment as part of your permit. This may or may not include things like a sleeping bag, stove, or fuel. Even if you are not obligated to bring these items, you may want to include them to avoid exacerbating any deforestation problems you may encounter en route to your destination.

SERVICE PROJECTS

Many parts of the world have been profoundly affected by mountaineering expeditions, commercial trekking groups, and tourists. Often everything from trash to used air canisters have been left to molder in the alpine environment, where they will remain

Find opportunities to connect with local cultures.

unchanged for hundreds, if not thousands, of years. If you have space in your pack after you complete your expedition, consider packing out some of the rubbish that has been left behind. A growing number of expeditions use these kinds of service projects to help raise money to support their efforts. These expeditions have helped to increase awareness of the problem of overuse and trash. Today, most guiding agencies have modified their practices to ensure mountaineering remains sustainable. They are now carrying out their own garbage, building latrines for human waste at base camps, and providing stoves and fuel for support staff. No one wants to climb a peak that is littered with trash, abandoned gear, human feces, and other signs of neglect or disrespect. So if you are going to a destination that sees a lot of traffic from climbers or trekkers, consider adding some sort of service angle to your expedition goals. It's nice to give back to the places and people that give you so much in return.

| **RECORDING YOUR ADVENTURE**

Sharing your adventure no longer means waiting until you're home and then simply sitting on the couch with your friends flipping through a photo album and reminiscing about your trip. Today's travelers are often plugged into the rest of the world every single day, blogging about their activities so their friends and families, as well as countless strangers, can follow them as they inch their way up a mountain or through the rugged outback.

We live in a world that expects—and often demands—instant and continuous communication. This may or may not be what you want from your trip. Many of us choose to head out on an expedition to leave civilization behind, but for others, the cyber connection is part of what enables you to take part in extended trips to remote locations in the first place. It permits you to maintain contact with your loved ones and to fulfill obligations to your sponsors. There's a wide range of ways to record your adventure with a daily blog being one end of the extreme and a postcard from Kathmandu the other. You may have certain requirements as a result of your funding; otherwise, you can choose just how much contact you want before, during, and after your expedition.

Before you go, consider what your goals are for recording and sharing your adventure. Do you simply want to help your family and friends understand your experience, or do you need to write a magazine article when you return? Do you hope to go on tour showing your slides and telling your story, or are you planning on selling photographs to catalogs or periodicals to help pay off your expenses? These questions can help you decide what kind of equipment you'll need and how much time and energy you'll need to put into the communications aspect of your trip. The least commitment

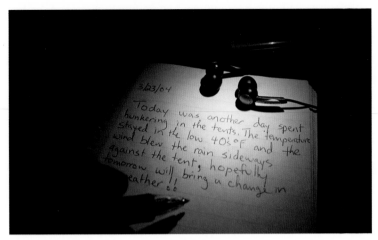

Journaling is a great way to keep track of your adventures. Later your journal can be used to tell stories to your family and friends or write articles promoting your success.

is to simply snap some photos with your point-and-shoot camera, write down notes and thoughts in a journal, and call it good. But if you are more ambitious or you have to meet certain obligations to sponsors, you'll need to invest time and money to ensure your work is professional and effective.

Photography and Video

Cameras come in all shapes, sizes, and prices, offering any number of features for would-be photographers. As with all equipment, don't expect to buy a fancy camera the day before you leave and think you'll be able to use it effectively during your expedition. If you are new to photography, you'll need to put some time into the activity before you head into the wilds to ensure your images are compelling and high quality, especially if you plan to do more than simply post them on your Facebook page.

DSLR VERSUS POINT-AND-SHOOT
What kind of camera should you carry? The answer is: It depends. Both DSLR (digital single-lens reflex cameras) and point-and-

shoot cameras have their pros and cons, but for simplicity sake, you can make the decision based on one calculation: If your priority is image quality, go for a DSLR. If convenience is your number one concern, nothing beats a 4-ounce point-and-shoot that fits into your pocket. A few more things to consider in determining which camera to carry include:

- Megapixels: Contrary to popular opinion, a camera's megapixel capacity does not necessarily determine its quality. A 10-megapixel point-and-shoot is not going to give you as good a photograph as an 8-megapixel DSLR because of the size of the image sensor in the camera. Sensors in point-and-shoot image cameras are smaller, which means that regardless of the number of megapixels advertised, their images will be grainier—especially when enlarged—than a DSLR image. For most of us, this difference doesn't matter, unless you plan to blow up your photos to poster size or to use them in a professional application, but it's worth understanding so you can get beyond the hype.
- Size and weight: DSLR cameras are heavier and bulkier, which makes them more difficult to pull out at a moment's notice. Plus you have to carry them along with the rest of

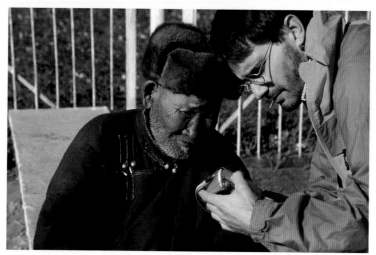

NOLS instructor Ant Chapin sharing photos from his point-and-shoot with a local man in Mongolia.

NOLS instructor Brady Robinson focusing in with his DSLR in Pakistan.

your gear. A point-and-shoot camera can be stashed in your pocket, and you'll barely know it is there.

- Adaptability: DSLR cameras allow you to change lens and are designed for manual operation, so you adjust the settings independently. Point-and-shoots usually come with built-in zoom lens and many have adjustable settings, but the range of adaptability is limited compared with that offered by a DSLR.

- Speed: Point-and-shoot cameras are notorious for their shutter lag, or the pause between the time you press the button and the time the shutter closes. This can mean you miss the action of your shot. Cameras are improving all the time, and shutter lag is less pronounced in today's top-of-the-line point-and-shoots, but it is still there. DSLR cameras do not have this problem.

- Price: DSLR cameras are in general more expensive than point-and-shoots. That said, they also tend to hold their value longer, so price may be a toss-up in the long run.

- Raw or JPEG: Again, for most amateurs, these words are meaningless. But if you hope to sell images for professional applications—catalogs, advertisements, and so forth—you will probably need to shoot RAW images. Check with the

companies you plan to work with to find out their requirements. Simply speaking, RAW images allow you to manipu-
late the final product more and, therefore, are preferred for
most professional use. If you need to shoot RAW images,
you will need to have a DSLR camera. Very few point-and-
shoots allow you to work in this medium.

A Word About Film

Film? Some people have no clue what film looks like, let alone how to use it. But
a few die-hard photographers still swear by film. Film does have its positives:
Slides last 50 or more years without degradation, photographs are dense and easy
to enlarge, and film tends to work better for long exposures, such as night shots;
but unless you have a personal preference for film, it's unlikely you'll ever use it
again (if you ever used it).

VIDEO

Most of today's cameras—both point-and-shoot cameras and
DSLRs—have video capability. This may be all you need for your
expedition if you want to capture a few moments of live action. If
your goal is to shoot a movie, however, you'll want a video camera.
These cameras are also able to shoot stills, so you can still snap a
few photographs to complement your movies. Video cameras come
in all sizes and shapes too. Do some research to determine what
will be most appropriate for the application you have in mind.
Remember things like temperature, moisture, storage capacity, bat-
tery power, and so forth will all be factors to contend with when
you are out in the field.

MEMORY AND POWER

While you no longer need to carry around hundreds of rolls of film
to record your adventure, you will probably need to bring along a
few memory cards to ensure you have enough storage capacity. You
can edit some photos in the field, but beware, it's hard to distin-
guish precise details sitting in a tent with the wind flapping on the

NOLS instructor Andrew Chapman taking video in India.

nylon and easy to accidentally erase images. Your best bet is to do most of your culling back in the comfort of your home, so bring along enough memory cards to tide you over for the entire trip. Store your cards carefully in waterproof containers so they are not damaged in transit.

You will also need to have sufficient power to operate your equipment for the entire trip. Use long-lived lithium batteries to get the most bang for your buck. You can also invest in a portable solar panel for recharging batteries in the field. This can help reduce the number of batteries you require, but make sure you have a few nonrechargeable batteries to use just in case the weather turns bad and you don't have any sunshine for recharging.

Accessories

If you are carrying a DSLR camera, you probably want some versatility in your lens choices. Dave's semipro setup includes a wide-angle and zoom lens and a tripod. Tripods can be small and inexpensive and are worth carrying to give you some flexibility in setting up photo shoots. If you plan to shoot video, it's worth investing in a video or fluid head, an attachment that allows you to pan the camera smoothly. Altogether Dave carries about 10 pounds worth of camera and video equipment. This allows him to take professional quality images that he has then sold for use in catalogs and other promotional materials.

GETTING THE SHOTS

It's one thing to carry a really nice camera in your backpack; it's another to actually pull it out and get quality images. Many of us lug around photography gear but never pull it out because it takes too much effort. If you want good pictures, you need to work at it.

Plan ahead. Think about your itinerary, where you will be and what you anticipate seeing. Think about lighting—lighting is often best early in the morning or around dusk. Gray days are also good for color saturation and contrast, and storms add drama to expedition photography. Make sure that your teammates know the importance of capturing good pictures and will cooperate. Shooting photography intrudes on people's privacy and can be annoying at times, so be considerate when you ask someone to model.

Not all photographs can be staged or anticipated. For those moments that develop unexpectedly—such as Galen Rowell's famous photograph of the rainbow dipping into the Potala Palace in Lhasa—you need to be able to pull your camera out and get in position quickly.

If you plan to take photographs of people you see and meet along the journey, do a little research on local customs. In some parts of the world, people do not want their pictures taken for all sorts of reasons, including the belief that you steal their soul when you take their photo. In other places, people expect to be paid for photographs. Learn how to ask if you can take a photograph in the language of the place you are traveling. Interact with people before you shove a lens in their faces to develop a rapport. People used to carry around Polaroid cameras so they could give people pictures of themselves, but you can't find Polaroids anymore. You can offer to send people copies of their pictures, however: Get their address or e-mail, and make a note of the date and place you took the image so you don't get confused. Remember, if you offer to send someone a picture, you need to follow through.

Blogging

Google "travel blogs" and you will come up with literally thousands of hits. Some people blog about their weekend visit to grandma's, others about their yearlong trip around the world. Many sponsored expeditions blog to help maintain hype for the athletes, their gear, and the goal. Most likely, unless you are professionally sponsored, your decision to blog will be a personal one. You can use your blog to stay in touch with friends and family and to help you keep track of your memories from the trip.

The primary issue with keeping a blog in the field is Internet access. Historically, most expeditions used satellite phones to connect, but the broadband width for this type of connection is very low, making it difficult to do more than send e-mails. A portable

Dave's expedition mates, Steph Davis and Jimmy Chin, filing expedition reports with the group's satellite phone and computer.

satellite modem is better for Internet use, but such modems are expensive (costing between $1,000 and $4,000), and using the device is also pricey. You can opt to use a smart phone—such as an iPhone—to connect to the Internet and post on your blog, but make sure that you can use your phone in the place you are traveling before relying on it for all your communication.

To ensure your blog is read, you need to include keywords—or common terms—that are likely to come up in Google searches. Keywords change with time, current events, and so on, but for expeditions, geographical locations, 8,000-meters peaks, first river descents, specific activity terms (climbing, skiing, hiking), special equipment (model of camera you are shooting with, type of climbing shoes or hiking boots), transportation information, and so forth are all likely to be strong keywords, as are your names if you have any cachet in the outdoor adventure world. It's worth doing a little investigating to learn more about how to use keywords effectively if you hope to generate traffic to your blog.

You can also include links to other Internet sites—corporate sites, geographical sites, people—to help create an audience for your blog.

Finally, your blog has to be entertaining, up-to-date, and relevant. The most popular blogs have a combination of personal reflections, amusing stories of mishaps, exciting adventures, dramatic photographs, historic or cultural context, and some videos to spice things up. It's a big commitment to do a blog right, so if you plan to use this tool to market your expedition, the whole team needs to support the endeavor. If you just want to have fun and stay in touch with your parents, you can scale back and tap a few words into your iPhone on a rest day.

Post-Expedition Media Tours

Many expeditioners will record their adventures as an obligation to a sponsor or grantor and then follow up with a tour upon their return. Even if you don't have sponsor obligations, though, slide shows are a great way to generate income once you've returned home. If you plan to charge a fee for attendance, you will need to put some effort into developing a compelling narrative supported by dramatic visuals and music. Slide show tours also require time spent booking venues and arranging for marketing. But if you do your work, you can pull in a few bucks and generate publicity for yourself and your accomplishments. Colleges and universities, outdoor shops, and outing clubs are good places to start if you want to go on tour. Try to book events close together to minimize your travel time.

| **PERSONAL REFLECTION AND HEADING HOME**

Some people say the hardest part of any journey is coming home, especially when the journey has been the culmination of months—even years—of planning. There's something anticlimactic about getting off the plane in your hometown and seeing that things are just the way you left them when inside you feel as if so much has happened, so much change has occurred.

Life is different on an expedition. You leave the humdrum reality of your everyday life behind. No more to-do lists, no more calendars full of meetings and activities, no more need to scrub the toilet or vacuum the carpets. Sure, you have chores on an expedition—cooking, packing up gear, cleaning dishes—but the scenery is ever changing, each day brings new experiences, and you are often pushed to test your strength, endurance, and intelligence by the challenges you encounter living and traveling in the wilderness or a foreign land. Many NOLS graduates talk about feeling more alive on their expeditions, and that feeling can be pretty addictive. Returning to "real life" is often a letdown, especially when your friends and family don't really understand what you've been doing.

There are some tricks to easing your reentry that help make coming home a fitting end to your expedition. Here are a few ideas.

In the Field

You are not alone in feeling some anxiety about the end of an expedition. If the trip has been a big deal for you, it has undoubtedly also been a big deal for your teammates. It helps to sit down and

NOLS instructor Steve Whitney taking a moment to enjoy a last sunrise in the Wind River Range before the end of an expedition.

share your feelings before you separate and return to your own homes. At NOLS, people talk about "group death" at the end of a course. It's a harsh term but hints at the very real emotional toil of breaking apart a team that has worked, played, laughed, and learned together for extended periods of time. Grief, loneliness, regret, and fear are often feelings you can expect to encounter as you leave behind your teammates and forge ahead alone.

So take time to debrief while you are still out in the mountains or away from civilization. Share highlights, take pride in your

A NOLS expedition takes some time to connect over the campfire in order to debrief their adventures.

accomplishments, laugh about the hardships or challenges you encountered along the way, congratulate each other for a job well done. Talk about your fears or concerns with regard to heading home. Come up with a plan for wrapping up the end of the expedition—for cleaning up gear, sharing photographs, finalizing finances, and so forth. It's easy for a team to splinter once you return to town. Phones, food, alcohol, and other amenities are tempting distractions, so bring closure to your expedition before these outside factors dismantle your team.

Tricks for Easing Reentry Back Home

1. *Give yourself time.* Don't rush right back into your old routines. You've undoubtedly been changed by your experience in some way. That change may be little more than having given up television or eating meat for two months. Give yourself a little time to ease back into life at home. Maybe you like the changes you made, in which case, by all means, don't give them up just because you've come home. Expeditions are all about personal growth. There's no need to lose that growth once you are back.

Don't rush every morning; your expedition will be over before you know it!

2. *Honor your experience.* It can be hard to share an intense experience with people who have no context or understanding of what you've seen or done. We've all seen our friend's eyes glaze over as we try to tell them about our adventures. Still, it is worth sharing. Make a slide show or a photo album. Invite a group of friends over to see the pictures and share a meal inspired by the place you traveled. You don't have to bore them with long, involved stories about the number two Camelot that made all the difference on pitch 33 of your epic wall climb. A few photos of the scenery, the exposure, the face of someone working hard will be enough to help them get a glimpse into what you have experienced.

3. *Celebrate your return with a special occasion.* Plan some sort of special event to honor your return, something you can look forward to on the flight home. It may be a nice dinner out at your favorite restaurant, or a glass of wine and a candlelit bubble bath—something to pamper yourself, something you could not do during your expedition.

4. *Honor the things you missed.* It's easy to take things for granted, but after two months without a bath in the same smelly clothes, it's worth reminding yourself how much you missed the feeling of warm

Once you get home, remember to explore your own backyard.

water running over your body and soft, fresh clothing against your skin. Pause and reflect on the beauty, comfort, and ease of some of life's luxuries you had to forgo on your expedition. Use this recognition to counterbalance the culture shock you are inevitably going to experience as you return to the world of cars, box stores, mass media, and pop stars plastered all over the tabloids. Be aware of the beauty of enjoying a cold drink with ice cubes floating in your glass, and the luxury of cool, clean sheets on a soft bed. Honor those things.

5. *Put time into your relationships.* Leaving for extended periods of time can put a strain on relationships, both friendships and romantic partnerships. People will have continued moving forward with their lives in your absence. You will have changed. You need to be patient with each other until you find your way back together. Make sure that you are as receptive to their experiences as you expect them to be of yours. Don't be condescending. Just because they have not ventured out on an extended expedition does not mean their life has not been full of its own challenges, excitement, and beauty. The people who are the most successful at maintaining relationships in spite of long absences are those who are as excited by their friend's stories of taking his kid to school for the first time as they are by tales of epic mountain ascents.

Molly Gets Back to the Grind

I pressed my face against the window and stared at the brown plains stretching out below—August in Wyoming. The land was dry and barren; it looked dead.

Our plane bounced and tossed as we made the final approach for landing. It was windy outside. Typical, I thought. When the plane door opened to let us out, a blast of hot air rushed into the cabin. I stepped out onto the stairs and down to the tarmac, feeling the heat, leaning into the wind. Home.

My car was parked in long-term parking where a friend had dropped it off. I loaded my piles of gear into the trunk, staring nostalgically at the backpack. In Canada, I'd been ready to come home: ready to sleep in my bed, shower every day, eat salads, and reconnect with friends and family. Now suddenly all I wanted to do was go back: to return to the rugged mountains, to feel the weight of the pack on my back, and hear the crunch of ice under my feet.

The drive to Lander took 30 minutes, and then I was back at my house: a small log ranch home perched in the middle of a flat, unshaded lot. The house smelled slightly musty from being closed up, and it was hot and stuffy inside. A stack of mail towered on the kitchen counter. My cat rubbed against my legs purring insistently, demanding I pay attention to her.

Nothing had changed. I might have never left. The couch was still shabby, and the paint in my bedroom still a putrid color I'd been meaning to change for years. I still had the same pile of bills to pay and junk mail to sort through. A red light flashed on the message machine. I turned it on and listened as voices droned on and on with long-irrelevant news. Delete, delete. Finally there was a message from the day before: "Welcome home! We've missed you. Call. . . ."

Suddenly everything in my life seemed so small, so unimportant, so boring and mundane. I felt as if I'd been yanked out of an amazing dream. All I wanted to do was go back to sleep again so the dream could continue.

Luckily I knew that feeling wouldn't last forever. As I worked my way through voice mails and stacks of mail, I remembered to count my blessings of not only having had a successful expedition, but of having a home and community to come home to. ■

Likewise, try to maintain contact with your expedition partners. They are sometimes the only ones that really understand your experience on the expedition, and it is nice to have that connection when you enter back into the hectic world.

6. *Get out and have fun.* What makes travel so exciting is that you are busy with new things all the time. Those new things may not always be fun, but they are different and keep you buzzing with a sense of life. Many people come home and find themselves overwhelmed by inertia. They cannot be bothered to get up and do things because they have done it all before. But presumably you've made your home somewhere for a reason, so get out and take advantage of those things that make life in your hometown fun: Go climb at your local crag, go for a run in a nearby park, return to the gym, hang out in a coffee shop with friends. Don't spend too much time lamenting the end of your trip. Every day is a new day, and just because you are back home doesn't mean you have to stop living.

7. *Take time to rest and recuperate.* While it's good to go out and have fun when you return home, remember not to overplan. You may be surprised at how tired you feel after a long trip, so give yourself a chance to chill out and recover. Keep your task list to a minimum, and gently ease yourself back into work. If you can, return home with a weekend or at least a day off before you have to go back to the office. Some quiet time helps you reflect on your experience and at the same time recharge your batteries.

Giving Back

Even the simplest expeditions have people behind the scenes helping make things happen and supporting you outside the actual expedition: your husband who stayed home with the kids, your girlfriend who went to work everyday, or your parents who stared at the phone anxiously for the whole six weeks you traveled. Show your appreciation for their support by giving back something upon

A great way to round out an expedition is to give back to the places you've visited by supporting humanitarian efforts (above) or helping with environmental conservation (left).

your return. Slide shows are a great way to share your story and say thank you. You can also give back twofold by bringing meaningful souvenirs home for your friends and family. Many developing countries have artisans' guilds designed to help promote local crafts. Try to support these efforts if you can. Often the proceeds go to a good cause—supporting traditional arts or giving work to unemployed women, for example.

You can also say thank you to the places you visit by supporting efforts to bring humanitarian aid to those in need or helping with environmental issues in areas of concern. You can do some research into the types of projects taking place in your host country—maybe there is a program to rehabilitate injured raptors or an effort to build schools that catches your attention—and volunteer to help after you complete your expedition. You may decide to bring over supplies for a hospital or a women's shelter that is supporting people in the place you visit. All these projects make a difference and can use your help.

You may also learn about a cause during your trip that you decide warrants your support upon your return, which is how a lot of the great humanitarian efforts began. Greg Mortenson's schools in Pakistan and the Sherpa climbing school in the Khumbu region of Nepal both had their roots in visitors seeing a need and finding a way to meet that need.

Whatever you decide, giving back to those who made your expedition possible is a karmic way to end.

Bibliography

INTRODUCTION

The NOLS Reference Library:

Gookin, J. 2003. *NOLS Wilderness Wisdom*. Stackpole Books: Mechanicsburg, PA.

Gookin, J., and B. Tilton 2005. *NOLS Winter Camping*. Stackpole Books: Mechanicsburg, PA.

Gookin, J., and T. Reed 2009. *NOLS Bear Essentials*. Stackpole Books: Mechanicsburg, PA.

Hampton, B., and D. Cole 2003. *NOLS Soft Paths*. Stackpole Books: Mechanicsburg, PA.

Harvey, M. 1999. *The National Outdoor Leadership School's Wilderness Guide*. Simon & Schuster: New York.

Howley Ryan, M. 2008. *NOLS Backcountry Nutrition*. Stackpole Books: Mechanicsburg, PA.

Lamb, J., and G. Goodrich 2006. *NOLS Wilderness Ethics* Stackpole Books: Mechanicsburg, PA.

Ostis, N. 2010. *NOLS River Rescue: Essential Skills for Boaters*. Stackpole Books: Mechanicsburg, PA.

Pearson, C. 2004. *NOLS Cookery*. Stackpole Books: Mechanicsburg, PA.

Pearson, C., and J. Kuntz 2008. *NOLS Backcountry Cooking: Creative Menu Planning for Short Trips*. Stackpole Books: Mechanicsburg, PA.

Powers, P. 2009. *NOLS Wilderness Mountaineering*. Stackpole Books: Mechanicsburg, PA.

Schimelpfenig, T. 2005. *NOLS Wilderness Medicine*. Stackpole Books: Mechanicsburg, PA.

Wells, D. 2006. *NOLS Wilderness Navigation*. Stackpole Books: Mechanicsburg, PA.

CHAPTER 1

Adventure Travel Report. http://www.adventuretravelreporter.com

Gump, B. B., and K. A. Matthews, 2000. Are vacations good for your health?: The 9 year mortality experience after the multiple risk factor intervention trial. *Psychosomatic Medicine* 62: 608–612.

National Agricultural Law Center, University of Arkansas. http://www
.nationalaglawcenter.org/assets/crs/RL31447.pdf

National Institute for Occupational Safety and Health (NIOSH).
http://www.marshfieldclinic.org/media/pages/default.aspx?page=
newsreleases&id=2831

Sung, H.Y., A. M. Morrison, and J. T. O'Leary 1997. Definition of adventure
travel: Conceptual framework for empirical application from the
provider's perspective. *Asia-Pacific Journal of Tourism Research*, 1(2):
47–67.

Underhill, P., P. Shen, A. Lin, et al. November 2000. Y chromosome
sequence variation and the history of human populations. Letters.
Nature Genetics 26: 358–361.

U.S. Forest Service. http://www.fs.fed.us/rm/pubs_rm/rm_gtr189.pdf

U.S. Travel Association. http://www.ustravel.org

World Tourism Organization. http://www.unwto.org

CHAPTER 3

Appalachian Trail Conservancy. http://www.appalachiantrail.org/site/
c.jkLXJ8MQKtH/b.851143/k.C36D/2000Milers_Facts_and_Statistics
.htm

CHAPTER 10

Peak Performance Sporting Excellence. http://www.pponline.co.uk/encyc/
0895.htm

Storen, O., J. Helgerud, E. Stoa, and J. Hoff June 2008. Maximal strength
training improves running economy in distance runners. *Medicine &
Science in Sports & Exercise*. 40(6): 1087–1092. http://journals.lww.com

CHAPTER 11

World Health Organization. http://www.who.int/entity/bloodsafety/GDBS
_Report_2001-2002.pdf

CHAPTER 13

Harvey, J. 1974. The Abilene paradox: The management of agreement.
Organizational Dynamics, Summer, 63–80. From *NOLS Leadership Edu-
cator Notebook*. Gookin, J., and S. Leach, 2009.Lander, WY: National
Outdoor Leadership School.

CHAPTER 14

Blanchard, K. 1999. *Leadership and the One Minute Manager*. New York:
William Morrow and Company. From *NOLS Leadership Educator Note-
book*. Gookin, J., and S. Leach, 2009. Lander, WY: National Outdoor
Leadership School.

CHAPTER 15

Felps, W. February 13, 2007. *Rotten to the Core: How Workplace "Bad Apples" Spoil Barrels Of Good Employees*. University of Washington. 236: Awareness Wheel.

Miller, S., et al. 1988. *Connecting with Self and Others*. Littleton Co: Interpersonal Communications Program. From *NOLS Leadership Educator Notebook*. Gookin, J., and S. Leach, 2009. Lander, WY: National Outdoor Leadership School.

CHAPTER 17

Torre, J. 2006. Joe Torre on winning. *Business Week*. http://www.business week.com/magazine/content/06_34/b3998401.htm.

Index

Access. *See under* Red tape
Accommodations
  airports, 169–170
  budget for, 67–68
  campgrounds, 168
  couch surfing, 169
  guidebooks, 173–174
  hostels, 167
  hotels, 167–168
  huts and teahouses, 170–172
  online researching/booking,
    172–174
  travel agents and, 174
Adversity and uncertainty, dealing
  with
  failure jinx, 242
  fun, having, 244
  Mount Logan anecdote, 238–240
  survivor, traits of a, 235–238
  turn around, deciding to, 241–242
Airports, 169–170
Alaska Mountaineering School, 139
Alpine Ascents International, 139
Alpine Club of Britain, 48
Alpine Club of Pakistan, 58
Alpine Ski Club, 74
Altitude illness, 141–142, 150
American Alpine Club (AAC), 30, 71
  detailed description of, 47
  Global Rescue and, 146–147
  grants from, 74
American Avalanche Institute, 139
American Canoe Association, 139
American Canyoneering Associa-
  tion, 30, 40

American Institute for Avalanche
  Research and Education, 139
American Mountain Guides Associ-
  ation, 139
American Society of Tropical Medi-
  cine and Hygiene (ASTMH),
  155
Antiquities Act of 1906, 65
Appalachian Mountain Club, 30

Banff Centre, 47
Behavior
  bad, 212–214
  crevasse anecdote, 215–217
  good, 209–212, 219–220
  sharing the load, 210–211
Blogging, 262–263
BootsnAll, 173
Budget
  equipment, 68–69
  fees, 71
  food, 70
  funding, sources of, 73–75, 77–78
  how to use your, 71–73
  support, 35–37, 41
  team selection and, 22–23
  travel and accommodations,
    67–68
Bureau of Indian Affairs, 56, 57
Bureau of Land Management
  (BLM), 7, 56
Bureau of Reclamation, 56
Burns, 151

Campgrounds, 168
Cash, obtaining, 189–190
Cell phones, 100, 231
Centers for Disease Control (CDC),
    143, 144, 148
Charity, adopting a, 75, 77
Civil unrest, 63–64
Climbing Magazine, 30
Commission Européenne de Canyon
    (CEC), 40
Commission Internationale de
    Canyon (International Associa-
    tion of Professional Canyoneer-
    ing Guides), 40
Communication
    awareness wheel, 217–219
    how to talk to each other, 218
    importance of, 217, 219–220
    Mount Logan anecdote, 219
Compasses, 96
Contact person, 31–32
Cooking, 124, 125, 127–128
Costs. *See* Budget
Crime, 63–64

Decision-making. *See* Leadership
Dehydration, 148
Diarrhea, traveler's, 148–149

Ecotourism, 42
Elemental Training Center, 142
Emergencies
    cash, obtaining, 189–190
    evacuation, 146–147, 231, 233–234
    fatality or serious injury/illness,
        234
    healthcare, 156
    risk management and planning
        for, 231–234
    support and, 36, 41
Endangered Species Act, 65
End of the expedition. *See* Returning
    home
Environmental protection, 64–66
    See also Leave No Trace

Equipment
    budget for, 68–69
    cell phones, 100, 231
    compasses, 96
    cooking anecdote, 92–93
    fuel, 124, 125, 127–128, 253
    Global Positioning Systems
        (GPS), 97
    group gear, 86–103
    jewelry, 86
    luxuries, 85
    maps, 93–95
    materials for clothing and bags,
        84
    personal gear, 79–84, 103
    personal locator beacons (PLBs),
        102–103
    radios, 99–100
    satellite phones, 100–101, 231
    tent, seam-sealing your, 89
Evacuation
    emergency planning, 231,
        233–234
    insurance, 146–147
Expedia, 173
Expedition News, 30
Exploration/expeditions
    brief history of, 1–3
    outdoor recreation, trends in,
        5–11
    overview of, xxi, xx, 11
    personal benefits of, 3–5
Explorers Club
    detailed description of, 48
    grants from, 74
Exum Mountain Guides, 139

Fatality protocol, 234
Fees budget, 71
Field Guides Association of South-
    ern Africa, 40
Food
    amount per person per day, 113,
        114
    budget for, 70
    cooking, 124, 125, 127–128

good/bad times anecdote, 106–107
international shopping, 121, 123
packing, 120
planning, 105, 107–111, 113–120
questionnaire, 108
resupplies, 123–124
Fuel, 253
calculating amounts of, 127–128
types of, 124, 125, 127
Funding, sources of
charity, adopting a, 75, 77
grants, 73–75, 77–78
sponsorship, 77–78

Gear. *See* Equipment
Global Positioning Systems (GPS), 97
Global Rescue, 146–147
Global Travel Clinic Directory, 154
Goals
known factors affecting, 12–13
Long Walk anecdote, 15–16
questions to ask yourself, 17–18
uncontrollable factors affecting, 15
variable factors affecting, 14
Google Earth, 47
Gore and Associates, 61, 74–75
Grants, 73–75, 77–78
Guidebooks, 173–174
Guided expeditions, 35, 37–38
Gym Jones, 142

HALT (hungry, angry, lonely, tired), 105
Health and medical issues
emergency evacuation, 146–147, 231, 233–234
emergency healthcare, 156
en route, 147–148
illnesses, 41, 141–150, 152–153, 232, 234
injuries, 41, 143, 145, 146, 151, 153–154, 231–234
insurance, 145–146
international healthcare, 154–156

medications, 144, 155–156
pre-expedition planning, 143–147
Health Hints for the Tropics (ASTMH), 155
Hostels, 167
Hotels, 167–168
How, When, Why Bad Apples Spoil the Barrel: A Theory of Destructive Group Members (Felps), 212
Huts and teahouses, 170–172

Illnesses, 41
altitude illness, 141–142, 150
dehydration, 148
diarrhea, traveler's, 148–149
fatality or serious, 234
malaria, 152–153
motion sickness, 149–150
pre-expedition planning, 143–147
rabies, 152
SOAP note template, 232
tetanus, 152
urinary tract infections (UTIs), 152
yeast infections, 152
Indian Mountaineering Federation, 19, 58
Indian Mountaineering Foundation (IMF), 61–62
Injuries, 41, 143, 145, 146
burns, 151
fatality or serious, 234
planning for, 231–234
SOAP note template, 232
sprains and strains, 153–154
tendonitis, 153–154
wounds, 151
Insurance, 145–147
International Association of Professional Canyoneering Guides (Commission Internationale de Canyon), 40
International expeditions
access, 58–63
attire and behavior, 176–178
civil unrest, crime, and traveler safety, 63–64, 179, 181
environmental protection, 64–66

food shopping, 121, 123
fuel, 253
healthcare, 154–156
history and culture, local,
    175–176, 251–252
language, local, 181–182
Leave No Trace and, 251–254
money issues, 186–190
red tape, 58–66
rich Westerner, the, 178–179
service projects, 253–254
staff, hiring, 183–186
terms and definitions, list of, 185
International Federation of Moun-
    tain Guides Associations
    (IFMGA), 39–40
International Porter Protection
    Group, 185
International Society of Travel Medi-
    cine (ISTM), 154
International SOS, 145

Jackson Hole Mountain Guides, 139

Kenya Professional Safari Guides
    Association, 40

Leadership
    case study, 191–194
    checklist, 208
    defined, 196
    designated leader, 194–196, 198
    roles, 197–198
    situational, 198–200
    skills, 200–203
    styles, 203–208
    team selection and, 23
Leave No Trace
    be considerate of other visitors,
        250
    dispose of waste properly, 248,
        252–254
    international travel and, 251–254
    leave what you find, 248
    minimize campfire impacts, 249
    origins of the movement, 245–246
    plan ahead and prepare, 246

respect wildlife, 249–250
service projects, 253–254
Talkeetna Mountains anecdote,
    250–251
travel and camp on durable sur-
    faces, 246–247
Leave No Trace Center for Outdoor
    Ethics, 246
Lonely Planet, 173
Long Walk, The (Rawicz), 15–16
Alex Lowe Charitable Foundation,
    186

Malaria, 152–153
Maps, 93–95
Medical issues. *See* Health and med-
    ical issues
Medications, 144, 155–156
Motion sickness, 149–150
Mountain Athlete, 142
Mountain Institute, The, 186

National Geographic, 15
National Geographic Expeditions
    Council, 74
National Outdoor Leadership
    School (NOLS), 16, 19, 59, 71,
    101, 108, 111, 114, 119, 120,
    127, 129, 138, 142, 216, 229,
    242, 245, 266
    leadership skills/roles/styles,
        196–208
*National Outdoor Leadership
    School's Wilderness Guide,* xix
NOLS Backcountry Cooking, xix,
    110, 128
NOLS Backcountry Nutrition, xix,
    105, 115, 128
NOLS Bear Essentials, xix
NOLS Cookery, xix, 124, 128
NOLS Cookery: Field Edition, 128
NOLS River Rescue, xix
*NOLS Soft Paths: How to Enjoy the
    Wilderness without Harming It,*
    xix, 246
NOLS Wilderness Ethics, xix
NOLS Wilderness Medicine, xx, 148

NOLS Wilderness Mountaineering,
xx
NOLS Wilderness Navigation, xx
NOLS Wilderness Wisdom, xx
NOLS Winter Camping, xx
overview of, xvii–xix
Wilderness Medicine Institute,
139
National Park Service/System, 7–10,
55–56
National Wilderness Preservation
System, 9
National Wildlife Refuge System, 7
NOLS. *See* National Outdoor Lead-
ership School

Orbitz, 173
Outward Bound, xviii

Personality, team selection and,
23–24
Personal locator beacons (PLBs),
102–103
Photography
accessories, 260–261
DSLR versus point-and-shoot,
256–259
film, 259
memory and power, 259–260
shots, getting the, 261
video, 259
Polartec Challenge Grant, 75

Rabies, 152
Radios, 99–100
Recording your adventure
blogging, 262–263
overview of, 255–256
photography and video, 256–261
tours, post-expedition media,
263–264
Red tape
access to private land in U.S.,
57–58
access to public land in U.S.,
55–56

Arunachal Pradesh peaks anecdote, 60–61
civil unrest, crime, and traveler
safety, 63–64
environmental protection, 64–66
international expeditions, 58–66
visas, 59
Research
importance of, 45
resources, 46–48
table for, 50–54
what to, 49
Returning home
advice for easing reentry, 267–271
giving back, 271–273
personal reflections on, 265–267
Risk management
avalanche anecdote, 222–223
emergencies, planning for,
231–234
environmental hazards, 225–226
human factors, 226
importance of, 221, 234
Risk Management Equation, 224,
225
risk management plan, 226,
228–230
understanding risk, 224–225
Rock and Ice, 30
Royal Geographical Society, 48
Rules and regulations. *See* Red tape

Safety
See also Emergencies; Risk management
civil unrest and crime and, 63–64,
179, 181
team selection and, 21–22
transportation, 166
Satellite phones, 100–101, 231
Shipton-Tilman Award/Grant, 61,
74–75
Skills
support and, 35, 36, 38–40
team selection and, 23–24, 27
training to develop, 138–139

South Pole, 2, 30
Sponsorship, 77–78
Sprains and strains, 153–154
Support
    budget, 35–37, 41
    choosing the right company,
        38–40
    deciding on level of, 35–36
    emergencies and, 36, 41
    guided expeditions, 35, 37–38
    Pine Barrens anecdote, 43–44
    self-sufficient expeditions with no
        outside, 35
    skills and, 35, 36, 38–40
    supported expeditions, 35, 37–38

Team, choosing your
    budget, 22–23
    contact person, 31–32
    finding people, 30–31
    larger groups, 20
    leadership and decision-making,
        23, 191–208
    liabilities and strengths, 32–34
    North Pole expedition, 28–29
    overview of, 19
    personality, 23–24, 27
    questionnaire for, 25–26, 214
    safety and style, 21–22
    skills, 23–24, 27
    smaller groups, 20
    solo, 20–21
    treasurer, 72–73
    tryouts, 30–31
Tendonitis, 153–154
Tent, seam-sealing your, 89
Tetanus, 152
Tours, post-expedition media,
    263–264
Trails Illustrated, 94
Training
    altitude illness, 141–142
    mental preparation, 129–132
    pace/preparation anecdote,
        136–137
    physical preparation, 132–136

resources, 142
    skill development, 138–139
Transportation
    air, 157–161
    budget for, 67–68
    buses and trains, 161–164
    hiring cars/vans/buses, 164–165
    Nepal anecdote, 160–161
    safety, 166
    taxis and rickshaws, 165–166
    travel agents and, 174
Travel agents, 174
Travel Guard's ProtectAssist, 146
Travelocity, 173
Treasurer, 72–73
Trip Advisor, 172–173

Uncertainty, dealing with. See
    Adversity and uncertainty,
    dealing with
Urinary tract infections (UTIs), 152
U.S. Adventure Racing Association,
    146
U.S. Army 10th Mountain Division,
    xviii
U.S. Department of State, 59, 181
    Overseas Citizens Services (OCS)
    Office of American Citizens
    Services and Crisis Manage-
    ment, 189–190
U.S. Fish and Wildlife Service, 56
U.S. Forest Service, 7, 56, 245, 246
U.S. Geological Survey (USGS),
    93–94
U.S. Ski and Snowboard Teams, 146

Visas, 59

Wikipedia, 47
Wilderness Act of 1964, 9, 245, 251
Wilderness Rescue International,
    139
World Health Organization (WHO),
    156
Wounds, 151

Yeast infections, 152